Drawing Fire

Drawing Fire

A Pawnee, Artist, and Thunderbird in World War II

Brummett Echohawk

with **Mark R. Ellenbarger**

Edited by Trent Riley

Foreword by Lt. Col. Ernest Childers

University Press of Kansas

© 2018 by the University Press of Kansas
All rights reserved

Published by the University Press of Kansas (Lawrence, Kansas 66045),
which was organized by the Kansas Board of Regents and is operated
and funded by Emporia State University, Fort Hays State University,
Kansas State University, Pittsburg State University, the University of Kansas,
and Wichita State University.

Illustrations are property of Mark R. Ellenbarger, unless otherwise noted
in caption.

Library of Congress Cataloging-in-Publication Data
Names: Echohawk, Brummett, author. | Ellenbarger, Mark R., author. |
Riley, Trent, editor. | Childers, Ernest, writer of foreword.
Title: Drawing fire : a Pawnee, artist, and Thunderbird in World War II /
Brummett Echohawk with Mark R. Ellenbarger ; edited by Trent Riley ;
foreword by Lt. Col. Ernest Childers.
Description: Lawrence : University Press of Kansas, [2018] | Includes index.
Identifiers: LCCN 2018027414
ISBN 9780700627035 (cloth : alk. paper)
ISBN 9780700627042 (ebook)
Subjects: LCSH: Echohawk, Brummett. | Pawnee Indians—Biography. | World
War, 1939–1945—Participation, Indian. | United States—Armed Forces—
Indians. | Indian artists—Biography. | LCGFT: Autobiographies.
Classification: LCC E99.P3 E25 2019 | DDC 976.6004/979330092 [B]—dc23.
LC record available at https://lccn.loc.gov/2018027414.

British Library Cataloguing-in-Publication Data is available.

Printed in the United States of America

10 9 8 7 6 5 4 3 2 1

The paper used in this publication is recycled and contains 30 percent
postconsumer waste. It is acid free and meets the minimum requirements
of the American National Standard for Permanence of Paper for
Printed Library Materials Z39.48-1992.

Dedicated to my Uncle Brummett
and the men and women of the Greatest Generation

—Mark R. Ellenbarger

Contents

Illustrations

Foreword

The true story you are about to read is one of the few books in print today that is written by a Native American about Native American actions in World War II. The depictions of war are not romanticized but instead are presented with straightforward honesty without embellishments. However, the events are given a unique "native" perspective since the people being described are Native Americans.

Native Americans look at this land as home, as their heritage, and could not hold any foreign country as "home." "Patriotism" isn't something Native Americans have to "create" or "discover" because Native Americans always have been here. For example, in places such as New York City people of different nationalities who have immigrated to America, such as the Irish, Italians, Puerto Ricans, Cubans, and Germans, have parades to show their pride in their homelands. Native Americans are always patriotic because this land has always been our only home. We are not "Irish Americans" or "Italian Americans"; we are Native Americans. Our heritage is this land, our land. Our ancestors are buried here, and when Native Americans fight for "this" country, we are doing so because we are protecting the lands of our forefathers, the only lands we call home.

Brummett Echohawk's description of events during World War II brought back memories as an eyewitness to these events as they happened. It is typical for Native Americans to try to see the humorous side of life, especially when the circumstances are very serious. Brummett describes a serious event, the landing on Italy by American forces, yet gives this monumental event a humorous twist as he relates the escapades of a Native American soldier planting a staff on Italian soil saying, "Columbus, we have arrived." Just as Columbus "claimed" the Americas for Europe, so the Native American soldier "claimed" Italy for the Native Americans!

His descriptions of Native American traditions, such as the "war whoop," reinforce the pride tribal people have in their heritage. For example, when attending a powwow, you know exactly which tribe someone is from by his "whoop," which can sound like a horse's whinny or a turkey's gobble. This is a part of tribal identity. This sense of identity gives strength to the Native

American soldiers. Native American boys aspire to become notable respected
warriors. This practice did not die with the coming of the "white man" but
instead evolved with these modern times as it continues to be dreamed and
realized. A Native American boy can endeavor to become a leader within
his community, work with the schools to help educate other young Native
Americans, or become a soldier willing to fight and possibly give his life for his
country's and his people's honor. In these ways, a boy can become a "warrior"
and in these ways earn the respect and admiration of his people.

*Lt. Col. Ernest Childers**
Medal of Honor Recipient
US Army Retired
Coweta, Oklahoma, August 1997

---

*Born in Broken Arrow, Oklahoma, in 1918, Ernest Childers would graduate from the
Chilocco Indian Agricultural School and, in 1937, join the Oklahoma Army National
Guard. In 1943, during the Allied invasion of Italy, he received a battlefield commission
from sergeant to second lieutenant in the 45th Infantry Division. For his meritorious actions
near Oliveto, he received the Congressional Medal of Honor, the US military's highest
decoration. Childers reached the rank of lieutenant colonel before retiring from the Army
in 1965. He wrote this essay several years before his death in 2005 at the age of eighty-seven.
See figures on pages 213–214.

Preface

The following account is a monument to the men of the 45th Infantry Division who fought through the campaigns of Italy during World War II. Considering this, Brummett Echohawk sought to tell this story without embellishment, noting that honor was paramount to portraying his experience. As he put his story on paper, Echohawk thought back to the men he served alongside: Shield Chief, Good Buffalo, Cheyenne, and Last Arrow. There were other American Indians: Two Hatchets, Medicine Man, and Leading Fox. Steeped in the traditions of elders, they all became what the Pawnee people call *chaticks-si-chaticks*—men of men.* Medals meant little to them, and fighting bravely in battle among their peers meant everything. There were other men from all walks of life who fought bravely alongside Brummett Echohawk: cowboys, farmers, roughnecks—all toughened by their coming of age during the Depression years. From Pawnee, Oklahoma, they emerged to be among the first to react to the Axis Powers in Continental Europe. This was B Company of the 179th Regiment.

This story begins on September 16, 1940, the day Major General William S. Keys federalized the 45th Infantry Division in Oklahoma from state control, one of the first National Guard units to be activated into a Regular Army force in the lead-up to World War II. Sensing the oncoming war in Europe, the United States boasted forces that could be ready to fight when the hour arrived. The 45th Infantry Division was one of four National Guard divisions federalized, alongside the 30th, the 41st, and the 44th Divisions. Originally called into active service for a one-year period, the men of the 45th Division were tough and plenty rough. Among its cowboys, hardscrabble farmers, American Indians, and others—drawn from Arizona, Colorado, New Mexico, and Oklahoma— the 45th had more than a thousand soldiers of Native American ancestry on its rolls. Oklahoma outfits such as the 180th and 179th Infantry Regiments contained the largest number of American Indians, with entire companies composed of young men of tribal heritage in some cases. Units formed at schools like Chilocco Indian Agricultural School and Bacone College produced some

---

*See Dramatis Personae on page 219 for more information on these men.

of the finest soldiers of the war, including two Medal of Honor recipients. Young men from tribes with strong warring traditions enlisted in great numbers in the 45th Division, aspiring to uphold tribal customs in the way many of their grandfathers had decades earlier on the Great Plains.

Brummett Echohawk was one of these young men. He fought and lived the warring traditions of Pawnee. Born in 1922 in Pawnee, Echohawk came from a family with a long tradition of military service dating back to the Indian Wars of the 1860s. It was then that his grandfather Howard Echohawk served as a famed Pawnee Scout. The tradition of military service continued with Echohawk's father serving in World War I, where Pawnee warriors earned their reputation as soldiers of the highest degree. As a young boy, Echohawk grew up hearing stories from elders who themselves had counted coup on the enemy in battle. Among the Pawnee, being recognized through brave deeds in battle gains a warrior the highest of honors. The Pawnee honor their veterans who return from battle by giving them a song that solidifies their story as a part of tribal history. It was a dream of one day attaining such recognition among their peers that drove young Pawnees to chase down the dream of becoming modern warriors of the twentieth century.

Growing up, Echohawk attended the Pawnee Agency Boarding School, where he first began experimenting with sketching and drawing. It was in these years that he first recognized his ability as an artist to sketch and paint scenes he instilled in his mind after the fact. Upon reaching the age of enlistment, Echohawk joined the Oklahoma National Guard with hopes of earning a steady paycheck while also offering service to his country. Like other young men in 1930s Oklahoma, he joined the 45th Division without any expectation that he might face a forthcoming war, and perhaps with a chance to fight and sketch the conflict as the warrior painted of old.

In 1941 the division began training in earnest, taking part in the noted Louisiana Maneuvers where the military initially evaluated the fighting capacity of some 400,000 Army personnel through mock battles in Louisiana and Texas. In these early days of training, funds to the unit were scarce, with the men training with broomsticks in place of arms, yet they still charged with the zeal of a warrior.

The following story was more than seventy years in the making. It starts at Chilocco Indian Agricultural School near Newkirk, Oklahoma, where my mother, Lucille Rose Johnson-Ellenbarger, spent time as a young woman. Through social circles of Native Americans my mother met a young Brummett Echohawk, with whom she became dear friends. Growing up in West Tulsa, I simply knew Brummett Echohawk as my "Uncle Brummett." He lived down the street and often visited with his wife, Mary Echohawk, for dinner, when he would jester me with old Indian jokes and stories about our heritage as Native People. I remember days sitting on the floor in complete silence as he painted with his knife, which, I learned years later, he had carried throughout the war. Growing up, I slowly began to learn more about Uncle Brummett's service. I knew he suffered wounds and visited exotic places; however, I was unaware of the deliberate documentation he developed of the conflict, where in great detail he offers one of the most unique accounts of any American fighting unit in World War II. Lost to time, his combat sketches completed during the war became a forgotten aspect of his career as an artist.

It was not until the early 1990s that he began to take down notes from his sketches and build them into a written exposé of his wartime experience. After completing chapters, Echohawk delivered his handwritten notes to his close friend Clyda Franks of Pawnee, who meticulously typed the pages of his epic. While Echohawk held an unflinching devotion to finishing this manuscript, his work as an artist demanded critical time and focus; he never gave up, though, and hoped to finish the work in his twilight years.

After suffering a debilitating stroke in 2005, Brummett Echohawk became unable to continue his work on World War II, leaving him shattered from the time he put in to telling the story of the brave men for whom he trained and served alongside, many who never returned home. It was then that he gave me a manuscript and an old intelligence case with instructions to share its contents with the world. The contents of the case included more than forty sketches concealed in wax paper, all completed by Echohawk during the war.

Using information gathered from oral history interviews and personal notes to supplement this manuscript, this work tells in its entirety Brummett Echo-hawk's story of World War II as he saw and lived it. The reader will experience Native humor, tribal traditions, and the grief of the actual events witnessed by Echohawk and the men of B Company. The use of Native American language will move you, offering a greater respect for how American Indians used it to baffle the enemy. Readers will get to know the role of a Choctaw Indian medic called "Medicine Man" and a forward scout of Lakota Sioux descent the men called "Cheyenne." You learn of other men like Phillip "Shield Chief" Gover, who led his men into some of the toughest battles of the war, and William "Last Arrow" Lasley, who fought with the same ferocity as his sta-tus—that of a Golden Glove boxer.

I want to thank many individuals who helped make this work a reality. Fore-most I want to thank my son Zachary Ellenbarger, who encouraged me to see this project through to completion. I also want to thank Dr. Herman J. Viola with the Smithsonian's National Museum of the American Indian for his interest and encouragement in publishing the story of Brummett Echohawk. Additionally, I want to thank Flint Whitlock for offering his insight and expertise on the 45th Infantry Division and the history of World War II.

I also want to thank the Language Department of the Pawnee Nation for their assistance in reviewing elements of the manuscript related to Pawnee linguistics. I would also like to recognize Kenny and Clyda Franks for sharing their knowledge and memories of Brummett Echohawk with me. I also want to acknowledge a veteran of B Company, the late Private First Class Robert Jackson, for sharing his memories of his time in World War II; his knowledge proved invaluable. Further thanks are directed to Elaine Childers for her interest and contributions to this work. I also want to thank Lawrence J. Hickey, author and historian, for providing valuable advice when called upon. Additionally, I thank the families of the individuals associated with the men featured in many of Echohawk's combat sketches and this book. The opportunity to share sketches and memories with these individuals was a special element of this project.

I express my eternal gratitude to Trent Riley for the endless hours of effort he put into this book. His skills as a historian and writer proved priceless during the course of the project.

Although much has been speculated about the "Indian Company" from Pawnee, this work serves the purpose of revealing for the first time what it was like for these young Native Americans serving among other American Indians in the European theater. This story provides an unflinching account of what it was like to be an infantryman of Native American heritage. It is my hope that this work serves to honor Brummett Echohawk and the brave men of the Greatest Generation while also offering a valuable contribution to the literature on the American Indian's experience in World War II.

Mark R. Ellenbarger

1

The Quill of the Thunderbird

The historical record before you is unprecedented. It carries with it the spirit of a man who spent his life holding to a level of accuracy and perfection for truth in everything he did. This was his legacy, and the thought of embellishment could not and did not enter his mind. These were his "brothers in arms"—men he would watch over and train to the best of his ability to fight and survive, yet knowing many would die. Now this story is shared with great honor, by the quill dipped in the blood of the Thunderbirds.

When I was young, growing up in Pawnee, Oklahoma, I used to listen to old-time Pawnee Indians tell stories of warriors and battles on the Great Plains. When a warrior distinguished himself in battle, the people gave him a name with great ceremony. The name was one of honor. Songs were composed describing his feats of bravery. Kept as history, the songs were handed down to the next generation. The warrior was held in honor all his life because he had defended his people and country. My grandfather had been a great warrior. He died when I was two years old; however, I got to see other old Pawnee warriors. In their twilight years, they still carried themselves proud. Seeing them and respecting them, I wanted very much to be a warrior myself.*

Also in my youth, I drew pictures and attempted to paint. My mother said that this was a gift from *Tirawa Uh-tius* (the Supreme Being, Father). I was moved when seeing old-time paintings on buffalo hides and shields. The paintings were done in line and earth colors. They told stories, and the figures bounded with action and life. The unusual thing about the paintings was that they were done by a warrior in battle . . . as he saw it . . . as he lived it.

Now more and more I wanted to become a warrior and artist. Grown up now, I am in a position to record a Pawnee warrior's story. Instead of eagle

---

*Pawnee, Oklahoma, is home to the Pawnee Tribe who relocated to this area of north-central Oklahoma between 1873 and 1875.

"The man I am to face in the coming war." Drawn from Life *magazine, Pawnee, Oklahoma, when Brummett Echohawk enlisted.*

feathers, I wear a steel helmet. I carry an M1 rifle instead of a bow and arrows. Instead of drawing on a buffalo hide or shield, I will draw on notebook paper. And, like the warrior-painter of old, I will tell and draw of battle . . . as I live it . . . as I see it.

—Off the southwest coast of Sicily aboard the troop transport ship USS LEONARD WOOD, JUST BEFORE H-HOUR, JULY 9, 1943

I am a twenty-one-year-old sergeant. It is July 9, 1943, and a couple of months ago the North African Campaign ended. My outfit is in a convoy on the Mediterranean Sea. This force of Allied battleships, cruisers, destroyers, tankers, and various invasion craft left North Africa a few days ago. The convoy has zigzagged and changed directions to confuse the enemy. It is announced that we will invade Sicily as we receive pamphlets titled "A Soldier's Guide to Sicily."

It is night. The ship is blacked out. Ours is the USS *Leonard Wood,*★ a troopship carrying the First Battalion of the 179th Infantry Regiment, 45th Division. The ship's loudspeaker calls the officers and noncommissioned officers (or "noncoms") of the First Wave to the strategy room. We climb from ladders and step through steel doorways manned by sailors. In single file we move through passageways lit with red lights. We wear life belts at all times. In the strategy room is a giant map of Sicily. An intelligence officer stands near with a cue stick. He gives an overall picture of the Allied invasion. Two armies will invade Sicily: the British Eighth Army under General Bernard Montgomery and the American Seventh Army under Lieutenant General George S. Patton Jr.† The British will land on the southeastern tip of Sicily. The Americans will land ashore thirty miles west of the British. In the American Seventh Army are II Corps and a New Provisional Corps. We of the 45th Division are in II Corps with the 1st Division. Commanding II Corps is General Omar Bradley. The New Provisional Corps is commanded by General Geoffrey Keyes.

I reach in my shirt pocket for a notepad and pencil to take notes. Crowded, the men of the First Wave stand shoulder to shoulder. All eyes are on the map of Sicily. I do a quick sketch of Sergeant Benning nearby. Out of C Company,

---

★The US War Department purchased the USS *Leonard Wood* in 1939 before converting it into an attack transport ship. The Navy decommissioned the ship in March 1946.

†The style used for unit designations helps identify their size. Units of division and smaller size (regiment, brigade, battalion, platoon, squad) are usually expressed with ordinals (45th Division, 179th Regiment). Corps designations are usually expressed with Roman numerals (VI Corps) and field armies written out (Seventh Army). In compiling his memoir Brummett Echohawk refers to Second Squad, Third Platoon, and First Battalion to advance his narrative portrayal of the soldiers' exchanges on the field. This book honors Brummett Echohawk's original system, but some passages describing unit operations follow traditional military style.

he had been a cowboy at the Oklahoma City stockyards. Benning is a hard-looking guy with a jutting chin. When addressing his men, he always bellows: "First off . . . I'm the toughest son of a bitch in C Company!" I switch to Sergeant Chauncey Matlock of B Company. Matlock is a Pawnee Indian. There are many Indians in B Company, and most are Pawnees. Except for his burr haircut, Sergeant Matlock resembles the chief on the Indianhead nickel.

I switch back to the map and listen. The 1st Division will land at the seaport town of Gela. On their right will be the 45th. The 45th will hit Scoglitti, a fishing village. The 3rd Division of the New Provisional Corps will land left of the 1st Division at Licata. Paratroops of the 82nd Airborne Division are to drop inland to cut enemy communications lines and block enemy reinforcements to the beach. We will have air cover throughout the landing. The American and British navies will shell the beaches prior to the landings. The officer says the HMS *Nelson* and the HMS *King George*, British battleships, will pour in fire with 16-inch guns.

"Now, Scoglitti, your objective," the officer says, raising his voice and pointing to the village on the map with the cue stick. We listen intently.

We can feel the USS *Leonard Wood* roll slightly. The officer says that the three Regimental Combat Teams (RCTs) that make up the 45th Division will land at Scoglitti. The 180th RCT will be on the left, the 157th RCT on the right. The 1st and 3rd Battalions will land abreast—the 1st on the right and the 3rd on the left, with 2nd Battalion in reserve. The 3rd will take Vittoria eight miles inland. The First Battalion will land, then veer southeast and take the beaches seven miles to Scoglitti. Three miles en route is an enemy garrison,★ Point Zafaglione. The First Battalion, the officer stresses, must take this garrison before it can take Scoglitti. On high ground, the garrison protects Scoglitti. We focus on Point Zafaglione. The USS *Leonard Wood* heaves and creaks. Sapper team leaders are called to a sand table depicting a relief model of the Scoglitti beaches. I am a sapper team leader. The sand table is a work of art, with miniature pillboxes, barbed wire entanglements, and stone walls, painted in natural colors. The First Battalion's beach is designated Yellow Beach. The officer tells us what to expect. He says three hundred yards inland is a small stone wall. Between here and the water are concrete pillboxes, which cover the beach, and fields of barbed wire. The naval barrage will destroy the entanglements and pillboxes. If any are left, it will be up to the sapper teams to finish them. The sappers will be equipped with the same explosives and hardware we trained with at Cape Cod. All will be loaded ahead of time by navy personnel.

★Garrison: a group of troops assigned to a particular location who are given the task of defending the area.

The officer asks if there are any questions. We study the sand table in silence. No questions. The officer puts aside the cue stick, then nods to staff officers. Some are British. A screen rolls down, covering the map of Sicily. The room darkens. A projector whirs. Projected on the screen are aerial photographs of a gleaming white beach. A British officer takes over in a dry and businesslike manner. He states that the Royal Air Force (RAF) has photographed the beaches three times a day for weeks. Shown now is Yellow Beach, where the First Battalion will land. Now, close-ups. Pillboxes are clear, and so are the barbed wire entanglements and the stone wall. Beyond the wall, inland, is a dark field, which the officer says is believed to be a cane field. He says that there has been no increased enemy activity here but that we should expect resistance. Flashing up now is an overall view of the garrison. The British officer emphasizes that we should "jolly well" expect resistance at Point Zafaglione. He cautions that we should be on the lookout for "Yank" paratroopers in the area.

Then the officer calls attention to the fact that Mussolini's fascist soldiers wear a similar color of cotton khaki as Yank paratroopers. The British officer, who talks like David Niven, the English movie star, has made a point. The German Afrika Korps wears this color of khaki too. The British summer uniform is cotton khaki. Only the Americans will be wearing woolen olive drab (ODs). It is well to know this because when hitting the beach there will be a lot of cowboys and Indians with buck fever. The officer states that the aerial photographs should help familiarize one with Point Zafaglione and its terrain. We study the buildings, roads, hills, and trails. Touching the cue stick to various places on the map, he gives the approximate distance from one point to another. The cue stick casts an arrowlike shadow on the bright screen. David Niven continues: "You should expect a fly-ming duel from the Eye-ties as they will be defending their homeland for the first time." He taps the cue stick against the screen for emphasis, holding it to the beach area. "And mark my word, Jerry will bloody well be there in force." The Englishman retrieves the cue stick, leaving us to stare at the screen with the same thought and pulse beat.

"Well, chaps. That's it. . . . Good show!" The projector clicks off. The lights come on. We notice the officer now. A Royal Air Force officer. Thin, medium height. An impressive figure in a starched RAF cotton khaki uniform with silver wings and campaign ribbons. Stepping aside, he nods to the American officer in charge. The American officer comes on like a Fourth of July orator, saying that we will have the honor of being the first Allied troops to set foot on Nazi-held Europe. He states that we will be under the command of General George S. Patton Jr. The officer wrings his hands and eyes us, expecting a reaction. We give none. "H-Hour will be at 0245 hours," he announces. The officer eyes us again. Then he says with heart, "Good luck, men." The staff officers echo the same. The RAF officer steps forward: "I wish you Yanks Godspeed."

The strategy room buzzes. We file out. We've come a long way since September 16, 1940. That's when the 45th Division mobilized into federal service. This National Guard Division was made up of men from Oklahoma, Colorado, New Mexico, and Arizona. The bulk of the 45th is from Oklahoma. Most of us are from small towns. Our B Company is from Pawnee, Oklahoma—an Indian Agency town. We return through the passageways lit with red lights. Sergeant Good Buffalo taps my shoulder. Grinning, he holds up the right hand, palm outward, shakes it, rubs two fingers in a circular motion on the left wrist, then points to me. Indian sign language: "What skin [tribe] are you?" Now, I notice that we Indians appear redder than ever in this red light. We enjoy a private joke. I glance back at the Indian faces in the eerie red light. Yup, Redskins all right . . . wonder what the Geneva Convention says about scalping.*

In the B Company[†] hold, the company commander addresses the men. In cramped quarters, we stand between steel bunks bulging with equipment and weapons. Beneath our feet, the steel deck of the *Leonard Wood* shifts and creaks. Captain Glen I. Lee, who mobilized with B Company, makes no pep talk, for the chips are down. Lee takes pains in explaining the situation. To the officers and noncoms, he stresses leadership. Then Captain Lee orders the platoon leaders to brief their platoons and check last-minute details. Ours is Second Platoon, led by Second Lieutenant Stewart Dobbins. Tall, thin, and slightly buck-toothed, Dobbins was assigned to B Company in 1942. An intelligent man, Lieutenant Dobbins is from Ohio. All sergeants in the platoon are full-blood Indians, except Right Guide Sergeant Robert Stone. Stone served in the National Guard prior to 1940. A sunup-to-sundown farmer, he is tough as a post oak and mean as a jersey bull. The First Squad in the platoon is led by Sergeant William "Last Arrow" Lasley. A Potawatomi Indian, he was one of the top boxers in Oklahoma. Though his eyes reveal otherwise, Last Arrow always smiles when the going gets tough, showing two gold teeth in front.

I have the Second Squad and am the youngest of the sergeants. Leading the Third Squad is Sergeant Floyd "Good Buffalo" Rice. This Pawnee is ramrod

---

*Although some scholars allege that scalping by Native Americans occurred during the war, no sources exist documenting such actions. Interviews conducted with veterans of B Company recall no incidents related to the scalping of the enemy.

[†]Sergeant Echohawk led the Second Squad (~9 men) of the Third Platoon (~42 soldiers) in B Company (62–190 soldiers). The Pawnee Company was assigned to 1st Battalion, 179th Infantry Regiment (Regimental Combat Team), 45th Infantry Division, known as the Thunderbirds. During the invasion of Sicily these units were part of the US Seventh Army.

straight with a barrel chest and slight paunch. He was a college wrestler and foot-ball player. The platoon sergeant is Staff Sergeant Phillip "Shield Chief" Gover. At thirty-seven, Shield Chief is the oldest man in the company. Powerfully built, he too had been a college football player. Intelligent and well respected, this Pawnee had been employed by the US Indian Service in his civilian days.

Lieutenant Dobbins briefs the platoon. We go at midnight. The Navy will load our hardware and explosives ahead of time. The platoon will load into the barge as it has done in amphibious training. Last Arrow and I will be forward behind the ramp. He's left. I'm right. The squads follow, with the Third in the rear. When beaching, the steel ramp will drop like a drawbridge. Leaving, we are to step on the ramp and dash forward. If the barge hangs on a reef, we step past the ramp chain then jump at right angles. No man jumps forward, for a wave could drive the heavy ramp into your back. Time is important. First Wave sappers must move quickly.

Lieutenant Dobbins tells us to double-check explosives when entering the barge. A steel helmet tumbles from a bunk onto the deck as the USS *Leonard Wood* rises, dips, and sways . . . taking us closer to Sicily. The password is sent down: "George Marshall." When confronting anyone on the dark beach you challenge "George." If it is one of our men, he will answer "Marshall." If not—kill him.

The ship's loudspeaker calls chow. The First Wave will be served first. That's us, and this is the last supper. We are served delicious steaks with all the trimmings. We eat standing at chest-high tables. Long tables, they are secured by steel poles, extending from the ceiling to the deck. The ship rolls constantly, causing trays of food to slide. Seasick soldiers sway from the tables, leaving un-eaten food. I steady myself and eat, knowing that this will be the last hot meal until the Lord knows when. I take an untouched steak, salt and pepper it, wrap it in a GI hanky, then stuff it in my shirt. Other Indians do the same. Food is energy . . . and, tomorrow, we'll need it. Back in the B Company hold, things pick up.

Ammunition, hand grenades, and K-rations are issued. We get 176 rounds of ammunition, which is a full cartridge belt plus two bandoliers.* Each man, one grenade. As a sapper team leader, I receive twenty-four blocks of TNT, a roll of tape, 25 feet of primer cord, and two automatic fuses, each with a five-second burn. I tape down the safety lever on my grenade. Don't want it to come loose with all the crawling I expect to do. We load weapons. I pull back the operating rod of my M1, opening the bolt, then press in a new clip. Come daylight . . . I'll be shooting at a human being . . . and will never walk the path of youth again.

---

*A bandolier is a belt with pockets used for holding ammunition issued to infantry soldiers.

I release the operating rod; it clangs forward, sending one round into the chamber. I set the sights for two hundred yards at zero windage. For quick aiming and night shooting, I stick an inch of white tape on top of the barrel and just behind the front sight. I put on my equipment. First, a lightweight gas mask, which is a mask and canister only. The fuses are stuffed into the gas mask carrier. Next, two bandoliers, crisscrossed over the shoulders. TNT is next. In blocks of big "pepper shakers," painted yellow, they are fastened to a "shingle" in two rows, twelve in a row. The shingle has cords at each corner to tie around the neck and waist. This holds TNT to the chest. I coil the primer cord like a lariat, taping it to hold its shape. After stepping inside the loop, it is pulled up, then adjusted above the life belt.

The combat pack is last. The shoulder straps are hooked to the web cartridge belt, which is heavy with ammunition, two canteens of water, wire cutters, and a first aid kit. The cartridge belt, now held up by the shoulder straps, is left unhooked. In an emergency, all can be discarded in one motion. This would leave the all-important life belt, gas mask, and explosives. On my belt is a Pawnee knife. The nine-inch blade is designed for stabbing, slashing, and throwing. There is no hand guard, allowing the knife to set deep in a Plains Indian sheath. The sheath is set under the belt next to the body. Made for mounted warriors of old, the sheath and knife do not hamper the movement of the body but move in unison with it. And there is no chance of the handle snagging brush. Upon drawing the knife, which rides left-center of the body, it is whipped out in one motion with the right hand, cutting edge up. The handle is straight and wrapped tightly with buckskin. When throwing, the knife is thrown by the handle. This ensures speed, control—and accuracy. Knife throwing is a mental thing. It is not "practice makes perfect" but "perfect practice makes perfect." I also carry a small knife at the small of my back.

This night, the First Wave men come out with all kinds of fighting knives: the Arkansas toothpick, the Bootleg frog sticker, the Blacksmith special (a dirk made from a heavy file), and the single-edge hunting knife. All of us have black, 15-inch bayonets, whetstoned to razor sharpness. In the combat pack are a raincoat, extra socks, handkerchiefs, soap, towel, toothbrush, salt tablets, and three days' supply of K-rations, and one mess kit with knife, fork, and spoon. My mess kit contains notepaper, pencils, matches, a Baby Ruth candy bar, a can of shoe polish for waterproofing boots, and a small coil spring, which we full-blood Indians use to pluck our sparse chin whiskers. None of us shave. In the pack too is a mosquito head net, used to protect the face at night from mosquitoes. Attached to the pack is an entrenching tool and scabbard with bayonet. Cradling a tommy-gun with a 20-round clip, Sergeant Shield Chief checks the platoon. He carries no knife, but stuck in his belt is a hatchet, which he calls his tomahawk. The Second Platoon is ready.

"The new M1-Garand Rifle," September 1942.

We settle. Crowded in the aisles, we lie propped against our packs. Lieutenant Dobbins comes from the officers' quarters and meets with Shield Chief. They talk in low tones. After a while Dobbins leaves. We try to sleep. Smell gun oil, which we use a lot, for we may end up in seawater. Our weapons must be in top working order. Feel the troopship dip and rise . . . seems to be rolling more. I am wearing new trousers and shirt. Was saving them for combat. My boots are saddle-soaped and shined. Got a fresh burr haircut. On my left shoulder is a new Thunderbird, the insignia of the 45th Division. I adjust my pack, TNT, and primer cord to get comfortable. Dang Germans stole our

Indian swastika. The swastika was the original insignia of the division. When
Hitler's Nazis goose-stepped over the face of Europe, the 45th changed from
the swastika to a Thunderbird.

A Thunderbird in gold is featured on a red diamond. The color gold rep-
resents sunshine and good luck. Red is for courage. The Thunderbird is a
mythical bird of the Southwest. Indians say that thunder is the flapping of its
wings and lightning is the flashing of its eyes. Sent by the Great Spirit, the
Thunderbird triumphs over evil. All spruced up, I feel good. General Patton
had his men in North Africa dress neat with ties, leggings, and insignias . . .
wanted to give the men pride. Maybe it did, I don't know.

I remember Patton in the Louisiana maneuvers and North Carolina maneuvers. He always appeared out of nowhere and cussed a blue streak.* The general
did this during our practice landing near Oran last month. It was night. We did
everything according to the amphibious training we got at Cape Cod. But the
Navy landed the Thunderbirds on the wrong beach. The battle dress rehearsal
was a flop. When things go wrong, they really go wrong. Our barge hung on a
reef. We lost time. We had to struggle ashore in deep water. We, the First Wave,
when reaching the beach, found other waves there. Landing barges, motors gun-
ning, were every which way in the surf. Men were yelling and cussing. Artillery,
antitank guns, weapons, trucks, jeeps, ambulances, and bulldozers crowded the
beach. Making things worse were curious Arab locals (whom we referred to as
"Ay-rabs") at the beach with carts, camels, donkeys, and a herd of sheep.

General Patton appeared. Knew it was him when catching a glimpse of his
pearl-handled guns in the dark. He was mad as a wet hornet. General Patton
tore into the men, cussing. Now, General Patton's voice was high-pitched and
weak. The voice did not fit the man. No one knew who he was. Tempers
were short. Wrestling with equipment and soaked in seawater, a GI exploded,
"Who in the gotdamned hell are you?" Then the GI, seeing it was General
Patton, gulped: "Oh . . . Sir!" Things got unscrambled fast. Our Indian Platoon
landed near a highway.

An "Ay-rab" came by riding a donkey and waving a long stick. He grunted
"Uh-dee, uh-dee!" as he whacked the donkey's rump with the stick. We Pawnees roared laughing. By coincidence, uh-dee is a Pawnee expression that de-
notes reprimand and disgust. Just then General Patton, still fuming, strode from
the beach to his command car. He heard our laughter and lit into us, cussing
up a storm. Now, in Indian country there is no bad-mouthing. No cuss words
exist in the language of the American Indian. We water-soaked Pawnees look
at the general with pearl-handled guns and utter "Uh-dee!"

---

*The Louisiana and Carolina Maneuvers were war games designed to test the wartime
abilities of United States Army personnel.

I hope this Sicily landing comes off better than the practice landing back at North Africa . . . hope the Brass got all the bugs out. Time drags. I say to myself in Pawnee, *Ti-ku-skipi* (I am sleepy). I close my eyes. *Ti-ku-skipi . . . Ti-ku-skipi*. This Friday night, July 9, is a long night. The USS *Leonard Wood* continues to roll, plowing through a restless Mediterranean Sea. A hornlike buzzer sounds: general quarters. We spring to life. The buzzer blares in prolonged bursts. The pulse quickens. Blares like an emergency. Through a forest of steel pipes and rods that secure the tightly spaced bunks, B Company is an activity of arms, elbows, legs, steel helmets, packs, M1s, tommy-guns, Springfield .03s, Browning Automatic Rifles, bazookas, mortars, and light machine guns. The buzzer stops. The loudspeaker tells all hands to stand by for the troops to disembark. I adjust my pack, TNT, primer cord, and life preserver belt.

Sergeant Shield Chief bellows: "Sergeant Last Arrow! Sergeant Echohawk! Sergeant Good Buffalo! Your men ready?"

"Ready!" we answer.

Good Buffalo adds, "*Aw-huh!*" (Yes) then gives a spirited "yes" in sign language. Other platoons sound off.

Sergeant Shield Chief turns to Lieutenant Dobbins, who has now joined the platoon. "Second Platoon is ready, Sir!" He snaps a salute. Lieutenant Dobbins returns it. In platoon order, the sergeants are at the head of their squads. I glance back. We are a mass of steel helmets, weapons, and bulging equipment.

We sway in unison with the roll of the ship, and we stand like packhorses, harnessed and ready. Two officers come down the ladder to our hold. They talk to Captain Lee. We wait. And wait. Men fidget with equipment. After a while, we unsling rifles. There are sighs. The old army game—hurry up and wait.

"Now hear this!" blares the loudspeaker. "H-Hour is postponed. H-Hour will be 0345. Now hear this. H-Hour will be 0345 hours. . . ." We uncoil. The hold buzzes. We slide out of our equipment, then lie down again. It is learned that the sea is too rough for landing barges. Might be getting rough for the big ships, too . . . and, we are packed in the hold below the water line. Maybe, I got claustrophobia . . . this makes me nervous. We couldn't get out of here if something happened . . . remember coming over; German submarines jumped our convoy near the Canary Islands. All ships zigzag routinely in a convoy to avoid being a target for the German U-boats, but now they zigzag more than ever as American destroyers hunt down Nazi submarines. Though the action was miles away, the explosions of American depth charges could be felt against the hull of the *Leonard Wood*. Being in the bowels of a troopship with things happening out there is scary.

I listen to the sounds of the heavily loaded USS *Leonard Wood* churning through the sea. Sounds like we are in a giant boiler room. I look at my watch.

It's after midnight. A few men talk in low voices. After a while, it is graveyard quiet. *Ti-ku-skipi* (I am sleepy). I drop off to sleep. The hornlike buzzer: *general quarters*. We get to our feet and grunt into our packs. Here and there a helmet bangs and rolls on the steel deck. We're going . . . going for sure this time. Fear grips me.

Over the rustling and shuffling activity comes the voice of Sergeant Shield Chief: "Last Arrow! Echohawk! Good Buffalo! Are you ready?"

"*Aho!*" we reply, which is an old Indian expression for "agreed."

Other platoon sergeants sound off. The hold rustles with activity. This time there is no waiting. We ascend an iron ladder in company order: Company Headquarters, First Platoon, Second Platoon, Third Platoon, and Fourth Platoon, which is the machine gun and mortar platoon. In single file, we move through passageways lit with red lights. We step through watertight doorways. Sailors stand by to man the steel doors. Each sailor pipes up, "Good luck." B Company emerges topside and into the open air. It is dark.

We can hear the sea surge against the hull of the ship, and we feel the moisture. Motors hum. Winches and cables creak. Chains rattle. Metal clanks against metal. Landing barges are swung into position at the railing. Navy personnel guide us to our respective barges. The ship isn't rolling now, and the fresh air feels good.

The loudspeaker: "All right! First Wave, boat one! First Wave, boat two! First Wave, boat three! First Wave. . . !" Army and naval personnel supervise loading.

Lieutenant Dobbins sounds off: "Second Platoon, load!" At the railing and near our barge is a chaplain. I see the small silver cross on his helmet. He shakes hands with all the men he can, saying, "God bless you and watch over you."

B Company legs over the side, which is latticed with heavy cargo rope, then clump into a swaying LCP (Landing Craft Personnel). A Company, C Company, and D Company do the same. The noise topside is continuous. We check explosives and hardware. The loudspeaker blares: "Lower away!" The barge jerks, then starts down. Standing shoulder to shoulder, we number about forty. With us is one medical aid man, a Choctaw Indian. He is known in the platoon as "Medicine Man." We descend along the side of the massive hull of the ship. In the blackness, a swell lifts and drops us. Released from cables, the LCP jerks as its motor fires.

The coxswain guns the motor, getting us under way.

Sergeant Stone hollers: "Take it away, Leon!"*

Others chime in: "*Aw-huh,* San Antone!"

Someone adds, "Sani flush!"

---

*The coxswain is responsible for steering the LCP.

Corporal Leading Fox shouts: "Katie bar the door!" Then he gives a piercing war cry.

Medicine Man yells: "Circle the wagons. Indi'ns are coming!"

As we sputter into the darkness, I look back at the *Leonard Wood*. She brought the First Battalion of the 179th RCT across the Atlantic from Hampton Roads, Virginia. We left on June 4. I will remember these days on the high seas. This Indian saw porpoises, flying fish, and hammerhead sharks. Some guys saw a whale. Sometimes, at night, a big silver moon appeared over the watery horizon. Sailors said it was silver because the atmosphere was clear at sea. Inland it's reddish because of dust from the earth. On June 24, we steamed through the Strait of Gibraltar. Saw the Rock of Gibraltar. What a sight!

2

Bureau of Indian Affairs

The Bureau of Indian Affairs (BIA) was established as a federal agency as part of the Department of the Interior in 1824. The primary goal, like the treaties before that failed, was to enhance the quality of life and "carry out the responsibility to protect the assets of American Indians, Indian tribes, and Alaska Natives." For the soldier on the front lines, serving with distinction, the phrase "Bureau of Indian Affairs" was used to describe the upper echelon of the military chain of command when orders were not clear or created unnecessary dire consequences.*

Our LCP bucks and rolls. Sergeant Stone hollers, "Ride 'im, cowboy! Outta chute number one!" The night is throbbing with the sound of landing craft. That's the 179th. Out there too are the 157th RCT and the 180th RCT. This invasion will be some show. Aboard our LCP are forty pounds of TNT, five bangalores, and two rolls of mesh wire, which we call "chicken wire." The TNT is for destroying pillboxes.† For blowing a path through a field of barbed wire, we have bangalore torpedoes. Each resembles an iron pipe, four inches in diameter and five feet long. Connected, and shoved pole-like under entanglements, the bangalores, now twenty-five feet long, can blow a wide path in the wire. The chicken wire is rolled around and fixed to a four-foot iron bar, forming a spool. At the other end, and on top, is another iron bar. Two men lug the chicken wire to the entanglements. They drop the top bar that anchors

---

*A vocational journal published by the BIA titled *Indians at Work* featured Echohawk and other American Indians of the 45th. The journal asserts that American Indians made for outstanding soldiers due to their "enthusiasm for fighting." Brummett Echohawk is provided as an example, described as "a 126-pound Pawnee [and] judo expert who, in a rough-and-tumble battle, could snap the back of an opponent twice his size. Sergeant Echohawk daily practices taking knives and clubs away from 'enemies' with the same fervor that Hoppe practices billiard masses." *Indians at Work* 10, no. 2-6.

†Pillboxes are concealed fortifications, often equipped with special holes through which to fire weapons.

the spool. Grasping the inner bar, the two men heave the spool over and across the barbed wire. The chicken wire unravels, forming a mesh wire footbridge.

Our barge bucks like a mustang. In the darkness, we catch a glimpse of another barge nearby. Aboard a sailor at the stern holds up a white board with the number four on it. He calls toward our LCP, "Are you number three?"

Our sailor at the stern answers, "No!" Another LCP appears. Then another. After much milling, the barges link up according to number. In single file like ducks, the LCPs churn in a wide circle. While the sea has calmed some, it is still rough for barges, especially when executing circling maneuvers. Now and then our barge idles to maintain interval.

This causes it to rock. Banging elbows and kneecaps, we thump into each other like football players making a goal-line stand. Then our barge sputters forward again. Pitching, splashing, and swaying constantly, we get seasick. Bangalore torpedoes roll and clatter. The chicken wire unravels. Loose, too, is the pack of TNT, which shifts and slides. Doubled over and vomiting, we wrestle with the hardware and explosives as we take on seawater. The miserable rodeo splashes on. Spewing vomit and doused with seawater, we hang in the saddle. The night air is filled with throbbing motors. More invasion craft rendezvous, forming circles. The slow-turning whirlpools of barges bide time until H-Hour.

After a while, the barges curl from the circle and pull abreast, forming a current. The current expands as barge motors roar. Now the First Wave of the American Seventh Army floods forward toward the beaches. On a straight course now, the rodeo is over. We secure hardware and explosives. Like old-time cavalry, the assault barges advance abreast and in a wavering line. Here and there a barge jumps ahead then pulls back in formation again. The cavalry line advances at a walk and champs at the bit. The barges rev motors in short bursts as if snorting. As the line is dressed, the cavalry then moves into a canter.

A destroyer looms at the right. It cuts the waves and glides up with a muffled roar. The destroyer escorts us inland through the early morning darkness. We can make out blue lights on her. Beautiful. A feeling of strength rises. The destroyer shepherds us in for several minutes. "Men!" booms a loudspeaker from the bridge: "Good luck . . . and God bless you!" The destroyer falls back from the line of barges, then fades into the darkness. Motors cough and roar. Then the cavalry springs into a gallop. I think of things we got to do. I picture in my mind the beach, barbed wire entanglements, pillboxes, sand dunes, and the enemy. There is a violent tearing of the air. We flinch as red balls of fire comet over and streak for the beach. Seconds later comes the sound of naval gunfire miles behind us. More red balls of fire flash over. The fireballs appear to slow down and float inland, becoming smaller and smaller until they look like a string of glowing red beads in the black night.

The dark coast of Sicily flickers and rumbles. Far behind we hear salvo after salvo.* The night air is filled with high-explosive naval shells whooshing over. Some projectiles streak by like giant Roman candles. Others pass, sounding like an express train. They skim over the dark swells like chunks of burning coals. We keep bearing in. Ahead are the beaches of Scoglitti, flashing and thundering like a summer electrical storm. We tense up. It's like we are in a canoe caught in a current that pulls us closer and closer to a thundering waterfall—and sure death. Then the naval barrage lifts. We keep bearing in. An enemy searchlight comes on. The searchlight lances the black night before it points a white finger out to sea. It probes, slashes, then picks us up. My heart pounds. "Son of a bitch!" screams the coxswain. We are framed in white light. Though the barge is bounding forward, we appear to be standing still. Salt spray twinkles like diamonds in the brilliant light. I glance back at the men. They crouch wide-eyed, mouths agape, drenched with seawater. Any minute now, we'll get blown out of the water. I am not a brave man . . . got to control my fear . . . got to control my fear. Then the light jerks away and sweeps the oncoming First Wave. What's that? An airplane! He's going after the searchlight. There is a crunching roar. The light goes out. We breathe easy; it is one of our Navy planes.

The First Wave kicks into high gear. The cavalry horses, given their heads, charge hell-bent for leather. Drawing sabers now, the LCP races toward the beach. Platoon Sergeant Shield Chief stands and shouts: "Fix bayonets!" Equipment rustles as bayonets click. Motors roar wide open. We bound over the swells. Wind and spray whip into our faces. Shield Chief gives a Pawnee war cry, "*A-a'e—ay, kiddi didde didde, kidde didde didde!*"

There is a piercing Cheyenne war whoop followed with "It's a good day to die!" Rising too is a Creek Indian war cry—the gobble of a wild tom turkey. From an adjacent barge comes the shriek of a gander goose and the neighing of a stud horse. Heard from another barge, hell-bent for leather, are cowboy yells.

"Stand by!" yells the coxswain. We buck over swells. "One hundred yards!" I finger the twenty-four blocks of TNT on my chest. "Seventy-five yards!" Fear grips me. "Fifty yards!" We hit something before bodies crunch forward. The barge hangs up and swings sideways. "Son of a bitch!" cries the coxswain. A wave slams us broadside. Bangalore torpedoes, chicken wire, TNT, steel helmets, and men clatter and clump. The coxswain guns the motor, trying to break free. Another wave wallops us. We almost capsize. I grip the life belt and prepare to ditch. Rocking violently, we bust elbows and kneecaps. Losing time, we're losing time. The coxswain guns the motor again and cries, "Son of a bitch!"

---

*A salvo is the simultaneous firing of weapons in battle. Typically used to soften defenses prior to amphibious landings during World War II.

"Get us outta here!" Shield Chief shouts. "Get us outta here!" Chains rattle.

The ramp drops. Sergeant Last Arrow and I, who are at the front of the barge, step on the ramp and jump into the water. A wave hits. "Son of a bitch!" The barge rocks, creaks, and rattles. Men splash into the sea. I struggle forward, holding my rifle above my head. The water is deep in places, so I bend my knees and "frog" forward. Ahead things are burning, giving the sea a red glow. I glance back. Men are barely visible in the dark surf. In shallow water now, I splash to the beach with hurdling strides, then dive to the sand at the water's edge. Fires blaze. The air is filled with smoke. A wave washes over my back, bulging my shirt with seawater. It's now or never.

Scared, I rise and shout, "Second Squad! Follow me!" I move forward.

A machine gun fires a long burst, but it is far down the beach. I reach the barbed wire entanglements. Much has been destroyed by the Navy barrage. I drop the life belt, then remove the primer cord. It's still coiled like a lariat; I loop the primer cord over my left shoulder and move through the shattered entanglements. My squad follows. The machine gun does not fire anymore. Here and there are shell craters with the smell of cordite. I keep my M1 and bayonet pointed forward with my fingers on the trigger. Fire and bellowing smoke create ghostlike images that slip soundlessly across the red-tinted dunes.

"Echohawk!" the voice of Shield Chief comes.

"Here!" I answer.

"Hold it!" Shield Chief calls, hustling up with his tommy-gun ready. "*Ka-rusu-terit?*" (Did you see that?)

"*Kah-kih.*" (No.)

"But it looks like the wire is blown away." Shield Chief is winded, as it was a struggle coming ashore. He is soaked with seawater from head to foot; his wet face reflects the red glow of the burning beach. "The pillboxes might have been destroyed by the Navy barrage, but we'll find out. Tell your men to hold and keep their eyes open. Don't bunch up. Hold till I can get everybody together."

"*Aho.*"

Shield Chief hurries off.

"Second Squad hold. Keep your eyes open. Don't bunch up!" Crackling fires send up red sparks and threads of burning grass. Odd, there's no shooting. Wonder what happened to that machine gun? Where's Lieutenant Dobbins? Wonder where the First and Third Platoons are?

Shield Chief appears with Last Arrow and Good Buffalo. "Let's move," he says. "Can't find Dobbins or anybody. We'll get killed if we sit and wait." Shield Chief looks at me, then nods in the direction of the dunes. "Brummett, go first. Bill, your squad next. Good Buffalo, follow. The company is bound to be near. We lost valuable time hung up on that reef. Send out a scout."

"Short Nose!" I call out for Private First Class Gilbert "Short Nose" Curtis, also known as "Cheyenne," who is a full-blood Cheyenne. He comes. "Lead out," I order. Cheyenne lifts his rifle to high part and moves out. I wait for interval. "Second Squad, let's go." The area is dark and smoky, the sand is deep. The pillboxes . . . they should be here, right here . . . the gunners . . . they're lying low and waiting for us. Maybe they were killed by the Navy barrage. Shield Chief positions himself at my left but keeps interval. I can barely see Cheyenne in the darkness ahead. Behind, I hear plodding feet and water jiggling in canteens. What the heck is wrong? No shooting. Nothing. Dang, this doesn't make sense . . . all that hard amphibious training and. . . . A man on a knoll! Right front, silhouetted against a red glow, crouching. That's not Cheyenne. "George!" I challenge. No answer.

Shield Chief and I both shout. "George!" We click off the safety locks and take aim.

"Marshall! Marshall! Marshall!"

"What's wrong with you, soldier?" Shield Chief explodes in anger. We check him out. A second lieutenant. He is badly shaken; the officer gapes at us, then hurries away without saying a word. "*Uh-dee! Uh-dee!*" growls Shield Chief. We uncoil.

Dang, we almost killed him. We lock our pieces, then push on. Got to keep contact with Short Nose. "What was all that hollering about?" comes the voice of Short Nose.

"Some second lieutenant, lost. Couldn't think of the password," I answer.

"We almost killed that Fort Benning idiot!" Shield Chief adds angrily.

"In the dark these white guys couldn't find their butt with both hands," the Cheyenne scoffs.

"*Aho*, for sure," Shield Chief says with his voice no longer reflecting anger.

We keep going. The ground is solid now. No sand. Shield Chief comes over. "Brummett, keep moving. I'm dropping back to see if I can find our own second lieutenant. It's just not the night for second lieutenants."

"*Aho*, for sure." Shield Chief fades into the darkness. The enemy . . . they could still be here. Probably pulled back to get away from the Navy barrage. But hollering "George" at the top of our lungs could stir anybody. Dry shocks of grass here, looks like prairie grass, buffalo grass. Still no pillboxes. The intelligence must have been wrong.

Cheyenne stops ahead. I signal "hold." Short Nose is crouched and poised like a bird dog. I slip forward. "What's up?" I ask, searching the darkness.

"I think we are in the wrong area," Cheyenne offers, lowering his M1 and bayonet. "'Member we're s'posed to come to a stone wall and cane field after the dunes . . . well, here's a field, but no stone wall. This is no cane . . . looks like kafir corn."

Short Nose stoops and takes a close look. "The stalks and leaves look like Indi'n corn."

"Maybe Intelligence has never seen Indi'n corn," I jest.

"They ought to go to the Anadarko Powwow and find out," Short Nose chuckles.★ "Or take in the Yuchi Green Corn Dance," I remark, stepping into the field for a look.†

This is a big field, with stocks just over knee high. "Echohawk, what's up?" calls Shield Chief, coming up. "Phil, there's no stone wall. And this is no cane field." Phillip Shield Chief lowers his tommy-gun, then studies the area. "No stone wall . . . and this resembles good ol' Indi'n corn. That's not important but what is, is that there is no stone wall."

"If we only had fried bread to go with this Indi'n corn," I chuckle. "I'd settle for good Indi'n camp coffee."

Short Nose adds, "Camp coffee brewed over an open fire of blackjack wood."

"Quiet," Shield Chief says. He removes his steel helmet. Cocks his head to listen. "No sounds. No stone wall. No pillboxes . . . they could have been knocked out by Navy gunfire. Things are just not right."

"Musta bin the storm," Short Nose offers. "Bet the Navy set us off in the wrong place like they did in North Africa."

Shield Chief puts his helmet on. "Right or wrong, I think we found a soft spot. Let's take the ball and drive. The rest of the company can't be too far away. Cheyenne, lead out."

In B Company, Short Nose is known as "Cheyenne." He is the grandson of a famous warrior, Chief Roman Nose. Proud of his tribe, Short Nose reminds all that it was the Cheyenne who defeated General Custer at the Battle of the Little Bighorn. I'll buy that. Cheyenne moves out. We follow with interval. In the distance, hills can be seen. Ahead I can barely spot Cheyenne—he is one brave Indian. On strange land, and in enemy territory, and he takes off like he is going to a powwow. Now the ground has stones from the size of marbles to baseballs. There are dark forms of cactus. Moving, I can see the horizon now. I glance back and see the trail of shadowy figures of men who follow. I pay attention to the sounds of the night, for Pawnees say the sounds of the night reveal more than the eye can by day.

The Morning Star is slightly to our right. We're heading northeast. The star twinkles brightly. Pawnees have a ceremony about this star. *Hupiri-Kucu*, the

---

★Sitting fifty miles southwest of Oklahoma City, Anadarko is a city in Caddo County.

†The Green Corn Festival (or Green Corn Ceremony) is a Native American celebration and religious ceremony. The dance is held by the Creek, Cherokee, Seminole, Yuchi, and Iroquois Indians as well as other Native American tribes.

Morning Star, is a messenger of *Atius Tirawa* (Supreme Being, Father). It is man with his body painted red. He wears a red downy eagle plume and signals *Tirawa*'s creatures of a coming new day. There, above the star, is a tiny cloud puff, making it look like a red downy eagle plume. *Tirawa* is creating a new day with *Hupiri-Kucu* signaling. The horizon looms broader. I keep Cheyenne in sight.

"Whatcha think, Brummett?" Cheyenne calls from ahead.

"Everything seems okay. Everybody's following. Keep moving!"

"*Aho!*"★

We expand interval in the dawn light. Communication is no problem as we use Indian sign language. *Hupiri-Kucu* reflects like a distant signal mirror. The Pawnee Morning Star ceremony is sacred. It involves sacred bundles, pipe, prayer, and songs. The songs are of *Tirawa*'s universe and his gift of life in a coming new day. At dawn back home in Pawnee, Oldman White Elk would be singing the Morning Song. Wearing a breech cloth and moccasins, he would slap his bare chest lightly with the palm of his hands in a drumbeat rhythm. Facing the breaking day, White Elk would sing with tears in his eyes; he would be thanking *Atius Tirawa* for a new day and the gift of life. And in the dawn sky, wearing a red eagle plume, would be *Hupiri-Kucu*, signaling: a new day is coming. I tell myself, *A new day is coming. A new day is coming.*

Ahead, hills of burnt amber bump against a rose-colored sky like a quiet herd of feeding buffalo. A soundless countryside is flooded in red light. Night shadows surrender to the advancing light of day. The air is cool as the Morning Star fades. Mother Earth awakens. Day breaks, and for the first time I see Sicily. Heck, it looks like west Texas. The land rolls with barren hills and very few trees. What trees there are resemble mesquites. Lots of cactus and dry shortgrass. Good for longhorns and Brahman, but no life. Something's wrong. I signal "hold." I pass the word for Sergeant Shield Chief. The men belly down and wait.

A big man, all shoulders and chest, Shield Chief approaches at a running walk. "What's up?" Shield Chief asks.

"Nothing. That's the trouble. Nothing is right. You think we ought to keep going like this? Where is Lieutenant Dobbins?" We drop to one knee and crouch to keep from skylining ourselves.

"The last time I saw Dobbins was in the barge when our guys were trying to get out of there," Shield Chief says. "Stuck on a reef, the barge was rocking real bad. Might have turned over. That's the last time I saw Sergeant Stone, too. Probably went to link up with the rest of the company and got lost.

★The Morning Star ritual is sacred to Pawnees, especially members of the Skidi (or Skiri) Band (meaning "Wolf Pawnee"). This band exclusively practiced this ritual among the tribe. Brummett Echohawk was a member of the Skidi Band of Pawnee.

The 179th Regiment enters Scoglitti. Image courtesy of the 45th Infantry Division Museum.

Probably lots of people lost, like that second lieutenant back there we almost shot. He was wandering around lost."

Shield Chief leans his tommy-gun against his knee, for none of us lays a weapon on the ground. He removes a canteen and takes a mouthful of water. He holds the water in his mouth, studies a while, rinses, then swallows, making the best of one drink. Kneeling, we cast long shadows in the early morning sunlight. "According to the briefing, we turn right southeast, after landing, then hit the enemy garrison, Point Zafaglione, then Scoglitti. The garrison is supposed to be three miles from the beach. Now, we can't be too far off the mark. I figure we can drive straight ahead, northeast, swing wide right, then attack the garrison from behind. However, there is one thing: we're not alone. The rest of the company and battalion will be riding hard to get there too. I'd much rather carry the fight to the enemy than sit and wait. Any minute now, the Luftwaffe will bomb the beaches."★ Shield Chief replaces his canteen. "We'll link up, we are bound to. All right, let's go hunting."

"*Ru-ra-chi-ra-u.*" (All right.)

I hurry forward to Cheyenne. I find him brushing the ground slightly with his hand and picking up tiny pebbles. I kneel beside him. He has two tiny

---

★The Luftwaffe was the aerial warfare branch of the German military in World War II.

pebbles in his hand. He puts one in his mouth, then gives me the other. I put it in my mouth and under my tongue. This keeps one from thirsting. "Had to stop and ask Phil what he thinks we should do. Dang, nothing seems right," I tell Cheyenne. "Phil says according to the briefing we are to turn southeast, take the enemy garrison, and then Scoglitti. The garrison should be three miles away; less now, probably. Phil thinks we can drive straight ahead, swing wide right and hit the garrison from behind. He says we can't be too far off and that we're bound to link up with the others. Go ahead. Use your own judgment."

"Okay," Cheyenne replies, glancing eastward. "I was thinkin' the same thing Phil was."

Short Nose stands, looks at the morning sun and the horizon. "Y'ah," he nods. "Y'ah, I can find it."

"Good," I respond, getting to my feet. "Where's Lieutenant Dobbins?"

"Lost. *Wuh.*" (*Wuh* is an Indian expression that applies to a comical situation.)

"And where's Stone?"

"Lost. *Wuh.*" Short Nose checks his M1, then takes off.

I jiggle the pebble in my mouth and wait for interval before flagging the men forward. Cheyenne moves like a prairie wolf, looking in all directions. He pauses, sniffs the air, and listens before continuing. Now and then like the wary wolf, he turns quickly to keep from being taken from behind. Short Nose veers from the line of march to investigate the folds of the ground. Then he trots back on course to maintain the overall pace. The morning sun feels good, as my uniform is still damp from seawater. The sky is clear, and I can see a long way. The land rolls with dry grass, like horse country. *I got a feeling we're too far ahead. Wonder where A and C Company are . . . wonder where—*Cheyenne dives for cover. Planes! I hit the ground. They flash over. Black crosses on the fuselage. Messerschmitt! The Luftwaffe! Hedge-hopping for the beach. Shield Chief was right. "Keep moving!" Shield Chief shouts. I spit the pebble out of my mouth, rise, and advance. I check the squad for interval and make sure they are in a staggered formation. Don't want an enemy shell hitting them bunched up or automatic fire raking them in a straight line.

We've worked on squad tactics and stay alive by Indian fighting. I'm not a hard-bitten sergeant. I explain, then lead. The men watch me. If I stop, they stop. I go down, they go down. I move, they move. When I signal, they hustle. The enemy is reacting now. I feel my heart pounding. Like a red-tailed hawk I scan the horizon for telltale movement. We reach high ground with cactus and mesquites.

Cheyenne signals me forward. I respond quickly. "Road," Cheyenne says, searching the area. "Thought we ought to check it. Might have something to do with the garrison." Ahead is a small dirt road, crossing our front. Fifty yards to the right, it turns parallel with our line of march. It hasn't been used, we learn, after reading the ground. Green grass with morning dew will glow when stepped on; so will dry grass, but it will flatten. Line the glow with the angle of the sun, and it will show the direction in which a person was walking. In this case, only one person passed here, running. It was a farmer, likely.

"What is it?" Shield Chief asks, trotting up with tommy-gun ready.

"Road, Phil. Might be a garrison road," I tell him.

"Communications road," Shield Chief says, looking it over. He walks around nearby mesquite trees and eyes the top branches like a hungry coyote that has treed a possum. "No communication wires. But it will lead to a main garrison road, it's bound to. You and Chey' watch it. Okay, move."

Cheyenne guides on the road but does not walk on it. I look ahead of him, left and right. Check for odd shadows under the mesquites. In the folds of the ground, I watch for a metallic glint that could mean a rifle barrel. A big explosion suddenly erupts. We hit the ground. A crack of thunder rocks us before another explosion. I take a quick "prairie-dog" look. Two clouds of dust mushroom up. Right front, three hundred yards. I hear the whooshing sound around me. I press my face to the ground. Thunder again. That's not field artillery, that's the Navy. The sound of low-flying airplanes. German fighter planes! Dang, if the Messerschmitts don't kill us, our Navy will. The Navy shelling stops. I raise and see Cheyenne. He motions "come." I signal the squad, hold, then sprint forward. Cheyenne has moved to the road and hides in tall cactus.

"The garrison!" Short Nose yells.

There in a valley is a long building, two stories. There, too, are smaller buildings with red-tile roofs. I turn and holler for Shield Chief. I crawl across the road for a better look.

Running hard, Shield Chief comes up and hits the ground.

"Phil! The garrison!" I call.

He scoots quickly across the road on his hands and knees. Shield Chief is wide-eyed and anxious. "That's it! Point Zafaglione!" he exclaims, without taking his eyes off the buildings. "Cheyenne, go get Last Arrow and Good Buffalo."

"*Aho!*"

"Phil, why do you suppose the Navy was shelling this road? There's nothing here."

"What happened is the Navy shelled this road to block enemy action, and to isolate the garrison," Shield Chief explains. Then there are explosions among the buildings. We see flashes of yellow, followed by rumblings and clouds of dust. "Now, the Navy is zeroing in on the garrison." Last Arrow and Good Buffalo come running. They zip across the road like a pair of roadrunners.

"The garrison! Point Zafaglione!" Shield Chief says with excitement. Last Arrow and Good Buffalo poke their heads up. They settle behind a few paces away to avoid bunching up.

They eye the garrison like hunters who have dry-gulched a ten-point buck. Shield Chief turns to us. "We'll swing right and hit them. They'll be stunned from the Navy barrage." He glances at the sun. "Made good time, even though we got delayed at the beach. Other units are probably already there in front of the garrison and waiting for the barrage to lift. The enemy saw the barrage hit this road, and they won't expect American troops here. And since we came up behind the garrison, we can surprise them. But we got to mount our ponies and ride before the enemy recovers."

"Phil," Last Arrow pipes up. "What if the Navy sees us coming from inland? They could take us for enemy troops coming to reinforce the garrison. The Navy would blow us off the map."

"Now, the Navy was shooting at prearranged targets. The Navy has spotter planes. They'd send one to check on us first. Remember how they launched one and knocked out that searchlight when we were about to hit the beach?"

"Okay, Chief. If you say so," Last Arrow concedes.

"Then let's take off at a high lope. Echohawk, you and Good Buffalo attack abreast. Bill, follow in reserve. Move!"

I zip back and signal my squad, pumping a fist upward three times—the signal for "on the double." They come up, scramble across the road, and belly down with interval. Good Buffalo maneuvers his squad into position at my right. Shield Chief settles between my squad and Good Buffalo's. The squad watches me, and I watch Shield Chief. He stands and bellows: "Bayonets! Gut the first ones. Show them we mean business! Second Platoon, let's go!" We advance.

About five hundred yards to the garrison. Not much cover. Cheyenne falls back to his regular position in the squad. I lead. I check for interval. Good Buffalo is at my right, thirty-five yards away, walking with a deliberate pace; his men follow. All bayonets point upward. We move down a slope and cross a shallow wash before emerging onto a field of dry grass and cactus. Small-arms fire at the garrison snaps and pops. Shield Chief begins to trot. We follow and do the same. Dead ahead, a long building, two stories, with many windows, and small buildings with the red-tile roofs. Smoke and white dust veil the garrison. Gunfire erupts: our guys are attacking. Men in gray-green uniforms come out of the main building. They appear to be regrouping but are facing the other way.

We keep dogtrotting. Shield Chief extends both arms outward, signaling "move abreast." Good Buffalo signals his squad. I do the same. Second and Third Squads swing abreast. Shield Chief gives the Pawnee war cry: "*Kiddi didde didde, Kidde didde didde!*" We lower bayonets and charge. The enemy soldiers turn in surprise, fire wild shots, and run. We go after them. Some drop weapons, thrust up arms, and jabber.

Short Nose gives a shrieking Cheyenne war cry. "It's a good day to die!"

A gobble of wild tom turkey comes from a Creek Indian, Sam Bear, who says, "*Uks-kotit! Retsu-kih!*" (Kill them! Use knife!)

Shield Chief shouts. Running hard, I go for a red-faced soldier wielding a pistol. He backpedals, whirls, and runs. Everywhere there is shooting, jabbering, and hollering.

More voices: "Hold it!" a voice rings out. "Hold it!"

"Hold it!" Shield Chief shouts, "Hold it!" We break off the attack. Captain Lee emerges from the right, waving his arms as if he were flagging a train. "Hold it! They're giving up. More in the buildings. Let them come out." Enemy soldiers are scattered in the fields. They drop their carbines and raise hands. Others huddle like frightened animals trapped in a prairie fire. More stream out from the buildings. They are Italian soldiers. "Watch them!" Shield Chief commands. "Don't bunch up!" Winded and soaked with sweat, we are still fired up after the running bayonet charge. I pant like a coyote breaking off chase with a jackrabbit.

Beyond the garrison, dark figures of men appear. They advance in three columns. Then they swing abreast and charge. Captain Lee jogs out, shouting: "Hold it! Hold it!" With his carbine at sling, he extends both arms upward and waves frantically. "Hold it!" The Italians look at Captain Lee. We get down to avoid stray shots. Good Buffalo and Shield Chief remain standing. The prisoners look at those of us who have bellied down. They look at the oncoming force. They look at each other. The Italian prisoners think to themselves that perhaps the approaching force are Germans coming to rescue the garrison. They whisper and perk up.

Then: "*Kiddi didde didde, Kidde didde didde,*" followed by a shriek of a gander goose and the neigh of a stud horse. The Italians turn to each other in bewilderment. They look at Good Buffalo. They eyeball Shield Chief, who is as big as Jim Thorpe. With quivering lips, one of them registers, "Americano Indiano!" With eyes bugged white, the fascist soldiers freeze. One drops to his knees, facing us, and cries: "Mussolini sonovabitch! Mussolini sonovabitch!" The attacking force is Sergeant Chauncey Matlock's Third Platoon. Viewed from the "receiving end," Matlock's bayonet charge could break any man. Having seen the signal, Sergeant Matlock brakes the attack.

At the garrison is confusion, milling, and jabbering. Captain Lee establishes order. The prisoners are herded into the open.

"Good Buffalo!" Shield Chief calls. "Your men okay?"

Good Buffalo signs "yes" and then answers, "Okay!"

Shield Chief turns to me. "Echohawk, your men okay?" I sign "yes." Signing "good," Shield Chief then points to the open field: "Move farther out. Watch your flank." Last Arrow, who is in reserve, watches from far behind. Seems like my whole body is shaking after that bayonet charge. I am soaked with sweat. A company runner appears. He says something to Shield Chief before both leave quickly. We get off our feet and drink water.

There is activity inside the buildings. Our guys calling for medics to attend the wounded. B Company men are scattered to our right. I wonder if the company is together now. Shield Chief and Cheyenne seemed to know where the garrison was and homed in on it. Shield Chief's attack was a complete surprise since we hit them in the rear. We watch the fascist soldiers being marched away. They wear gray-green woolen uniforms with wrap leggings that bag at the knees. At the start, some wore small "Mussolini" helmets; now they've discarded them for field caps.★ The Italians are small compared to us. Somehow, I expected their fighting men to be as big as Primo Carnera.† The garrison, with its stone buildings and red roofing, looks like a government school for Indians. Since there is no breeze, a haze of white dust hangs over the buildings, caused by the naval shelling. I reach for a notepad and pencil, deciding I will do a drawing of this before planes roar in from the heavens. And like clockwork: more Messerschmitts! We duck, sweating, realizing it's going to be a long day.

I hear footsteps approach. "Echohawk! Good Buffalo! Over here on the double!" orders Shield Chief as he pumps the "on-the-double" sign to Last Arrow. We squad leaders meet with Shield Chief. We stay a few feet apart to keep from bunching up. Shield Chief says that we are to advance to a road junction on the high ground beyond the garrison. It's about a mile. Enemy troops are believed to be there and could be preparing to jump us. Sergeant Matlock's Third Platoon will be on our right. Captain Lee wants us to move fast.

"Where's Lieutenant Dobbins?" asks Last Arrow.

"They think he is with elements of the First and Fourth Platoon," Shield Chief replies. Part of the First Platoon is with Captain Lee, also strays from Battalion. Lee says Battalion is now getting organized after last night's landing. Battalion is dropping off one company to mop up, and B Company is to swing left. "Okay, Third and First Squad move abreast. Echohawk in reserve. Maintain interval. *Wees-kah-chuh*" (Hurry up).

★During the war, the Italian dictator Benito Mussolini wore the uniform of the Royal Italian Army, often appearing wearing military-style helmets.

†Primo Carnera, nicknamed the "Ambling Alp," was an Italian professional boxer and world champion in the 1930s.

In a short while we are moving at a brisk pace for the high ground. I glance at the sun. We've swung in an arc and hit the garrison at the rear, and now we're heading east-southeast. I'm glad we didn't sit and wait. The Luftwaffe would have torn us to pieces. Wonder what happened to that officer we almost killed. Guess a lot of guys got lost, and maybe some drowned in the surf.

More dry grass; it is knee deep now. We flush grasshoppers and flying insects, sending them springing about. I don't feel as tense now since my squad isn't leading. In reserve, I move behind other squads at point ready to assist as needed. Walking at a consistent pace, I follow what resembles a wagon trail that doglegs in front of us, then straightens. We guide on it but don't walk on it. We arrive at what looks like an orchard. In the orchard are bundles of wood stacked in neat piles. The wood has been cut in lengths of four feet, thick as pick handles. Each bundle is about three feet thick. The bundles resemble the bundles of wood used in the peyote religion by Indians of the Southern Plains. During peyote meetings, the bundles are stacked near the entrance of the tepee. In the tepee is an earthen fireplace. Shaped by hand, and partially encircling the fire, it is called the Moon. Resembling a new moon, it is four feet across and twelve inches high at the center. The wings of the moon taper to points. With ceremony, the peyote is placed on the apex of the moon. The wood is set in ceremonial order within the moon and fired. The bundles of wood here give a good feeling, and also a feeling that a peyote tepee is near, where there is peace.

Shooting surprises us from ahead. We hit the ground as gunshots that sound like .22s ring out. I recognize that they are not ours. I listen and sweat. I hear Shield Chief calling me. I acknowledge seeing he is ahead and behind a knoll. Shield Chief points left and swings his arm in a hooking motion. Fingers extended, he taps his rib cage, signaling: "Move left, hit flank." I break left. "Second Squad, follow me!" We dash through the orchard and sidestep bundles of peyote wood. Ahead is a ridge with cactus. Scrambling, we make it to the top.

Beyond is a dry gully; I follow it upstream where it bends right. We keep hustling, sounding like pack ponies galloping up a dry gulch. The gully flattens, then forks with the main branch, turning left. I take the right. It leads to the high ground. Coming to the high ground, I remember that I must not skyline myself. I hit the ground and crawl fast. I hear the squad thump to the ground, following close behind; using a grove of cactus as a blind I race forward.

Ahead are sandbags and freshly turned dirt. I hold as fear hits me. I raise my M1 to shooting level, then advance. On the ground is field equipment and bloodstained bandages. I pass shallow trenches and huge shell craters. In one crater are two dead soldiers. Badly torn, the bodies lie face down, covered with white dust and clods of dirt. I stare momentarily, then check for tripwires that could trigger a mine. I find none. Coming upon more craters, we see they are filled with shattered artillery pieces with old-fashioned wagon wheels. Mussolini helmets lie here and there. Walking near a mangled body, I disturb a swarm of flies. The stench is awful; I keep moving. The squad follows. Advancing further, a road junction appears to our far right. Near it is a grove of trees. From this high ground we can see Last Arrow's and Good Buffalo's men attacking the road junction. From our view they are specks. We turn right for the enemy's flank and the road junction. I look to the right rear. My God, the sea! All kinds of ships. They are miles away on the hazy horizon.

Moving down a long slope, we pick up a road that leads to the junction. At the junction, there's gunfire. I check interval and make sure we are in a staggered formation, ready for any attack. With bayonets pointed forward, we advance with steel springs in our backs. The land rolls with dry grass that stands like wheat.

Someone calls from the right: "Hold it!" A Second Platoon runner flags us down. He looks in every direction, then ducks below the grass line. We wait. I glance back at the high ground, then study our position. We can see the ships at sea from here . . . which also means the Navy can see us too. They may not have been told that we are up here. If they spot activity here, the Navy might blow us to pieces. The way things have gone, I don't trust anybody . . . better tell Shield Chief.

I call to Cheyenne, who is a few yard behind. "Chey', I'm going to see Phil, want to talk to him. Be right back!"

"*Aho!*"

I take off.

Grasshoppers rise in my path. I drop below the grass line now and then to avoid being up too long. Could get picked off. I wonder why we've been ordered to hold. Trotting, I follow a gully downstream. It is filled with brush and cactus.

"Echohawk!" The voice of Shield Chief.

"*Ka?*" (What?)

"*Siks-a!*" (Come here!) Near the gully, in a forward position, is a stand of small thorn trees. I get a glimpse of dark faces in the shadows. It's Shield Chief and his brother, Grant. Grant is a sergeant in Matlock's Third Platoon. With them is Corporal Leading Fox, who is well hidden too.

Grant Shield Chief greets me with "*Nawa*" (Pawnee greeting). Leading Fox greets me too.

"*Nawa*," I reply.

"*Six-pettit*" (Come, sit down). We are glad to see each other. We haven't seen each other since leaving the ship last night.

I turn to Phil. "What's the score? Why the hold?"

"Battalion. They passed the word. That's all we know."

"Phil, from the high ground, we can see a lot of ships out there. I was thinking, suppose no one told the Navy that we are up there. They might take us to be the enemy, and they'd blow us to pieces . . . don't think it's a good idea, running around up there. Tell Captain Lee, so he can let Battalion know!"

Shield Chief rises to one knee and looks at the high ground. "Captain Lee has a walkie-talkie radio. He's in touch with Battalion. Battalion and Regiment are in contact with the Navy, the Navy coordinates fire with ground troops. They also have spotter planes. I am sure Battalion knows where we are."

"Well, okay. But you got to admit things got fouled up with that storm and beach landing."

"Everybody's fouled up," Grant pipes up. "We haven't seen the rest of the platoons, and there's part of a cannon company on the right lost. Their half-tracks are thrashing around in the brush like a spooky herd of buffalo."

Leading Fox, who used to work for the Bureau of Indian Affairs, snipes: "Fouled up like the Bureau of Indian Affairs."

"That's not all, either," Grant adds, scooping up a tiny pebble. He puts it in his mouth and jiggles it as though it were hard candy. "Some stray paratroopers have joined us. They dropped in the wrong place last night. They are bushy-tailed and fouled up." Grant grins, showing a gap in his upper front teeth, something from his college football days as quarterback. "Then to top things off, we got two sailors with us. I know dang well they are fouled up. I don't know about this war party. Maybe the Big Chief doesn't have all the feathers in his war bonnet."

"Just like I said, Bureau of Indian Affairs," snickers Leading Fox.

Then Grant turns to me. "*Tiwat*" (Nephew/Cousin), he says in a serious note, "your men okay?"★

"Yeah, they made it okay."

Thinking our brothers might run into trouble, Matlock ordered my squad to come help. Battalion is expecting bad medicine at the road junction.

"Yes, but soon as we get on our ponies and close on them—" Phillip Shield Chief adds, taking a twig and breaking it. "Battalion orders hold." He eyes the road junction, then throws the broken twig to the ground. "I don't understand."

"Bureau of Indian Affairs," nods Leading Fox. "Bureau of Indi'n Affairs."

We hear an airplane approaching. A biplane. Funny looking. It has pontoons. A seaplane!

★*Tiwat*, meaning "nephew" or "niece," was used interchangeably by Echohawk to mean "cousin."

"Navy spotter plane," Shield Chief says, glancing at me with an I-told-you-so look.

"A catapult bomber!" Leading Fox exclaims. Heading straight for us, the seaplane noses into a dive. Now what? It releases a bomb. The bomb passes over and thunders beyond. He's hit that road junction. The biplane climbs, then banks in a blue and cloudless sky. A curtain of dust hangs over the road junction. Hot dang! Hooray for the US Navy! What do you know, a two-wing job. Sure don't see those anymore. Looks like Captain Eddie Ricken-backer.* The biplane returns, rocking its wings at the infantry in the fields. There is wild cheering.

We hear another plane. Messerschmitt! The cheering stops. Having seen the German fighter, the American seaplane tries to escape. It drones out to sea, where the Navy can offer protective antiaircraft fire. The German fighter flashes straight for the seaplane. A tense moment ensues as we watch and pull for that American pilot. I find myself leaning forward, trying to urge him on. The pontoon biplane is painfully slow. The swift German fighter closes like a falcon streaking to a helpless pigeon. In a few pounding heartbeats it's over. "Killed on the wing," the seaplane spirals downward and falls into the sea. Then, like a nighthawk, the Messerschmitt swoops low and sunfishes between destroyers and cruisers, avoiding antiaircraft fire. In no time, it's gone.

"*Ah-ka*," utters Grant Shield Chief, looking where the seaplane went down. "He sure tried to help." A Pawnee expression, "*Ah-ka*" covers lament and disappointment depending on the situation. In this case it is lament, for we felt great sorrow for that brave Navy pilot.

Word comes to move out. "Ecky, keep bearing in at the flank," Shield Chief calls. "Turtlehead will hit straight ahead. Flop will drop to reserve."

"Okay."

Shield Chief is in good spirits since seeing his brother Grant. He calls us by our nicknames. I'm "Ecky." Last Arrow is "Turtlehead," and Good Buffalo is "Flop." Good Buffalo earned the nickname as a football player. He was a bone-jarring tackler; when this Pawnee hit a ball carrier he went flop! I take off.

At the squad area, Corporal Ira Ingalls meets me. The way things have been going, I had forgotten him. He is the assistant squad leader and has done well at bringing up the rear and making sure the men have interval.

"What's up, Sarge?" Ingalls inquires. Cheyenne asks the same.

I kneel and keep my head down. "That was Battalion. Had to hold till that Navy plane came up to bomb."

---

*Edward V. Rickenbacker was an American fighter ace in World War I and a Medal of Honor recipient.

"G'damn, that Navy plane blew them to hell. But, too bad he got it himself," Ingalls remarks. "G'damn, it's gittin' rough for everybody." I move to the squad, which is dispersed and bellied down.

I raise my voice so they can hear. "That was Battalion. They called for a bomb strike. The First and Second Squads will drive for the road junction. The Third will—"

Messerschmitts! We sink into the grass and don't move. Looking up, beads of sweat get into my eyes. The day is getting warm. Where is the air cover our Big Chiefs were bragging about? The Luftwaffe is going to eat us alive at this rate. One thing is for sure, the Navy is here . . . and poor "Captain Eddie." There is a distant rumble, like it is in the bowels of the earth. A grasshopper lands on my sleeve. I brush it away. The rumble continues. I get to my feet, then motion the squad forward. Glancing back, I check interval. Good God! The Germans hit one of our ships! A giant column of smoke billows on the Mediterranean horizon miles away. Comets of ammunition trailing smoke, hurled by explosions, rise, arc, and fall into the sea. Like Fourth of July fireworks, explosions twinkle against a mountain of smoke. At this distance things appear in slow motion and without sound. Moments later the sound arrives. Sleek destroyers move in, laying smokescreens. Today is Saturday, July 10, 1943. I will remember this sight as long as I live. We've witnessed the drama and tragedy of the air war, and now this awesome spectacle at sea. However, the drama of our ground war had not even begun to play out.

3

Van Gogh Countryside

In retrospect, much of the embattled Italian landscape still held its awesome beauty, created thousands of years before it became entrenched in war. For Brummett Echohawk, the unexpected splendor of nature discovered on the battlefields encouraged the young sergeant to find inspiration in the chaos surrounding him. He noted that the landscape of Italy reminded him of great impressionistic works by artists like Vincent van Gogh. Yet, as the war grew more serious, this beauty began to fade, offering no sanctuary for the Thunderbird to escape the horrors of combat—not even for a moment. Destruction, set against a backdrop of the stunning natural sceneries, created a conflicted perception of beauty and its relationship with mankind, a perception that both inspired and terrorized those who laid witness to its power. Sergeant Echohawk, caught in the moment, is transformed as he witnesses the bloating bodies of dead soldiers floating abreast. The beauty is lost...

The ground war again. We make for the road junction. The enemy has withdrawn. We hold before we move again. A road here runs in line with our march. We guide on it with First Squad on the right and Second Squad on the left. Third Squad follows in reserve. We place no scouts out; we are able to see a long way, and the land is flat. It simmers in heat waves as we move across the barren land. Abreast, we advance in a long and wavering line. Olive-drab uniforms present dark figures on a sea of white grass. Crouched and moving past wind-carved thorn trees, we appear like natives on an African lion hunt in a Martin and Osa Johnson documentary. Now walls of cactus screen the sides of the road as we continue to move. Mesquite trees limit our vision. The road turns often, causing men on the flanks to run and catch up. Shield Chief stops and studies the front. Then he signals: "squad column."

From abreast positions, the men fall into squad columns. Now there won't be any running to catch up at turns. Squad leaders now turn to signal their men. I turn and motion to the men staggered squad column. On the ground is peyote wood. It's hotter'n heck. Sweat gets into my eyes and runs into the corners of my mouth. *Where in the heck are we going? Why doesn't Battalion call hold? We had made the road junction. Maybe there's another junction with the main one further on . . . if the main one is ahead, why did the Navy plane bomb that road junction back there? A mix-up . . . Bureau of Indian Affairs.*

The walls of cactus that surround us are about eight feet high. Now and then there is a break in the cactus. Out there too are mesquites and thorn trees. I scan things ahead, searching for any signs of movement. The road takes a sharp turn, then snakes through mesquites. Ahead I don't see Last Arrow's squad, which I know is there. I realize then that I have fallen behind; I should have maintained contact but was busy searching elsewhere.

Ahead I spot green shrubbery with two stone pillars beyond. The shrubbery runs to the pillars like a gate to a big cattle ranch. As we continue moving, a road junction comes into view, and it is a big one. Beyond, a haystack . . . but there are no hayfields that have been cut. Odd-looking haystacks. Poorly stacked—very poorly stacked. I think to myself, *This is no—*

"Look out!" Machine gun fire erupts. I hit the ground as machine gun bullets rip the land around me, kicking up dust. It creates a zing and whine as bullets buzz around. Terrified, I flatten out and close my eyes tightly. Another machine gun fires to our right front. I spread my arms and legs in an effort to get lower, but my chest is propped up on a rock. I reach for it. It's the TNT! I still got the twenty-four blocks of TNT tied to my chest. Oh, God—*Tirawa*! If a tracer bullet hits this, we'll blow up like that ammunition ship. Fear grips me; I've got to get control of myself. I take a deep breath, exhale, and settle. Now, the first thing is to get rid of is this TNT. Not wanting to make an eye-catching move, I ease out of the TNT and shove it aside . . . breathe.

I turn my steel helmet around backward to see better. The grass is knee deep. I grasp the forearm of my rifle with the right hand and then pull it over the crook of my arm before I begin bellying forward. The M1 with bayonet is parallel with my body and causes no waves in the grass. Spotting a thorn bush, I peer through it at the grass line. Ahead, and to the right, is a pillbox disguised as a haystack, around sixty yards away. It sets back from the stone pillars. Between me and the hedges are bundles of peyote wood.

"Cheyenne!" I call as the pillbox gunners continue fire. I jam my face to the ground.

"*H'yo!*" Cheyenne's voice is muffled. His face is down too.

"Where's the BAR?" (Browning Automatic Rifle.)

"Pinned down. But Ingalls is crawling up!"

"Come on. Tell him to follow you, watch the TNT!"

"TNT! Got dog!" Cheyenne exclaims.

Now, let's see. First, the bundles of peyote wood, the row of hedges, then pillars. I shed my pack. Can't risk being seen. Keeping in mind where everything is, I slide forward, facedown. A burst of machine gun fire churns at the right front. Reaching the first bundle of wood I spot a couple of hands higher than the grass line. Four more bundles ahead. Two are in line of sight with the pillbox, making a blind . . . seems the best approach. Barely visible in the hedges is a low wall. Beyond is the pillbox.

"TNT! G'damn!" shrieks Ingalls. Glad he's coming. He has an antitank grenade launcher. The machine gun at the right fires a long burst. M1s answer. Carbines hit back. They sound like .22s.

I finally reach the last bundle of wood. Still facedown, I inch my way to the wall. I follow it and pass in front of the pillbox and under the nose of the gunners. They fire two short bursts as I move under them; I freeze. I move again, making it to one of the pillars, where I get on my knees and wipe the sweat from my face. The stone pillar is eight feet high and five feet square. Shielded from enemy fire, I stand and look for a way to get to the pillbox.

I look back. Everybody is pinned down in a barren stretch of land. Ready with hair triggers, both sides watch for the other to move. In this charged atmosphere, it is as if I were standing on a prairie under a summer thunderhead. I will attract lightning by just being here—and suddenly it strikes. Bullets assault the pillar as they whang and ricochet. Chips of stone fly as I hit the ground. The fire is coming from the far right, Third Platoon's area. They take me for an enemy soldier before Last Arrow's men shout, "Cease fire!" The pillbox machine gun sends a chain reaction of rooster-tailing dust across the barren flat, raking the area.

At the instant the pillbox gunners cut their burst, I rise and peek around the pillar. The pillbox is solid concrete with a deep gun port.

"Ecky," Cheyenne calls in a voice none too loud. With his body pressed against the wall, Short Nose strains toward me. Not far behind is Corporal Ingalls. Both have discarded their packs. They are less than ten yards away—yet it might as well be a mile and an eternity. Shielded by the massive pillar, I squat and hold the butt of my rifle out. He grabs it and I pull him in. He wipes the sweat and threads of grass from his face. Cheyenne huddles against the pillar and sighs. Ingalls worms forward, chin down. The gunners fire a long burst. Ingalls freezes. His eyes widen. Muddy rivulets of sweat run down his face.

I nod, then move my lips. "Come on, come on." Ingalls's knuckles whiten and his hands shake as he claws forward. I pull him in. Breathing heavily, he wears the facial expression of a coal miner that has just been rescued from a certain-death cave-in. Our guys don't fire now; they know who we are.

We hug the stone pillar. "The pillbox," I tell them. "It's just around this pillar, fifteen yards. Ing, we'll use your antitank grenade launcher. We can hit the opening from here."

Face streaked with muddy sweat, Ingalls grins. "That's why I came up." He pats his Springfield rifle, which has a grenade attachment on the muzzle. "Figures we'd need ol' Zuzu here to do the talking." He removes a special blank cartridge from his ammunition belt, one used to launch the antitank grenade. Ingalls checks the grenade attachment. "G'damn, Sarge," he exclaims with his jaw dropping. "Them antitank grenades are back there in my pack!" Wide-eyed, we look at each other. "We're up shit creek," Ingalls says, voice quivering.

Like shipwrecked men on a desert island, we gaze hopelessly back at the sea of grass. The air snaps with enemy carbine fire. Now the pillbox gunners rake the platoon area with a long burst. As soon as the gunners cut their burst, I peek around the pillar and jerk back. "The gun port is stair-stepped inward," I tell Ingalls and Cheyenne. "All concrete."

I reach in my pocket for my grenade. Had forgotten that I had taped the safety lever down as a precaution. I tear at the tape with my fingernails, but it is stuck fast. Since I'm on the throwing side, Cheyenne hands me his grenade. I stuff the taped one in my pocket. I yank the safety ring, take a half step out, then pitch the grenade with a side-arm delivery. The hand grenade pops the safety lever and clanks into the opening. I jerk back. Seconds later, the grenade explodes harmlessly on the ground, having hit the stair steps and bounced back. Ingalls gives me his grenade. I yank the safety ring. Machine gun fire rivets the pillar at my side, exploding bits of stone. "G'damn, they know we're here!" Ingalls cries. With little elbow room, we press ourselves against the pillar.

Another burst stitches the wall, splinters the hedges, and clangs into the wrought-iron fence. I hold a firm grip on the grenade. Abruptly, a ripping sound with an explosion makes us all flinch. That was near the pillbox. Another ripping and explosion, followed by an instant echo.

"G'damn! Here comes a half-track!" Ingalls screams. The American half-track approaches from five hundred yards away. From a cannon company, this armored vehicle carries a 75mm cannon. Rumbling forward, the half-track fires again. Cheyenne and Ingalls drop to the ground and double up. I dive away from the pillar. The 75 shell slams in. Having seen me, enemy riflemen take potshots. Bullets kick up the dust, and I wiggle back to the pillar. In the field, even though they can't stand up, men shout at the top of their lungs to stop the half-track. Dust rises from the concussion and the strikes of bullets. *Tirawa*, help us.

I hang on to the grenade with a death grip. "Throw that thing away, Sarge! If they get you, we'll all blow up!" Ingalls shrieks in panic. A 75 shell can't penetrate the pillbox. A grenade in the opening is the only chance. The gunners in the pillbox fire at the oncoming half-track. Our guys are still shouting at it to stop.

With attention directed at the half-track, the pillbox gunners won't notice me. I step out, cock my arm—and then an explosion! Like facing a flash camera with no time to blink, the explosion knocks me back. Shrapnel whirs, sending bits of concrete buckshot everywhere. Shaken, I grip the hand grenade with both hands, for it is still live. The half-track scored a hit but is veering right. The pillbox gunners do not fire. Their heads are down.

I move out and rifle the grenade into the gun port. I pull back. "The grenade went in! Get ready!" There is a "rain barrel" explosion. I step out and fire as fast as I can into the gun port. Ingalls and Cheyenne blaze away too. We draw carbine fire, sending Ingalls diving to the ground.

Cheyenne and I charge with bayonets. We dash for the rear of the pillbox yelling: "Hands up! Hands up!"

Cheyenne drops his rifle, picks up a rock the size of a basketball, and shouts— "It's a good day to die!"—then heaves the rock into the entrance. More carbine fire. Cheyenne falls. Lead zings off the concrete. I duck into the entrance, a stone staircase going down into the pillbox. At the bottom of the stairs is an enemy soldier, curled up. I aim my M1 at him, but he does not move—no signs of life in the pillbox. I take a quick prairie-dog look. Cheyenne is on his back with blood on his temple and side of his face. Shaken, I stay down.

The enemy soldier groans. He props up on one elbow. Head drooped, the man has difficulty breathing. The front of his tunic is soaked with blood. In the heavy air, flies drone about him. Though he is the enemy, I feel sorry for him. . . .

I remember a picture show, *All Quiet on the Western Front*, where Lew Ayres, playing a young German soldier, was in a shell crater with a French soldier he had just killed. Frightened and regretting having killed the poilu (French infantryman), he huddled next to the dead man. Ayres listened to the sounds of war outside the shell hole—the crack of rifle fire and the chatter of machine guns. The same is happening to me. Outside are the sounds of rifle fire and machine guns. I study the man at my feet before he stops breathing.

From outside: "*A-a'e—ay! Kiddi didde didde, Kidde didde didde.*" I bolt from the stairs. Cheyenne springs to life. He grabs his rifle and gives a war cry with "It's a good day to die!"

Much relieved, I shout, "It's a good day to play possum!"

The Second Platoon charges with Shield Chief leading. On the right the Third Platoon charges too. Enemy soldiers stand, drop weapons, and raise hands. Shield Chief shouts: "Second Platoon! Hold it!" Then he and some Third Platoon men flag the prisoners in. "Don't bunch up!" bellows Shield Chief. "Any funny business from these guys, kill them!"

There's a lot of activity on the right. I check the squad. No one is hit. Check Cheyenne. "You hit bad?"

"Nah. Ricochet. This kind . . ." he answers, popping the right fist into the palm of the left hand. Touching the right temple, he rolls the right hand downward. Meaning: hit in temple, went down. Many Indians in Oklahoma, when explaining things, accent it in sign language as they talk. Since lying face-up, Cheyenne's right ear and shirt collar are covered with blood. I look at his temple. "Let's make sure." I turn and call: "Medicine Man!" Word is passed.

"You guys all right?" It's Corporal Ingalls, coming on a jog. He lugs the packs we discarded. "G'damn!" he exclaims, seeing the blood on Cheyenne's ear and shirt collar. "You okay, Cheyenne?"

"Y'ah, I'm okay," Short Nose replies.

Checking the Platoon, Shield Chief approaches, walking fast. Having heard the call for Medicine Man, he asks, "Who got hit?"

"Cheyenne got a ricochet," I answer, nodding at Short Nose.

"Bad, Cheyenne? Let's see," Shield Chief says, stepping up to examine Short Nose.

"Naw. Nothing. Ricochet jus' rang my bell was all," Cheyenne remarks, snapping a finger and whipping it by his temple.

From the right I hear in a hushed tone, "Sergeant Shield Chief!" It's Captain Lee.

"Ecky, stay with Cheyenne till Medicine Man looks him over," Phillip Shield Chief says with fatherly concern.

"*Aho.*"

Shield Chief takes off in the direction of Captain Lee, where Third Platoon has its hands full with the prisoners. There, the prisoners are herded to the road and formed in columns of twos. Cheyenne and I take our packs from Ingalls and put them on.

"G'damn, that pillbox was a booger!" Ingalls remarks, gulping water. The chained cap clinks against the aluminum canteen. Ira Ingalls, a ranch hand from the Oklahoma panhandle, wipes his mouth with a sleeve and replaces the canteen. "Bet that pillbox could hold a lot of potatoes and white lightning. Also would make a jim-dandy tornado shelter."

"For sure," I nod.

"Make a good sweat lodge too," Cheyenne says, wiping sweat and blood from his face.

Returning from a powwow with the company commander and platoon sergeants, Shield Chief calls the squad leaders. I turn to Corporal Ingalls. "Ing, make sure Medicine Man takes care of Cheyenne."

"Okay, Sarge."

I join Shield Chief. Last Arrow is with him. Good Buffalo, who is in reserve, arrives a few minutes later. "Who called for Medicine Man?" he asks. "Somebody get hit?"

"Cheyenne," I answer. "A ricochet crossed his temple." The three Indian sergeants look back at the pillbox and stone pillars. Our medics, with the help of prisoners, remove limp figures from the pillbox.

"Ecky, you guys did all right," Shield Chief says, getting to his feet and wiping the sweat from his face. "Even with both sides shooting at you. Worse, was our own half-track firing on you with a 75. Thank *Tirawa* you guys made it. Brave warriors make their own luck." Saying nothing, I turn my steel helmet around forward again, then rub my skinned elbows.

"Now," Shield Chief says, facing the front. "Captain Lee wants B Company to be aggressive and take the next high ground. He says the rest of the regiment is strung out behind but will follow. Runners have been sent back for contact. He also says Battalion is coming together and everybody is moving forward." We three squad leaders study the high ground. Barren hills about a mile ahead. "Since this road runs that way, we will guide on it," Shield Chief continues, keeping his eyes fixed on the high ground. "The Third Platoon will be on our right. Turtlehead and Flop will lead. Ecky, reserve. Okay, move out!"

Calling us by our nicknames, Shield Chief feels good since he found that his brother, Grant, made it okay in the Third Platoon. We return to our squads and fill them in on the situation.

Captain Lee, who is between Second and Third Platoons, waves his .30-caliber carbine, which looks like a BB gun compared to our M1s. "Move out!"

"Second Platoon! Let's go!" Shield Chief yells.

"Third Platoon! Let's go!" Matlock yells.

"B Company! Let's go!"

Everybody sings out. "Anchors aweigh!" Anchors aweigh? A wave of laughter. The company moves, straddling the road.

On the right, one squad from Third Platoon remains in reserve. My squad is in reserve for the Second. Approaching from the right is Sergeant Matlock with two American sailors. In blue dungarees and blue-gray steel helmets, the sailors carry Springfield rifles. At the road Matlock stops and talks to them. Then the sailors straighten to attention and salute him. Matlock flicks a salute and nods. The sailors turn to join a few B Company men who are marching the prisoners through the stone pillars and down the road. Matlock's reserve squad near the road explodes in unison, "Yea!" Then they hit the strains of "Anchors Aweigh." Like prizefighters introduced in the ring, the sailors clasp their hands above their heads and shake them. With Navy pride, the seamen pick up the step like the midshipmen of Annapolis. My squad joins the singing; there is laughter by all. The column of prisoners trudges down the road. At their heels, and enjoying the spotlight, swagger the two American sailors. With M1 at sling, and hands on hips, Platoon Sergeant Chauncey Matlock watches. A haze of white dust rises from the column. Matlock turns toward us, drops his hands, palms out, and shrugs his shoulders: "These white boys can't behave." We enjoy the joke.

In reserve, we wait for the platoon to get strung out. I check Cheyenne. He and Medicine Man are sitting in knee-deep dry grass. Cheyenne has a bandage on the right temple. Medicine Man scribbles in a notepad. With a cigar in his mouth, he sits cross-legged, Indian fashion. Medical aid bags are open with things spread out. A pair of scissors reflect in the sunlight.

"How are things at the US Indian Hospital?" I ask Medicine Man as he shifts the cigar in his mouth.

"Just like the US Indian Hospital at Pawnee. Admitted in the morning, discharged in the afternoon . . . pneumonia, broken arm, TB, green apple two-step, all the same. But first you gotta fill out a lot of papers. Then they get mixed up, and you do it again. Bureau of Indian Affairs, you know."

"Yeah, I know, I know."

Cheyenne looks at Medicine Man and chuckles. "He's too much."

"He'll live." Medicine Man smiles. "Making notes for the record in case there are aftereffects, like dizziness and having double vision. He could get hit by concussion later, which might bring something up that we overlooked here . . . never know. Right now, it's not all bad, but I better keep an eye on him."

"Fine, Shield Chief wants you to look him over good."

Medicine Man puts away the notepad, then looks at Short Nose. "Cheyenne, you're supposed to go back to the Battalion Aid Station. You're entitled to the Purple Heart. . . ."

Private First Class Gilbert Short Nose stiffens. "Purple Heart! Now, look out!" he exclaims, shaking his head. "Naw, naw. Jus'a scratch. We Cheyennes got pride. Rather earn an eagle feather. Besides, if the Indi'ns in the Company knew I got the Purple Heart for this, they'd laugh—especially the Pawnees." Short Nose looks at me and grins.

He is referring to the time when the Cheyenne and Pawnee were enemies on the Great Plains. Intertribal wars often flared. However, at times, the wars were games of skill and courage aimed at humiliating and demoralizing the enemy. To shame the enemy in battle was to scar him for life. Brave warriors earned eagle feathers—and wore them proudly. They were men of honor. Today, this Cheyenne warrior earned an eagle feather. And he could wear the Purple Heart with pride too.

"Say, that was some shootout back there," Medicine Man says, changing the subject. He packs the medical bags. "Everybody was shooting at you guys, including an American half-track with its 75. All I can say is that the Cheyenne and Pawnee have good medicine."

"We didn't have a choice," I reply, feeling scared again. "They caught us in the open and pinned everybody down."

"Saw the pillbox," Medicine Man adds, drawing on a dead cigar. "Theoretically"—he draws harder on the cigar—"it would take naval gunfire to destroy it. Our medics took the wounded out of there with the help of some prisoners. One was dead. The others were more dead than alive. We help them when we can. Hope someday their medics help our wounded."

On the move again, Second and Third Platoons advance. Medicine Man takes the medical aid bags and saddles up. Cheyenne fingers the bandage on his temple. "Cheyenne, you guys go on," I say, glancing back. "I'm going to look at that pillbox. I'll catch up."

"*Aho.*"

Medicine Man lights his cigar. He and Short Nose move out.

The platoon likes Private First Class Moses Bowlegs, our Choctaw medic. He has a round face, full lips, and narrow slits for eyes. When smiling, his eyes appear to close. And Medicine Man has perfect white teeth. Removing my pack, I take pencil and paper folded in the mess kit. The flat lid serves as a drawing board. I sketch Medicine Man and Cheyenne, walking across the dry fields. Medicine Man is talking as they walk on. Now and then he pauses with "Theoretically. . ." then continues. Short Nose is tall and broad-shouldered. Moses Bowlegs is stocky. Slung at each hip are medical aid bags, which cause the Choctaw to walk with arms curved out from the body like a gunfighter in a western movie who is about to draw. Now and then Medicine Man sends up a puff of cigar smoke.

I jog to the pillbox. The thing is round and built of solid concrete. I can't tell the height with all the hay on it. The gun port is three feet wide and six feet tall. It curves with the contour, giving gunners an excellent traverse. The port funnels inward with stair steps to deflect fire, grenades, and shrapnel. Medicine Man was right: it would take naval gunfire to get this. The pillbox bears a nick from the 75, no damage.

Close by is the gateway with the stone pillars. The stone pillar that we were behind shows it has been through a storm of lead and shrapnel. I enter the pillbox. As I enter, stepping in from the sunlight, it is dark. The interior is about ten feet in diameter with a round stone table in the middle. A machine gun is sighted through the port. The view, and field of fire, are commanding. As my eyes adjust to the dark, I notice that the ceiling and walls are scarred by grenade fragments. Ricocheting lead in here would be murder. On the floor are spent brass, field equipment, and cooking utensils. Starting with the machine gun, I sketch the interior. The bunker grows warm with little fresh air, and I continue to sketch as the flies drone. Then I notice that I'm standing in a pool of blood specked with the flies. I scramble out to fresh air and sunshine. Like a buffalo bull pawing dirt, I try to get the blood off my boots. I run, pick up my pack, and rejoin the squad. The first day of battle. I was almost killed and am still

shaking. I want to be a brave warrior, but I must never, never look back. . . .
Yet there is an urge to draw this. We push forward.

Ahead, we spot haystacks. Real ones. Gun-shy, our scouts check them out.
At the right is the road we're guiding on. Beyond this road is an orchard and
then a mansion. Partly hidden in mesquites, it is landscaped with green shrubbery and cedars. The mansion features pink adobe houses with red-tile roofs.
Probably belongs to one of Mussolini's officials. It is in the Third Platoon area.
No shooting. Nobody at home. Pangs of hunger hit me, but there is little time
to eat. Then I remember the beefsteak taken from the ship's mess hall. It is still
wrapped and stuffed in my shirt. In seawater, running, and crawling has caused
it to settle at the small of my back.

I see scouts from First and Third at a distance, far ahead of their squads.
We're on a grassy plain, and there are the occasional thorn trees. It looks like
rhino country in the *Trader Horn* movie. We flush grasshoppers as we move
across the area. They flutter ahead, circle, and settle. In this Mediterranean
heat, everything is dry. Like a day out of the Dust Bowl when the Southwest
wilted under a drought. As a little boy, I walked a bone-dry prairie to catch
grasshoppers to use as fish bait. Creeks and ponds in Oklahoma had dried up,
but the springs had not. Here one could fish for perch. *Perch is good with brown
beans and fried bread.* I keep thinking of food. . . . getting hungry.

I watch for hand signals. Ahead, the column stops. We move. We stop.
We move. Suddenly gunfire erupts from the far right front. We hold. Everybody gets down. From the front, a hand signal. Then word comes: "Echohawk. Forward!" I signal the squad "hold," then I hurry forward. At a distance are Shield Chief, Good Buffalo, and Last Arrow. With them, sitting in
the grass, is a blond man. Maybe we captured a German soldier. Arriving, I
find the blond is an American paratrooper. A little guy, wearing a tan jump-
suit with an armband bearing the American flag. The paratrooper has an M1,
but no helmet.

Shield Chief is drinking water with one hand and holding his tommy-gun
in the other. "Ecky, this is Private Flowers," Shield Chief says, pursing the lips
and thrusting the chin forward at the paratrooper. He often gestures with the
lips and chin to call attention to someone, or to indicate a direction. Pawnee
call this "pointing with the lips." In the old days, they did this during a conversation if their hands were full. "Flowers, this is Sergeant Echohawk," says
Shield Chief, putting away his canteen of water. "You stick with his squad
until you find your outfit."

The little paratrooper eyes me, nods: "You guys all Indi-yans, yeah?"

"Most of us," I reply. "Some are cowboys."

"I didn't know Indi-yans were—"

"Ecky," Shield Chief interrupts. "Flowers says there are Germans ahead."

Private Flowers cuts in: "There's a bunch of 'em! My outfit got scattered all over hell last night. My sergeant landed on a stone wall and broke both legs before the Germans got him. What was left of us fought Italians—they're a game bunch. We were scattered too damn much, so hell, it was everybody for himself. Had a buddy with me this morning, but when them low-flying German planes came over, he took off. Since then, ain't seen nobody but you Indi-yans."

"Phil, I heard shooting to right rear a while back," I inject.

Disturbed, Shield Chief glances to the rear: "It's the Third Platoon," he says. Good Buffalo and Last Arrow look back too.

"There's a lot of cactus groves and brush in Matlock's area . . . the Third Platoon could be anywhere now."

"Did you have contact with the Third Platoon, Ecky?"

"*Wuh.* No. Thought they were up and to the right of you guys. Captain Lee was for a while, then didn't see him anymore. I took it the captain knew where he was going!"

"*Ah-ka*" (an expression of disappointment).

"I'm sorry, Phil." Shield Chief frowns, shakes his head, then looks to the front. The little paratrooper follows the conversation with his eyes. He is squatting near Shield Chief, who is standing. At six foot one, and with massive shoulders, the Pawnee makes the little paratrooper look like a child. "Let's go hunting." Shield Chief says. "Bull and Flop abreast. Echohawk in reserve. Move out."

"*Aho!*" we respond.

"Echohawk," Shield Chief says, pointing his lips to Flowers, "*Suks-ti-wata*" (Watch over the little boy).

I reply "yes" in sign language. I turn to Flowers, who is all eyes and ears. "Okay, follow me."

We fall back to a knoll where I signal the squad: "forward." "What did the chief say, Sergeant Elk Heart? That was Indi-yan talk, wasn't it?" His eyes follow Shield Chief, who is moving away.

"Aw, it's nothing," I answer. "He was referring to the Germans."

"But, what did the chief say?" he persists. "What did the chief say?" I step up on the knoll and pose like a cigar-store Indian, cross my arms, and lift my chin: "Big Chief—he says—Palefaces up front—not Pilgrims."

"Uh . . . oh."

I sit and wait for the squad. Flowers sits close to me, rustling equipment as though building a nest. "I understood the chief to say that you Indi-yans are from Oklahoma . . ." Flowers leads.

"That's right."

"And I think the chief said you come from a town called Pawnee."

"Right."

"Where 'bouts in Oklahoma is Pawnee?"

"Fifty-five miles west of Tulsa, and one hundred miles north of Oklahoma City."

"Is it a reservation?"

I explain, "There are no reservations in Oklahoma, only tribal reserves for schools and hospitals. However, there are allotments."

"What's an allotment?"

Annoyed, I look down and put a hand to my brow, covering my eyes. "It's a long story."

Flowers fidgets with a strap that holds a knife and sheath to the calf of his leg. "You Indi-yans are different kinda warrior-soldiers . . . are you scared, Sergeant Elk Heart?"

I look at Flowers and sigh. "No. Up front here, I just shake with patriotism."

"Uh . . . oh." The squad comes up. I fill them in but don't introduce Flowers. He'll get in their scalps soon enough. We move out.

Grasshoppers rise in our path. We're hunting now. At hunting, Indians have no equal. Better the hunter than the hunted. Leading us are three excellent hunters: Shield Chief, Good Buffalo, and Last Arrow. Though the land is alien to them, their eyes won't miss a thing. We stop and watch for hand signals. I remove my helmet and wipe sweat from my forehead. The steel pot is warm from the sun. I take a sip of water before putting my helmet back on. At the right front is an orchard, a grain field, haystacks, and rows of cactus. Once in a big city library when we were stationed on the East Coast, I saw a print of a painting by an artist named Van Gogh. It was of an orchard and grain fields under brilliant sunshine in southern France. This countryside resembles the Van Gogh painting: azure sky, green orchard, golden fields, and brilliant sunlight. Even the heat waves out there suggest the wavy brush strokes of Van Gogh. Beautiful.

Word comes: "Echohawk! On the double!" I signal the squad to hold, then hustle forward.

The road we guided on turns left. Ahead are big hills. Everybody is hidden; I sense something's up. Last Arrow and Good Buffalo are bellied down, looking to the right front. I don't see Shield Chief. I crouch down a few paces away to keep from bunching up. "What's up?" I ask, panting.

"*The enemy is coming*," Good Buffalo replies, pointing with his lips to the horizon. "Phil went to look over the lay of the land."

"Take a look," Last Arrow says. I crawl forward, rubbing sweat from my eyes, and search the Van Gogh countryside. Struggling to see, I cup both hands over my eyes to shade them from the sun; still nothing. "Use the blue and green like the old scouts did," says Last Arrow. I set my eyes on the green orchard for about thirty seconds, then shift to the blue sky above the horizon.

Cool colors, like green and blue, are restful to the eyes. This makes it easier for the eyes to pinpoint something at a distance. Fixing the eyes too long on a distant point in a bright sun strains them. I scan slowly. There they are: small specks coming this way. Now and then they fade in the heat waves.

"Wish we had field glasses," I remark.

"Who needs them," Last Arrow scoffs.

"Nobody's chasing them," Good Buffalo notes. "They are taking an easy path."

Running footsteps are heard approaching. It's Shield Chief. "All right. Come on. I'll explain the layout." Shield Chief turns and dogtrots ahead, keeping off the skyline. We follow and hustle up a rise.

Shield Chief gets on his hands and knees and we do the same before emerging on a shoulder of ground that overlooks a wide valley. We belly down. In the valley are trees and underbrush, and I figure there could be a riverbed. At the immediate front, two hundred and fifty yards or more, is a dense stand of trees. To where we are, the ground slopes with dry grass, cactus, and thorn bushes. "Okay, we'll lie for them here," Shield Chief says. "It is barren here, like an empty pasture where a man wouldn't look for horses. They will follow the drift of the land and pass here. The way these people walk tells a lot. When hunting, they're relaxed, the same as animals. These people skyline themselves and have no interval. They don't expect anything. Like a herd of deer, when you come upon them downwind, their movements are predictable." Phillip Shield Chief, one of the best hunters in the Pawnee tribe, studies the stand of trees and grins mischievously. "On this hot day," he says pointing with his lips, "that grove of shade trees will act as a watering hole for our game."

Lying still, we eye the approaching enemy. "There's a tiny glint on them," Last Arrow notes. "Dust goggles. German motorized troops wore them in North Africa. You guys will remember that we were issued dust goggles, then they were recalled because the goggles reflected too much. They'll reflect like a mirror when the angle of the sun is right, and right now, it is."

"It's a reconnaissance outfit," Good Buffalo speculates. "Bet our Air Corps destroyed their vehicles. Now they have to act like infantrymen. Infantrymen are hunters, and these guys are not hunting."

"Deploy here," Shield Chief says, rising to one knee. Avoiding movement, he points with his lips, "Bill, left. Flop, middle. Ecky, right. Have the men put the mosquito head nets over their helmets. We must blend with the ground. Okay. Move. *Wees-kah-chuh*" (Hurry up).

"*Aho*," we reply.

Having the farthest to go, I run back where the squad can see me. I sign: "Come, on the double." They hustle. Grasshoppers fly before them. Without bunching up, I fill them in on the situation, then mention the mosquito nets.

The men take the nets from their packs. Lifting the steel pot from the helmet liner, they cover it with the netting. The edges of the netting are tucked under the steel pot, then it is placed back over the helmet liner. Strands of grass are stuck into the mosquito netting for camouflage.

I call to Medicine Man, who is at the rear of the squad: "Medicine Man! Stay behind! Keep under cover!" Medicine Man does not cover his helmet, for it bears the international sign of a medical aid man—a red cross in a white circle. We move out quickly. On the run, I swing my squad to the afternoon side of the hill, where I locate Good Buffalo and Last Arrow, who are well hidden. I position my squad on the morning side of the hill, to the right of Good Buffalo. Here the ground has what looks like rundown terraces where dry grass stands like ripe wheat; no cover. But Shield Chief said a man wouldn't look in an empty pasture for horses. Shield Chief calls for a last-minute check; we are ready.

The enemy approaches as Shield Chief predicted. "They don't have scouts out. In Indi'n country, you gotta have scouts out. Boy, howdy, right now this is Indi'n country."

Cheyenne chuckles. "All I can say is welcome to the Little Big Horn!" The grove of trees ahead are good shade trees, and they look inviting on this hot day. Connecting the grove are more trees of various sizes with underbrush. They become dense as they march upstream to the left front. At the extreme left are hills, with fewer trees. The right front, which is downstream, is lined with trees and groves of cactus. Lying in knee-deep grass, the heat is stifling.

"*Tara-hak tudah-heh, Karoo-rot Kuda-oo?*" (Good Buffalo, where is Medicine Man?), the voice of Shield Chief comes.

"*Ti-ros-a luri-hi-ru pa-huh*" (He is far behind the hill), replies the voice of Good Buffalo.

"*Tudahe*" (Good), Shield Chief says.

"That's Indi-yan talk! What did the chief say?" asks Private Flowers.

"Aw, shut up!" Cheyenne scolds.

Focusing back on the job at hand, I separate the grass in front of me slowly. The enemy does not appear to be hunting as Good Buffalo said. I look left to Shield Chief, who has placed himself in a commanding position. His head and shoulders are above the grass line. Hidden from the front, he blends with a thorn bush and a stand of cactus. His helmet has mosquito net, with strands of grass for camouflage. "All right, men," Shield Chief says. "Faces to the ground. Don't move." As a pureblood Pawnee, Phillip Shield Chief eyes the oncoming enemy. He puts a pipe in his mouth and lights it, keeping his head and shoulders motionless.

At thirty-seven, Shield Chief is one of the older soldiers in the company. Steeped in Pawnee tradition, he draws on the pipe, lifts his face, and sends a puff of smoke. Then he sends a puff of smoke to the ground. The first puff is to

Tirawa (the Supreme Being), the next is to Mother Earth. Lastly, he puffs to the four winds. Then Shield Chief says, without turning his face: "Men, wait for my command. Fight bravely!" He empties the ashes from the pipe, then speaks in the Pawnee tongue. It is difficult to hear because he faces the front. I make out these words: "All men are clay. All men return to clay. We were formed by the hand of *Tirawa*. On earth for a short time. We must prove ourselves in life, especially on the path of war. We crossed the great waters to fight. So fight like the Pawnee warriors that went before us. We are *chaticks-si-chaticks,* men of men." I am moved.

As a small boy I heard stories, told by the old ones, about Pawnee warriors. For every story there was a song, which told about a warrior or an incident in battle. Pawnee history was kept this way. The bravest of the brave led the war party. He was called *Raáwiirakuhkitawi'u*—the Leader. Before battles the *Raáwiirakuh-kitawi'u* would address his men as Shield Chief has just done. The words are the same except for the part about crossing the great waters. Every young Pawnee warrior has heard this. My father spoke these words to me before our division came overseas. He told me his father said the same to him in World War I. Mounted on a war pony, Grandfather, as a young warrior on the Great Plains, heard the *Raáwiirakuhkitawi'u* speak the same.

The enemy is getting closer; now and then I see a reflection. I hear a rustle of equipment and the sound of water in a canteen jiggling. It's Private Flowers, wiggling up near Cheyenne and me. Flowers adjusts a knife that is strapped to the calf of his right leg. He points his rifle upward and sets the sights. Rolling to one side, he fishes into a baggy leg-pocket and pulls out a small automatic pistol. He clicks the receiver, then puts the pistol back into the leg-pocket.

"*Tiwat, peduski tah-kah, pahetuh!*" (Cousin, tell that white boy, quiet), Shield Chief growls as I glare at Flowers.

"All right, soldier, settle down." He settles. The July heat is fierce. Out there, the cool shade trees offer torturous temptations. Shield Chief said that the grove will act as a watering hole. Now, as we wait patiently in the brush, the game approaches the watering hole. They sniff the air for danger. Their leaders check the watering hole and the surrounding area for hazard. As they evaluate the area, the other Germans crouch with weapons ready. Finding the area secure, the enemy ambles to the shade trees. With the watering hole free of predators, the game pauses and drinks. Salty beads of sweat run down my face and into the corners of my mouth. After a while the enemy emerges from the cool shade trees. Here they will turn upstream or come our way. They pause and start to bunch up and then come our way. Relaxed now, their guard is down. We click off the safety locks of our M1s.

"Stillness is camouflage," Shield Chief cautions. "Don't move!"

There are about thirty of them closing in, some two hundred and fifty yards away. They are Germans. The Germans that dropped the Poles with one punch, knocked out the French in the first round, floored the British at Dunkirk, and had them on the ropes in North Africa. They shamed the Americans at Kasserine Pass, and now they are beating up on the Russians. Though the Allies have pushed them out of North Africa, the Germans are still the bull of the woods. Suddenly, the leaders stop and crouch with weapons ready. Something's up. Did one of us move? I swallow hard. Sweat runs into my eyes. I blink to clear my vision. The leaders gesture and look to their left. Maybe they spotted Third Platoon. The sun reflects on dust goggles worn by a tall soldier who appears to be doing the talking. The tall one extends an arm and points left. Then with a sweeping motion turns and points our way. All look in our direction, but we remain motionless.

When a hunter approaches a deer in the woods, the buck will lower its head into the brush, eye level, to blend its rack. A doe with its protective coloring stands motionless even at bow-shot range. I remember: stillness is camouflage. The hunter's eye, as well as a predator's, will pass over. The hunter has programmed himself to see the correct image, while the predator watches for movement. Both search where game is expected. As for us, we're not where the enemy expects us to be. There are no horses in this empty pasture.

The Germans regroup and come on. The tall one with the dust goggles has blond hair and is sunburned. The soldiers wear gray-green tunics with black leather harnesses. Most wear field caps, and a few have steel helmets. Because of the heat, their sleeves are rolled up. One shoulders a machine gun with a belt of ammo draped around his neck while another lugs two boxes of ammunition. Metal gas mask containers and entrenching tools clink and rattle from their hips. Jackboots. Moving, they sound like farm horses, harnessed and plodding through a harvest field. Grasshoppers flitter ahead of them.

We lie still as they come closer. I can hear some talking. Fear grips me as I begin to sweat. My heart pounds, pulsing throughout my body with every breath. A grasshopper lands on my shirt collar.

"Now!" Shield Chief shouts. We spring up. War cries sound out. In a wild heartbeat, the tall one's jaw drops as our eyes meet. Gunfire erupts before the man's blond head snaps in a spray of blood. Caps and goggles fly, and their machine gunner's face explodes, then the ammo carrier falls. Another German soldier flips backward like he was clotheslined. M1 fire continues as the sound of war cries rises over the battlefield accompanied by the sound of tommy-gun fire. The only audible sound becomes ejecting clips and men screaming. Before us the enemy is mowed down, leaving tumbling bodies littering the ground in front. What's left of the enemy runs.

"*Uks-ko-tit. Ru su kih!*" (Kill them. Use knife!), Shield Chief yells.

We go after them running at a full sprint. Ahead, I spot pounding jackboots, flashing hobnails, rattling equipment, pumping elbows, and bobbing heads. With ears ringing, and running hard, I jump a ditch. Two soldiers huddle there. I cut back for them. "Go on, *Chibonni!* I'll take 'em!" Sam Bear comes running, lowering his bayonet as he leaps into the ditch. I turn and keep going. Our guys fire on the run so as not to let up on the enemy. From behind comes the gobble of a wild tom turkey—the Creek Indian victory cry! The Germans run for the heavy woods upstream from the watering hole and vanish.

"Hold it! Hold it!" Shield Chief hollers; we break off chase. I drop to one knee, panting, sweating, and with my heart beating like a war-dance drum. I look to Shield Chief, who is crouching, wide-eyed. With his tommy-gun ready, he studies the wooded area.

A shot rings out. We hit the ground as I realize there is no cover here. "Echohawk!" Shield Chief calls. "Right side of creek! Good Buffalo, the left! Last Arrow, reserve! Move! Quick!" We move fast as I keep my M1 with bayonet pointed forward, one finger on the trigger. The woods are much bigger than they look. There is a dry creek with lots of trees and tall grass with underbrush. If we had stayed in the open to head them off, they would pick us off. Better stick to Indi'n fighting and stay in the woods.

I signal the squad: "extended column" (a staggered column, each man guiding on the man ahead of him). Vision is limited. We come to a small stone wall, about three feet high. We spot fresh blood on the wall. We leg over.

"*Wees! Wees!*" (Hurry! Hurry!) The voice of Shield Chief urges us on. "Don't give them a chance to get organized!" We step up the pace. The creek bed fades among the trees. Moving uphill, now we bear right. Glancing back, I check the squad, where I can make Cheyenne out in the brush. He has a bandage over the right eye and temple; I also catch a glimpse of Bear. The rest are following. I spot a clearing ahead, a donkey trail; I cross over. The squad follows. We settle as enemy fire comes from the left front in Good Buffalo's area. The enemy rear guard is holding him up.

"Move! Move!" The voice of Shield Chief shouts. We wade through waist-high grass, past trees with spreading branches. The leafy branches touch the top of the grass, obstructing the view. The enemy won't stand and fight, as some are wounded. And the blood on the wall back there indicates that one of them is bleeding like a gut-shot buck. "*Wees!*" Shield Chief urges.

We come upon another clearing. It's a wide passageway; I dash across. As I sprint through the clearing, I take fire from the left. Seeing a wall, I dive over, then crawl forward to some trees, waiting in their shadows. The enemy fire increases. *It sounds like .22 carbines,* I think to myself. *It must be the Italians!* They must have heard our fire when we were ambushing the Germans. Now the

Italians are moving on us; my squad has not crossed that clearing, and they're pinned down. What to do? I ease up close to a tree trunk and spot a man about forty yards away. Angling left, he stoops under low-hanging limbs and wades through high grass. He is armed with a carbine. Beyond, and through the brush and leaves, is another man following the first. I take aim at the first man and fire. I feel the M1 kick; he falls. The second man dives behind a bundle of peyote wood. I pump seven rounds into the bundle of wood. The clip clangs and ejects, empty. I shift positions, lie low, and reload.

Heart pounding and sweat pouring down my face, I come up under a branch, making sure to keep eye-level with the grass. A slug blasts a limb inches away, sending splinters of wood into my face: *That guy spotted me.* I duck and get behind the tree trunk. Two shots whack into the trunk as bark flies around. He's really after me. I scoot to another tree with spreading branches. Removing my helmet, I ease up in front of the tree, maybe the width of a man's face. In the shadows, the tree trunk is blurred. With dark hair and skin, I'll blend like a quail. Ahead are more trees in the sunlight; their shadows are heavy and the dry grass appears like snow. Beyond the trees the ground rises; this is where the sniper will be. I pick three spots out there, forming a triangle, then move my eyes from point to point, searching. If there is movement, peripheral vision will detect it.

M1 shot! On the right front I spot movement. The sniper reacted to the shot, moving his head. He is still again. Like me, the man is on the forward side of the tree trunk in the shadows. Well hidden, he has his helmet off. His forehead is white, and his face is sunburned. He looks like a wheat farmer in the summer. *Thought that pale spot looked odd. He's just over a hundred yards away.* I aim, squeeze the trigger, and fire. The M1 kicks. The man's head snaps before he rolls over.

I slide quickly to another place as carbine fire opens on the right front. Lead strikes the tree branch as I notice I am in what looks like a deer-lay. Blood on the ground and the flattened grass show that three people were here—one wounded. On the left: heavy gunfire. I hear Shield Chief's tommy-gun. I call out: "Cheyenne?" No answer. M1 fire rings out from the right front. Carbines answer. I figure it can't be anyone from Second Platoon, as we're on the left. From under a spreading branch, I take a quick prairie-dog look. A man scrambles from right to left and then disappears. Someone from Third Platoon, perhaps, but he's not wearing woolen ODs. The man rises, runs like a halfback, sidestepping peyote wood and trees. He pitches a grenade and dives for cover. I duck.

The grenade explodes. I look. An enemy soldier tumbles from behind a bundle of peyote wood. The man, an American paratrooper, dashes up and fires at the soldier on the ground, who is screaming. Then the trooper pumps shots into the immediate area. As I continue to observe, a burst of automatic fire drops the paratrooper. I hit the ground.

The fire came from the left front. *That was quick.* I come up slowly to the grass line. The paratrooper struggles to his feet, clutching his stomach before he falls and drags himself to a nearby tree. With his back against the tree, using it as a shield, he wraps his arms around his knees, then rocks back and forth. His head rolls like a man about to fall asleep. I spot three enemy soldiers advancing on the wounded trooper. Crouching, they steal through low-hanging branches. Suddenly the leader stops, stands, and cranes his neck, searching for the American paratrooper. I spring up and shoot him in the face. I then drop the second man before the third man and I fire at the same time. Splinters of wood explode at my right shoulder. The man tumbles backward. I duck, scoot right, then crawdad away. Hearing no automatic fire, I lie low. My left breast stings as I notice that across my breast is a red streak: I'm bleeding. The flap of my left shirt pocket is shot away; got lucky there.

Hedge-hopping German planes roar over as I hug Mother Earth. Someone is calling from the left rear; I listen. Gunfire crackles across the left front. *That automatic fire . . . it's moving left.*

"Ecky! You all right?" The voice of Cheyenne comes. His voice is muffled as he is in deep grass. Glad he made it.

"Yeah, I'm okay," I reply.

"Heard all that shooting, is that the Third Platoon?"

"No. It's an American paratrooper. He's been hit!"

"Could get Medicine Man to help him, but he's way back there somewhere!"

"Where's the rest of the squad?"

"Pinned down. Bear was following me, but I don't know what happened to him!"

I glance back and don't see anyone. Nothing but trees and underbrush. "We might as well wait for the squad to cross over."

"*Aho!*"

This place is an oven with no breeze. The wounded paratrooper remains still in the same position. No fire comes and can only be heard at the left front. I check the underbrush and tree trunks ahead, then rise to help the trooper. I notice blood all over me. From the deer-lay. I rub dirt on my pants and shirt front to get rid of the blood. The stench makes my stomach churn; I turn my face to vomit.

An M1 shot from the rear. Ahead of me a tree limb snaps, sending a man tumbling through leafy branches before he thumps to the ground. Insects rise as leaves float down.

"*Tiwat*," Corporal Leading Fox shouts. "Watch it!" he scolds. Jolted, I recover from the nausea and get down. Leading Fox had shot that man out of the tree. Crawling up, he calls: "Ecky, Phil wants you to protect the flank and rear. We're moving left."

"Okay. Will do. Anybody behind you?"

"Bear's back there, he got grazed on the left cheekbone, but he's okay. He has taken cover behind a wall. I followed the same wall from the left to get here. We're fighting a mixture of Germans and Italians. Everybody is pinned down. Phil has called Bill from reserve to help Good Buffalo. Okay, I'm going back to report to Phil. In the meantime, *Tiwat*—watch it!"

"I will. I will!" I reply, still shaking from the man in the tree who could have killed me.

Several yards away, among trees and deep grass, Cheyenne calls Leading Fox: "Hey, my fren'! You okay?"

"Cheyenne! I'm okay. You?"

"I'm okay. Hey, that was a good shot you made!"

"I'm an ol' squirrel hunter. You guys watch it!"

Planes roar in the distance before more Messerschmitts flash over. I stay down. "Cheyenne!"

"*H'yo!*"

"Go back to the wall. Check on Bear. See if any of the squad made it."

"*Aho!*"

On the left beyond where Cheyenne vacated, carbine fire erupts. I hear an M1 hit back before more carbine fire, followed by M1 fire. Finally there is more carbine fire. Then: "Mussolini get you! Mussolini get you!"

"Shit!" Leading Fox shouts back, blazing away with a full clip. Silence comes; I sweat. Leading Fox calls back, "*Tit kotit, tawit!*" (Killed three!) At the left front, in Good Buffalo's area, the fire dwindles to sniping. There is no fire from the immediate front.

If the squad has made that clearing back there, we could advance and flank them. Don't think anyone is behind, so why wait to protect the rear like Shield Chief wants us to?

"Ecky!" Cheyenne says.

"*H'yo*," I answer.

"Bear's all right. He got a ricochet and bits of stone from that wall. Nicked his cheekbone and corner of his eye. Some of the squad made it. They've taken cover behind the wall too. Ing and the rest are still way back there."

"Stay put. I'm going ahead. There's no fire up there. It's all on the left front. Maybe I can find a way for us to get around behind them. I'll be back."

"Watch it, Ecky!"

"Oh, I will."

I come upon the man Leading Fox shot out of the tree. He lies face up, tangled in a broken tree branch. He has eyes with a blank stare, and he has bled through the nose and mouth. In this heat, flies swarm over his face. Caught in briars is his carbine. The carbine has a folding bayonet attached to the barrel. I move and eagle-eye everything. This time I look in the trees. I spot a waist-high wall and crawl over. A limb snags the bayonet on my M1 and deflects it downward, and it pierces my right boot at the sole and little toe. Suddenly automatic fire erupts, sending me scrambling to get down next to the wall. The fire is at the left front, on sloping ground. It's firing into Good Buffalo's area; there is no fire here.

Suddenly I hear voices. Germans? Italians? I pull my M1 up to ready and click off the safety lock. These people are crawling along this same wall, coming this way. Then: "Pass the word: 'Hold!'" It is our guys. I uncoil and lock the M1 again before running down in places where the wall has cracks in it. I turn to one of the cracks. I hear a man crawling as his equipment rustles. Water in canteen jiggles. I look through the crack and see Pawnee eyeballs.

"*Wuh!*"

"*Wuh!*"

"*Nawa, tiwat. Kitte kesu toddi?*" (Hello, cousin. What are you doing?), I ask.

"Hunting deer," Grant Shield Chief replies with a twinkle in his eyes. "The other kind of deer—*chu-wat*" (girls).

"*A-ay.* That's the way you are. Always thinking of girls."

"Ecky, you're on the wrong side of the wall. There's a machine gun up there. I was going up there to take a look. I might be able to get close enough for a grenade. My squad is behind me."

I stand and roll over the wall. "Hey, Eck! How's Good Buffalo, Last Arrow, and the rest?" someone calls from down the wall.

"Hold your voice down!" Grant Shield Chief barks. "Good to see you," Grant says. "The Second Platoon okay?"

"Yeah, we're okay. How about the Third Platoon?"

"We're okay. The Second Platoon is moving fast. Has a hard time keeping up. The enemy delayed us for a while. The going is slow in this place . . . there are too many trees and underbrush." German fighters pass over—more Messerschmitts.

Hugging the wall, I am lying in front of Grant. He taps my feet: "Ecky, your foot. It's bleeding. You been hit? Does it hurt?" Grant is concerned. "And here you are weathering the storm. The old ones say Pawnees are men of men." As though congratulating me, he pats my foot gently.

"It's nothing, Grant." Embarrassed, I can't tell him that I stuck myself with my own bayonet. I feel ridiculous. It's like an Indian shooting himself in the foot with his own bow and arrow.

Automatic fire comes again. I can tell it is definitely firing at Good Buffalo this time. There's M1 fire, carbine fire, and tommy-gun fire. "*Tiwat*—let's go," Grant urges. "Maybe we can spot that gun."

We follow the wall for some time, then come to another. Where they meet are cracks and fallen stones. Grant turns his helmet around backward and looks through a crack. He peers with the intensity of a submarine captain eyeing his victim through a periscope. There is a long burst of automatic fire. "I see them, on a brushy knoll, about sixty yards or more away." He takes a grenade and pulls the safety ring. Grant Shield Chief, an ex-quarterback, rises, then heaves the fragmentation grenade like it's a long forward pass. He ducks behind the wall. I peek through a crack to see if it is on target. The grenade has popped the lever and spirals to an arc, trailing a ribbon of smoke. Then an explosion and a puff of dust on the brushy knoll. "Did I score, *tiwat?*" From the brushy knoll comes silence.

"Yea! 'Atta way to go!"

The husky Pawnee springs to his feet, turns, and shouts: "Let's go, men! Let's go!"

On the left, hollering and war-whooping can be heard. Good Buffalo and Last Arrow's men attack. M1 fire rings out, but no carbine fire is returned. I limp back and shout: "Second Squad! Let's go!" In a short while the squad comes up, and we join the attack. The immediate front and the left front rises with knolls and washouts. At the right, war cries, cowboy yells, the shriek of a gander goose, and the whinny of a stud horse can be heard. It's Matlock's Third Platoon, charging with bayonets. Figures in dark uniforms, with hands raised, dot the knolls and washouts. Those on the right scatter as Matlock's men close in before taking them prisoner. It takes minutes to collect all the prisoners, attend the wounded, and reorganize.

I check the squad and check Bear, who holds a blood-smeared GI hanky to his face. A slug hit a wall, grazed his left cheekbone, and exploded bits of stone into the corner of his eye.

"Medicine Man! Medicine Man!" Minutes later Medicine Man responds. He has been checking Good Buffalo and Last Arrow's men. Medicine Man has Bear sit on the ground, then attends to him.

Having heard the call, Shield Chief appears. "Is he okay?" he asks, looking at Medicine Man, then to Bear. Examining Bear's cheekbone and eye, Medicine Man replies, "Yeah, he's okay. But the enemy almost got a wild turkey gobbler. Boy, that was close."

Sam Bear looks at Medicine Man and grins. Suddenly a runner scurries from behind: "Sergeant Shield Chief, Captain Lee wants all platoon sergeants." Acknowledging, Shield Chief nods. Then he steps closer to Bear and looks at the cheekbone and eye as Medicine Man swabs the wound with cotton. The runner and Shield Chief take off. I stay.

I tell Medicine Man about the wounded paratrooper. "The battalion medics, coming up from the rear, will find him. We'll take good care of him," he says, carefully going over the eye with cotton. Seeing that Bear is well cared for, I rejoin the squad. The First and Third Squads are dispersed beyond. In this

heat, the men have unbuttoned their shirts and pulled shirttails out. Some lie
in the tall grass, while others stand. Most drink water and watch the prisoners
being marched off.

Corporal Ingalls checks with me. I tell him about Bear. "Damn, it's getting
rougher," he says, shaking his head. "And the day ain't over yet."

Shield Chief, Lieutenant Dobbins, Sergeant Stone, and three men from
Second Platoon approach. "Sergeant Echohawk," Lieutenant Dobbins says:
"You and your squad all right?"

"Two men were hit, Sir. Not bad. They are patched up and still going
strong."

"Yes, Sergeant Shield Chief told me about them!"

"It's good to see you, Sir."

"Good to see you too, Sergeant." Lieutenant Dobbins has a slight limp on
the right foot. He looks at Sergeant Stone: "Sergeant Stone, have the squad
leaders assemble here."

"Yes, Sir," he replies. Sergeant Stone turns and walks hastily toward the
platoon and bellows: "All squad leaders! Got *damn* it! All squad leaders! Over
here!" Dispersed, the men turn when they hear Stone's voice: they know he
is back. In a short while three squad leaders, Platoon Sergeant Shield Chief,
and right guide Sergeant Stone assemble. Lieutenant Dobbins, the platoon
leader, briefs us. I notice that the bottom of his right legging is rolled up to the
top of his boot. On his face are muddy rivulets of sweat. Like ours, his shirt is
sweat-soaked. Lieutenant Dobbins tells us Captain Lee has brought B Company together and that we are to turn and drive north. A Company will be on
our right and C Company in reserve. Battalion is on track now. He passes on
to us that Scoglitti has been taken and that the Italians are giving up all along
the coast. Lieutenant Dobbins also relates that the Germans have also pulled
back but that there are still pockets of resistance. Second Platoon falls in for the
long trudge to come.

Brummett Echohawk sketches in late 1943. The pad he is sketching on was a gift from the actress Madeleine Carroll, whom he met at the 17th General Hospital at Naples, Italy. Carroll appeared in films directed by John Ford and Alfred Hitchcock in the 1930s. Image courtesy of Elaine Childers.

Greek soldier. Private First Class Paulis Diamanbis, Greek 50th Infantry. Captured by Germans, Diamanbis escaped after cruel treatment. March 29, 1944.

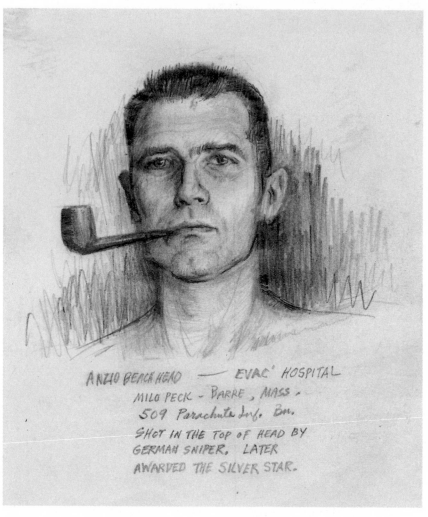

ANZIO BEACH HEAD — EVAC' HOSPITAL
MILO PECK - BARRE, MASS.
509 Parachute Inf. Bn.
SHOT IN THE TOP OF HEAD BY
GERMAN SNIPER. LATER
AWARDED THE SILVER STAR.

Portrait, Corporal Milo P. Peck of the 509th Parachute Infantry Battalion. Peck, from Barre, Massachusetts, was shot in the top of the head by a German sniper. He later received a Silver Star for action in France.

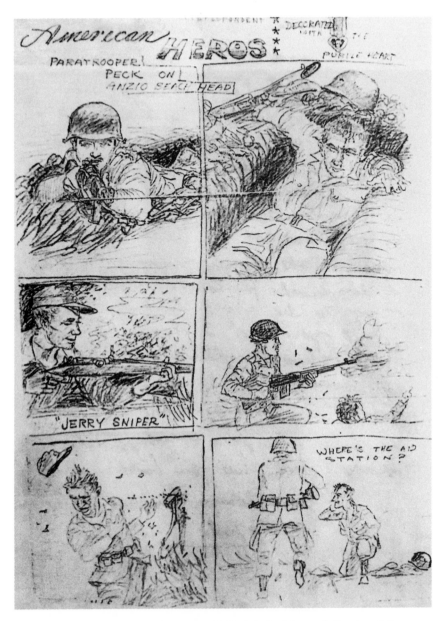

Echohawk sketches documenting the actions of Milo P. Peck of the 509th Parachute Infantry Battalion.

Echohawk sketches documenting the actions of Milo P. Peck of the 509th Parachute Infantry Battalion. Peck received a Silver Star for his actions depicted in these sketches.

Platoon Sergeant Phillip "Shield Chief" Gover poses for a Brummett Echohawk painting in traditional Pawnee regalia; the painting hangs today at the 45th Infantry Division Museum. Image courtesy of the 45th Infantry Division Museum.

OPPOSITE: *Brummett Echohawk paints a portrait of Platoon Sergeant Phillip "Shield Chief" Gover at his home in Tulsa, Oklahoma.*

Cathedral at Venafro, Italy. Image courtesy of the 45th Infantry Division Museum.

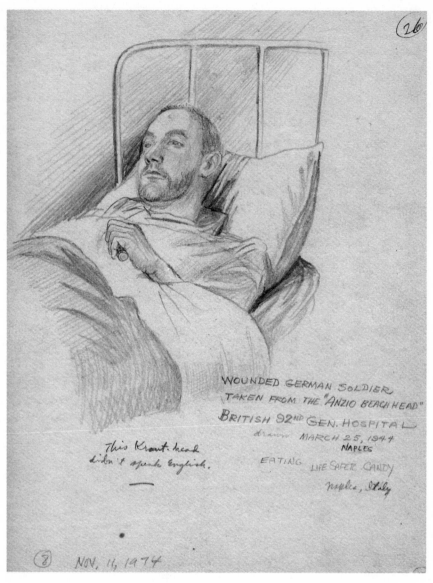

"Wounded German soldier taken from the Anzio Beachhead. This Kraut head didn't speak English. Eating Life Saver candy." British 92nd General Hospital, Naples, Italy, March 25, 1944.

B Company veteran. Private First Class Robert B. Jackson stands next to Echohawk's commissioned work on the USS Anzio *during a 2011 change of watch ceremony in Newport, Virginia. Image courtesy of Robert B. Jackson.*

4

Father, Bless Our Soldiers

Sergeant Echohawk's faith was paramount in his duties and leadership. Knowing that the minds of his men and himself were vulnerable to the horrors of war, his faith was both his strength and his shield. Fear was always present, but he knew of the spiritual river from which to drink and refresh his soul. After the war he would read the Bible through many times. The mark of war on this Thunderbird created a resolve of his Christian faith and devotion that, at the end of his life, was evident beyond words.

Setting out, Shield Chief has us take the same order we were in before: Second and Third Squads lead, with the First in reserve. Lieutenant Dobbins and Shield Chief place themselves between the two leading squads. Sergeant Stone, who assists Shield Chief, brings up the rear of the platoon. B Company moves out with First and Second Platoons abreast. The Third Platoon is in reserve, followed by the Fourth, with light machine guns and 60mm mortars. As scout of Second Platoon, Cheyenne leads the pack. We leave the dense trees, tall grass, and underbrush. I think to myself, *It must have been a river basin or tributary.* Ahead, barren hills with dry grass protrude from the horizon. *Must be about three in the afternoon. . . .* I'm hungry and haven't eaten since last night and it's hot—real hot. There's no conversation between the men as we continue on. Tired, we keep moving. As we plod through fields the grasshoppers rise, circle, and settle in front of us. We come upon them again, and again they rise and flitter until they thin out. Gunfire sounds from the front before we hit the ground. The fire came from the right in First Platoon's sector, but nobody is firing on us. I rise and signal Cheyenne "forward," and we advance.

There is an exchange of carbine and M1 fire on the right as we move. Suddenly an eruption of machine guns opens up at the immediate front, raking the area. They have the whole front covered, which is a vast field of wheatlike grass with washouts, cactus, and sparse trees. They were waiting for us to pass through here: textbook ambush.

"Cheyenne!" I call. "You all right?"

"Y'ah, I'm all right!"

"Did you spot anything?"

"I saw movement up there, about three hundred yards. Didn't see that gun, though." At the right front the firefight continues.

"Ecky!" Shield Chief yells. "*Siks-a! Wees!*" (Come! Hurry!) I run and get down near Shield Chief and Lieutenant Dobbins. They are lying a few yards apart. I stay a few paces away to keep from bunching up.

"Sergeant Echohawk," Lieutenant Dobbins says with his head above the grass. "Take your squad around the left flank. We'll lay down a base fire to cover you. I take this to be just a delaying action; they've been doing it all day. Our troops are building up and pushing inland fast. All right, sergeant . . . move out."

I wonder why the lieutenant doesn't send First Squad, who is in reserve. My squad's done all the end runs so far. I look at Shield Chief, who knows what I am thinking. He turns his face to the left and points with his lips, meaning "go."

Lieutenant Dobbins looks at me. "Any questions, Sergeant?"

"None, Sir." I take off and call Cheyenne before we double back, picking up the rest of the squad. I look the ground over for an approach where we won't be seen. If they see us moving left, they'll know what we're up to. We run at an angle that is more to the rear than left. Good Buffalo's men start to shoot, laying down base fire for us as we move. First Platoon on the right is swapping lead for lead. We dip into a shallow draw to find cover. We can hear the squad running blind. My right foot hurts from stabbing myself, but I must keep going. We come to an old wall that stands just above the knee-deep grass. Ahead of it there is no cover. We cross the wall and turn right. Crawling, we follow the wall a short distance, where it turns left parallel with the immediate front. From here on, the wall becomes a trail of stones that fade in the grass and lead to mesquite trees. We hold.

Good Buffalo's men are still firing. First Platoon has let up. Ahead is a hill. On the right is the immediate front and a hill higher than the rest, commanding the ground. This is where that machine gun will be. The squad can't cross here, though—it's too open. If they see us that gun will cut us to pieces, and they're sure to be watching their flank. Two men might make it. I pass word that Cheyenne and I are going forward and that everybody is to cover us. We leave our packs and follow the trail of stones. Inching forward, we reach the mesquite trees. Here, a part of the wall still stands, goes on a short way, then fades again. The ground leading to the hill above us is bare save for clumps of cactus and thorn bushes. It's around a hundred and seventy-five yards to get up there.

I wipe the sweat from my face and eyes. "Chey' . . . cover me. The ground up there is awful bare. Maybe, one can make it. I'll go."

"Okay," he says. "But watch it, Ecky . . . watch it." I slip through the eroded wall and make for the hill before pausing at a thorn bush to look things over. I see nothing and keep crawling.

Ahead I see a small wash that meanders up the hill. There is no more firing: could be that they pulled back. The lieutenant said it was just a delaying action. I get up and move in a crouching position. Nearing the top of the hill all is quiet; all that running and crawling for seemingly nothing. I stand upright and immediately spot movement. At the right, men in the grass are lying down and facing the other direction. Fifteen yards away is a machine gun, and these two men are behind it. Standing still, I ease out a grenade. It is the one with the lever I taped down. I claw at the tape with my fingernails without taking my eyes off the enemy. The man with the ammunition at the gun sees me. He shouts as I duck. I nearly bust my kneecaps crawling down the draw as machine gun fire churns up the ground around me. Lead zings as I move like a lizard running from a red-tailed hawk. A grenade explodes, then another. My heart is pounding. I glance back and see two men with carbines skyline themselves in the afternoon sun. I slam two quick shots at them and take off. I sidestep cactus, hurdle thorn bushes, and run like a scared deer. Reaching the wall where I started, I dive over it and roll. Recovering quickly, I crawl back to the wall for cover as machine gun slugs rivet the other side. Carbines kick up the dust, and M1s hit back: the squad is covering.

A Browning Automatic Rifle opens up as I press myself against the wall and shake. "Ecky, you okay?" Cheyenne calls with concern. He's a few yards down the wall.

"I'm okay!" I force myself to take a deep breath, ease it out, and relax. "Came on the blind side of that gun. Since there was no fire I thought they had pulled back. I took a grenade but it was the one I taped the lever on. You remember, I had it back at the pillbox. I was standing up, and when I tried to get the tape off, they saw me. Luckily, I ducked as they shot at me."

"Heard that gun," Cheyenne says, and adds, "And heard grenades. Spotted two men too. When I started to shout, I heard you shoot. The two men went down and then everybody started shooting." The machine gun fires no more as our guys cease fire.

Someone calls. Cheyenne picks it up. "It's San Antone!" Private Gilbert Santana, a Comanche from San Antonio, Texas, crawls up to Cheyenne. *Maybe he has a message*, I think to myself.

Expecting word from the lieutenant, I listen. San Antone says, "Ecky, I have an idea. I know a way we can get them." Cheyenne and I look at each other. San Antone continues: "Look at the sun. It's past midafternoon. We could get on that hill at the left and shoot at them. They can't see us because the sun will be in their eyes. Another thing: the sun will shine on their faces.

Being white men, their faces will stand out like Hereford cattle. We'll pick them off; it's an old Comanche trick."

San Antone beams, awaiting an answer. I look to Cheyenne. "What do you think, Chey'?"

"Sounds good," Cheyenne replies. He looks at the hill, then the sun. "That's a long way to go over bare ground, but the sun is right."

"Hey, Sarge!" Corporal Ingalls says as he crosses the open space toting our packs. "You guys all right?" Ingalls gets down before reaching us to keep from bunching up.

"Yeah, we're okay. Just stirred up a hornet's nest was all."

"Damn," Ingalls says, eyeing the hill where the machine gun was. "Sure glad none of you guys got hit. Lieutenant Dobbins sent a runner to us. We're moving. The Second Squad will link up with the Third Squad. Here's your packs. Looks like I'm always bringing up your packs!"

"Okay, let's go," I say, putting on my pack. I tell San Antone that the Comanche trick is good and that we'll use it later. Disappointed, he smiles.

Hungry, I remember the beefsteak wrapped in a GI hanky. I reach in my shirt, but it's gone. It could be anywhere, with all that crawling and running. Most likely where I dove over the wall. I tell the guys that I'm going back for something I lost and that I will catch up. I return to the wall and find it. It has strands of grass on it that I brush off before putting the beefsteak in my shirt. Happy, I jog back and rejoin the squad. Cheyenne, our scout, is far out ahead. First Platoon, on the far right, has a scout out too. Advancing in extended squad column, I look back to make sure my column is staggered with interval. Ahead is a range of hills. The sun is past midafternoon, and it is still hot. I adjust the shoulder straps on my pack. As I move my pack I can feel the sweat run down my back. I pick up a tiny pebble and put it under my tongue to stay cool.

Cheyenne stops at the top of a hill. He signals: "come." I signal the squad to hold, then jog forward. My legs are tired, and my foot still hurts from the incident. I run slowly like a tired packhorse to make it up to Cheyenne.

Far to the right, the First Platoon scout has stopped too. Reaching Cheyenne, he says, "We better get the lieutenant up here. Look!" I turn to look forward, spotting dead ahead—about half a mile—buildings with terra cotta houses with red-tile roofs. Mesquite trees, green shrubbery, and cedar trees surround them.

I wipe the sweat from my eyes with my sleeve and take another look. "Chey' . . . wonder if that's a garrison?"

"It's got to be military," Cheyenne offers, jiggling a tiny stone in his mouth. "'Cause that bunch that delayed us with that machine gun had to fall back to something."

"I better get Lieutenant Dobbins." Just as I turn to leave, I see the lieutenant and Shield Chief coming up the hill at a running walk.

"What's up, Sergeant?" Lieutenant Dobbins asks, his face red with sweat.

"Sir, take a look."

"That's got to be a command post." The lieutenant takes his field glasses and looks: "There are no vehicles." He focuses the binoculars and keeps looking. "Sergeant Shield Chief, the platoon will keep moving. There could be fire. If any, it won't be in an organized manner." Lieutenant Dobbins puts the field glasses away. "Let's move out."

Shield Chief steps out where he can be seen by the men. He signals "forward" to Good Buffalo, who is watching. Good Buffalo answers "yes" in sign language. Then Shield Chief turns to me: "Okay, Ecky . . . move out." I move into the open, then signal the squad: "forward." The squad responds. Cheyenne falls back to his position, and I take lead. Lieutenant Dobbins and Shield Chief position themselves between my squad and Good Buffalo's squad. Far to the right, First Platoon advances. The squads move forward and down the slope of the hill; I check our interval. We reach the bottom of the hill leading to the buildings. As the ground levels off we spot the buildings ahead. The main one is two stories and does not have a deserted look. Carbine fire and M1 fire can be heard in the distance as we inch closer to the complex. We look to Shield Chief: he extends both arms outward and motions us forward. Good Buffalo relays the signal to his squad before I relay the same to mine. Second and Third Squads swing abreast. We dogtrot with M1s and bayonets at high port. Dust kicks up as carbines snap. More dust kicks up. "*He-doohl!*" (Go!) Shield Chief shouts. "*Kiddi didde didde, Kidde didde didde!*" We lower bayonets and charge.

Running hard, we give war cries. Cheyenne hollers, "It's a good day to die!" From Sam Bear comes the gobble of a wild tom turkey. We shoot up doors, windows, and walls as we reach the structure. Plaster, glass, and chips of stone fly through the air. Powdery dust rises at the base of walls. There's a lot of M1 fire coming from the right.

White flags appear in the windows and doors. "Hold it! Hold it!" Shield Chief shouts. We hold and cease fire. Italian soldiers stream from the building with hands up, eyes wide, jabbering. They discard their Mussolini helmets and put on field caps. Shield Chief shouts: "Don't bunch up! Don't bunch up!" I check my men to see if anyone got hit. "Ecky, go around the back and check it out!" Shield Chief orders. I take Cheyenne and San Antone. In the back are three small buildings. I kick in the door of the first building as Cheyenne and San Antone cover me. Inside are desks, cabinets, and a drafting table with all kinds of drawing instruments. On the drafting table are sheets of drawing paper. I take several sheets and stuff them in my shirt. I also take some pencils.

San Antone and Cheyenne come in. They look around too. On the wall
are maps, a calendar, and a huge picture of Mussolini in a small helmet with
his chin jutting forward. "Mussolini sonofabitch," Cheyenne says; we have a
laugh. The drawers of the desks and cabinets have been opened and emptied.

San Antone quips, "They left in a hurry, saddled up, and headed for the
border."

I raise my M1 to ready: "Let's check the whole place out." We check the
other two buildings and find nothing. We look in a shed, and on the dirt floor
is a bloodstained paratroop jacket bearing the 82nd Airborne insignia. Scattered about are first-aid packets that are torn open. And there's blood, with
flies droning about. Partly hidden in a mound of straw are three Musette packs
worn by paratroopers. In them are seven hand grenades, shaving kits, a pair of
barber clippers, and buckskin gloves with the trigger finger out. In the straw,
too, are odd cartridges. Instead of lead, the bullets look like wood and are dyed
purple. None of ours, that's for sure. I take a Musette bag and put the seven
grenades and barber clippers in it.

Leaving the shed, we see men from First Platoon searching the buildings.
We enter the rear of the main building and go up a flight of stairs to the second
floor. The walls are riddled with bullet holes, and the windows are broken.
Glass and plaster crunch underfoot as we move. There are desks, chairs, and a
table about twelve feet long. On the table is paper money, banded and stacked
in neat rows. We look at each other, then help ourselves. Last Arrow comes up
the stairs. He, too, helps himself to the money. Last Arrow flutters the edges of
the currency and laughingly remarks, "Hot dang, I'm rich as an Osage, and I
don't even have oil wells!" We laugh. It feels good.*

Sergeant Matlock appears at the head of the stairs. "Hey, Phil is looking for
you guys." He is standing in sunlight coming from a broken window.

"Okay," Last Arrow replies, holding a bill to the light for a closer look. The
paper money is yellow and bigger than ours.

"What you guys got?" Matlock asks.

"Sicilian money," Last Arrow answers, still examining the bill.

"Aw, Turtlehead, the money's no good," Matlock scoffs. "We were issued
invasion money when we left North Africa. They told us everything else was
no good. Might make good souvenirs, though."

"Well, let's just say I'm taking some souvenirs," replies Last Arrow.

Matlock wipes the sweat from his face. The late-afternoon sunlight hitting the side of his face reveals character. This Pawnee has a powerful nose

---

*By 1939, Osage individuals had received and shared a total of more than $100 million in
royalties and bonuses from the rights to oil on their land. See Corey Bone, "Osage Oil,"
www.okhistory.org/publications/enc/entry.php?entry=OS006.

and cheekbones and a firm mouth; he resembles the chief on the Indianhead nickel. Matlock removes his steel helmet. His stern, Indianhead-nickel look vanishes: "Phil said you ran into a lot of fire," he says with heart. "Glad you made it. You all right?"

"Yeah, I'm all right," I reply. Matlock and Shield Chief are the oldest men in the company. Both have concern for their men. Matlock looks at Cheyenne and eyes the bandage on his temple: "Cheyenne, did you get hit?"

"Naw," Cheyenne waves off the question. "Just a scratch, it's nothing; Medicine Man fixed me up."

Matlock looks at San Antone. "San Antone, you okay?"

"Okay? Us Comanche got good medicine."

"Good," says Matlock, smiling. Matlock puts his steel helmet back on. That Indianhead-nickel look returns: "All right, men. Let's move out!"

We rejoin the platoon as the prisoners—about fifty—are being marched off. Our guys are high with excitement, making sure to eyeball everything. Medicine Man checks everyone and learns no one has been hit. Lieutenant Dobbins, who has met with Captain Lee, as other platoon leaders have, assembles the squad leaders Shield Chief and Stone. Other men of the platoon stand close by to hear what the lieutenant has to say about the overall situation. He says that B Company is to keep pushing north. Vittoria has been taken by Third Battalion, but there is still patchy resistance. He relates that we haven't heard anything on how the 180th is doing. And there's nothing on the 157th either. "Bureau of Indian Affairs," Leading Fox says in a hushed tone.

Lieutenant Dobbins takes off his steel helmet and, with a GI hanky, wipes the sweat from his face and neck. "The company will move in the same order, First and Second Platoon forward, the Third in reserve, weapons last." Lieutenant Dobbins puts his helmet back on: "Sergeant Shield Chief, move the platoon out."

Shield Chief, munching on a K-ration biscuit, says, "First and Third Squads lead. Ecky, since you've made all the end runs, the Second Squad will be in reserve."

"*Aho!*" we squad leaders reply. B Company moves out.

The platoons take interval. It's about five in the afternoon and there's not a cloud in the sky. It's still hot, like the July heat in Oklahoma, especially about five o'clock. That's when we gather for the Pawnee Powwow. It's July 10th— yes, the powwow is going on right now back home in Pawnee. I can hear the drums and the singing, and see the dancers. The heat is fierce. We stop. We move. We stop. Move again. I shift the Musette bag with the seven hand grenades and barber clippers, then adjust my pack. My shoulders are tired: it's been a long first day, and I'm feeling the sweat run down my spine. I look back at the men. They're plodding along like tired packhorses. Occasionally, grasshoppers rise in our path. We stop, and I get a box of K-rations from my pack. I take a K-ration biscuit and powdered coffee. I then remove my canteen and canteen cup to make a cup of cold coffee.

A hand signal comes. I start to take a quick drink of coffee and find a grasshopper in it. I remove the grasshopper and gulp the coffee anyway. I move forward at a running walk, carrying my cup. I reach Lieutenant Dobbins, Shield Chief, Good Buffalo, and Last Arrow. They are sitting, but they keep a few yards apart to avoid bunching up. Lieutenant Dobbins says we are to dig in, set up defenses, and hold for the night. That's all he says before dismissing us. His face is sweaty and red with heat; he looks beat. All of us are tired: we've been going nonstop since hitting the beach at H-Hour.

Evening comes, but the heat lingers. "Sergeant Shield Chief, let's look the ground over; then we'll deploy the platoon," Lieutenant Dobbins says, rising slowly to his feet. His right legging is still rolled to the top of his shoe, and he still has a limp.

"Okay, Sir," Shield Chief replies. "Ecky, bring your squad up." I move where the squad can see me. I signal for them to come. I sit, drink coffee, and down another K-ration biscuit. Good Buffalo and Last Arrow chomp on K-ration biscuits too. In a short while my squad comes up. Then Lieutenant Dobbins and Shield Chief return. Shield Chief shows us where to dig in. Our area overlooks a shallow valley about three hundred yards away. In the valley are groves of cactus. Beyond it are hills with white grass. Shield Chief says the lieutenant wants all three squads abreast, for there is a wide front to cover. The weapons platoon will support with machine guns and mortars. I show each man where to dig; our slit trenches will form a staggered line, linking First and Third Squads. I have each man pick an object in front of him, fifty to seventy-five yards out, as an aiming point. At night, if a man moves near the aiming stake, you know the range. Without this, the distance of a moving object at night is deceiving. I also instruct them to aim low, for at night there is a tendency to shoot high. Aiming low also creates a ricochet, which is equally effective.

Shield Chief talks to the squad leaders: "First and Third Squads' automatic rifles will cover the flanks. They will also lay down a crossfire in front of the platoon. Ecky, at center. Keep your automatic rifle in reserve, but close enough for quick commitment. The First Squad will put out two men for a listening post. Two men in each squad will stay awake two hours. At 0500 everybody is up, ready for a possible counterattack. Same password: 'George Marshall.' Okay, check your men's feet for blisters. If they have any, have Medicine Man take care of them." I check with Corporal Ingalls about what Shield Chief said. We set a two-hour watch in the squad, with Cheyenne and me taking the dawn shift. This way I can have control should the enemy counterattack. We check the men for blisters and find none. We dig in.

Some men are equipped with a small shovel, others with a pick mattock. For the sake of efficiency, the men exchange entrenching tools: the shovel is for scooping, while the mattock is for hacking. The grassy hills are candy pink with lavender shadows. The cactus groves are purple as the blue twilight settles over the strange land. I pull drawing paper from my shirt and take a pencil from my breast pocket. The eraser has been shot away. Partly shot away, too, is the shirt's flap. I attempt to sketch using the flat mess-kit lid as a drawing board. The paper is damp with perspiration, so I give it up. Now to eat: I unwrap the beefsteak I retrieved earlier. I pick off the threads of grass and wolf it down—still salt-and-peppered. *Hot dang . . . it's delicious*! I wipe grease from my mouth, then get the Baby Ruth bar from the mess kit. It's melted, but I eat what I can and chew the wrapper for flavor. I also drink water; it feels good. A wolf howls in the valley.

San Antone, dug in a few yards away, calls over: "Hey, didn't know there were wolves in Sicily."

Cheyenne answers from the dark, "That's no wolf . . . I heard an echo. That's a Pawnee!"

"Hey, Cheyenne," I call. "Let's go visit Phil." Good Buffalo and Last Arrow are with Shield Chief when we approach. They are talking about what happened on this first day of combat. We join up.

"Say, Ecky," Shield Chief says. "Medicine Man was here a few minutes ago. He had been to the battalion medics. We asked if he had any news. All Medicine Man said was what Lieutenant Dobbins told us. Mentioned the wounded paratrooper in your area. He had taken a burst of machine gun fire in the lower body that tore up his groin and privates. He lost a lot of blood. Medics figured by the time they got him to the beach . . . then taken by barge to a hospital ship . . . the trooper would die. They gave him a lot of morphine. Our medics did their best to save him."

"All paratroopers are brave," Shield Chief adds. "When they jumped, the troopers were scattered all over the coast and had to fight in small groups. But they raised heck with the Italians and Germans anyway and kept them off balance."

Footsteps at the immediate front approach fast, startling us. Shield Chief reaches for his tommy-gun. "Are you one of us?" he says in a loud voice.

"I am," comes the answer. Sergeant Louis "Ruling His Son" Eaves steps from the darkness.

"Thought that was you after hearing the *skiri*" (wolf).

The rest of us greet Ruling His Son. "*Nawa*."

"*Nawa*," he replies.

"*Six-pettit*" (Come, sit down), says Shield Chief. Ruling His Son sits down cross-legged, then sees Cheyenne. "Hey, Cheyenne, let's get drunk."

"*Aho*, um ready," Cheyenne chuckles. "Heard a wolf call. San Antone said he didn't know there were wolves in Sicily. I tol' him that was no wolf. It's a Pawnee. Old-time Cheyennes said Pawnees were tricky because they signal each other by wolf calls. Old ones say the way you tell it's a Pawnee is that a man's voice echoes. The howl of the wolf doesn't . . . and I heard an echo."

Ruling His Son tells us he was scouting country where he found tracks from a small car. He says it parked north-to-south to make shade from the afternoon sun. Around the car tracks were heel prints from jackboots, indicating that the men sat close to the car for shade. For the sun to throw that tight a shadow puts the time at about three in the afternoon. Short cigarette butts meant they had been there quite a while. They were nervous, too: there were attempts to start grass fires. I saw places where fires were started but went out. Ruling His Son figures the small car was a German jeep equipped with a radio. They might have been watching us as we moved; they could be preparing a counterattack. Ruling His Son gives another wolf call in the valley to let the Pawnee know that it was another Pawnee.

Clumsy footsteps come from the rear. "Got *damn*, Phil, you guys holding a powwow?" Sergeant Stone asks.

"Bet you all would like to be back home with the Pawnee Powwow going on about now."

"For sure," Good Buffalo remarks.

Stone looks around as if to find him with us. "How's Lieutenant Dobbins?"

"He's sacked out," Shield Chief answers. "Thought I'd see how he was. I believe he sprained his ankle leaving the barge this morning. Them got-damn bangalore torpedoes was a-rollin' around on the floor of the barge. He stepped on one as it rolled and twisted his ankle. It was dark as hell, and the barge was a-pitchin'. We and some of the Third Squad were in the back and were the last to leave. We jumped into the water up to our necks . . . the barge got hung up sideways. Suddenly a big wave hit. The barge driver hollered, 'Son of a bitch!' I believe the barge turned over. I didn't look back to check, and then, well . . . we got left behind. The lieutenant was limpin' bad, but he kept a-goin'. We joined part of the Fourth Platoon. Everybody was mixed up."

"Lieutenant Dobbins is a good officer," Shield Chief adds. "I just came from the First Platoon. Sergeant Newby shot himself in the foot today."

"*Uh-dee*" (an expression of disgust), Shield Chief and Good Buffalo snort. Newby was a gambler, bootlegger, and a man who lent money at highway robbery interest rates. He exhibited no leadership in the field and showed little concern for his men. The Pawnees in the company called him *Chaticks-takah ta kitti wis* (White man who cheats). No wonder Shield Chief and Good Buffalo both growled "*Uh-dee.*"

Sergeant Stone continues: "Lieutenant Langley just about had a heat stroke. The First Platoon got delayed some. But the lieutenant came out of it."

Stone picks up a clod of dirt and crumbles it in his big fist. "Freddie Roland was killed today." He looks down at his hands and lets the dirt trickle through his fingers. "Y'all knowed Captain Roberts over at C Company . . . well, he was killed today too. Hear'd he was shot in the stomach with a wooden bullet. The bullet splintered and hoogered up his insides."

We remain silent. Shield Chief stands. "Well, let's get some shuteye. You guys get your men up at 0500. Want them bright-eyed and bushy-tailed."

"*Aho!*" we chorus, and return to our slit trenches.

I lay out my cartridge belt, then get into my slit trench. I drive my Pawnee knife into the wall of the trench where it can be had in one movement. At my side is my M1, its fifteen-inch bayonet propped against the front edge of the trench. I keep my steel helmet on; the liner cushions my head like a pillow. Freddie Roland . . . the first man to be killed in B Company played shortstop on the company ball team when we were in Abilene, Texas. Real good guy. Captain Roberts . . . killed by a wooden bullet. I remember seeing those wooden bullets back where we found the bloodstained American paratroop jacket and Musette bags. Captain Roberts was from Oklahoma City. We went to spy school together. They took me because I could remember things and sketch them in detail later. One officer said I had total recall. Captain Roberts was given the code name "Mistretta Red." I was "Mistretta Blue." We could use any telephone, give the code name, and be connected to Intelligence immediately. The term "an officer and a gentleman" fit the captain perfectly.*

The first day of combat—this morning—I almost got killed at that enemy pillbox. Later Corporal Leading Fox shot a man out of a tree ahead of me. The enemy soldier had seen me stand and move—he could have killed me there. I got careless and didn't look in the trees. While advancing, I engaged a machine gun, and it almost got me too. Enemy soldiers threw hand grenades at me. *I want to be brave like the Pawnee Indian warriors. Chaticks-si-Chaticks*—Men of Men. I get scared . . . awful scared. But I must not show fear, for I am a *Raáwiirakuhkitawi'u*—a leader.

---

*Although it is unknown what spy school Echohawk attended, it is believed that he received formal training in espionage and intelligence due to his photographic-like memory, which enabled him to sketch detailed scenes after the fact.

This has been the hardest day of my life. I look up to a Mediterranean night with millions of stars.

Father, bless our *ra-ri-pa-ku-su*. Father, bless our soldiers.

I pull my shirt collar up, shift my shoulders, and let the clods of dirt settle. Exhausted. I drift off to sleep.

5

The Second Day

The war carries on. . . . Fear is an absolute, not a movie scene to excite the emotions. This is the reality of war as each man draws on his training and the grace of God to carry him through each day. Humor is a part of the experience; without it sanity may slip away. The thoughts of home bring a balm of relief, if only for a moment.

"Ecky."

"*A-ay*," I respond from sound sleep. Take my M1 and sit up.

San Antone has a hand on my shoulder. "It's four o'clock," he says in a low voice.

"Anything happen during the night?" I ask, getting out of the slit trench and stretching.

"No, nothing." My throat is dry as I move from the trench. I drink water; the air is cool.

"I'll go wake Cheyenne," San Antone says, yawning and rubbing the back of his neck.

"Okay." I do a couple of deep knee bends to get the kinks out of my knees. Then I hold my arms above my head and lean backward a few times to get the kinks out of my back.

Cheyenne approaches: "*Aho*."

"*Aho*."

"Sleep good, Ecky?"

"Fair," I answer. "How about you, you sleep good?"

"Y'ah. Dreamed I was sleeping in a tepee at the Anadarko Powwow. Was jus' rolling over on my Indi'n side when San Antone woke me." Cheyenne still has the bandage on his temple, and his bayonet is fixed. We sit in silence and watch the front for any movement.

The eastern sky grows light before the Morning Star comes out. It changes color and reflects like a looking glass. Short Nose fixes his eyes on the Morning Star and utters something in Cheyenne. I think of *Hupiri-Kucu* as a man with a red eagle plume. He is a messenger from God, signaling the coming of a new

77

day . . . I wonder what this new day will bring. "Chey', why don't you sleep awhile? I'll watch."

"Naw, Ecky. You sleep. I'll watch."

"Well, okay," I reply reluctantly. The Sicilian countryside is without sound. No farm dogs barking, no roosters crowing, no birds cheeping, and no owls passing over on silent wings. I doze.

"Ecky," Cheyenne says, touching my shoulder.

I hear Shield Chief calling: "Second Platoon! Everybody up! Last Arrow, Good Buffalo, Echohawk! Get your men up!" It's the hour when all of B Company rises and prepares for a possible counterattack. Cheyenne stands, stretches, then ambles to his foxhole. The men in the platoon stir, taking M1s and fixing bayonets. I check the squad. They're ready. Everyone is in his slit trench. The area is quiet—all eyes are on the front.

Sunup comes and goes and nothing happens. Shield Chief calls: "All right, men, let's eat!"

The men get out of their foxholes. Canteen cups and mess kits rattle. Medicine Man walks up. "The grand dining room is open. Coffee, cream, and sugar. Don't soil the tablecloths, watch your pinky, and keep your cufflinks out of the K-ration. And you Indi'ns don't steal the silverware. You can't make tourist jewelry out here!"

"Dang, he's too much," Cheyenne remarks, coming up with a box of K-rations and with his canteen cup handy. I reach in my pack and get a box of K-rations labeled "Breakfast." The box is a bit larger than a Cracker Jack box. In it is a small can of dehydrated chopped ham and eggs, two flat cracker biscuits, powdered coffee, and two cubes of sugar. I remove my Pawnee knife from the wall of the slit trench, then dig a small hole the size of a man's fist at the base of the hole. "Get your cup ready," I say, placing strips of the K-ration box in the small hole. The heavily waxed box tops go on last. I strike a match to it. The hard waxed paper throws a small but steady flame. The flame is not visible since it is inside the slit trench. We hold our canteen cups of water and powdered coffee over the flame, which is good for two cups, then burns out. We each use one spoon to stir coffee and eat with. We drink hot coffee while the chopped ham and eggs are eaten slowly because they are dehydrated.

I tell Cheyenne about Freddie Roland and Captain Roberts, but I'm sure not to tell the rest of the men. They'll hear about it as we move along. Cheyenne shakes his head, stares into his coffee, then drinks. "I'm going to Medicine Man to see if he heard anything about the Second Battalion. My cousin Two Hatchets is in E Company." I tell him to ask about the Third Battalion; there are two Pawnees in I Company. Cheyenne answers "*Aho*," then leaves.

I take some of the drawing paper I found; most of it is wrinkled and soiled. I take a pencil and pick the cleanest sheet. The mess-kit lid acts as a drawing board, offering a firm and stable surface to sketch on. Looking to the platoon area, a few men have their shirts off and are picking weeds from their shirts and undershirts. Some lie on the ground with their shoes off, while others snooze in their foxholes. I look to the front. This land is barren. I start sketching.

"All squad leaders! Over here!" The voice of Shield Chief: "All squad leaders! Over here!" The voice of Sergeant Stone follows. I put my pencil and paper aside and head for Shield Chief. Good Buffalo and Last Arrow respond. We move to the back side of a slope where Lieutenant Dobbins is dug in. The lieutenant looks better than he did yesterday. His right canvas legging is laced over the right shoe again. Lieutenant Dobbins greets us warmly and tells us to sit down, take it easy, and smoke if we wish. We sit.

None of us Indian sergeants smoke, except Shield Chief. He has a pipe, but I feel he uses that as a prop—for sure it's a prayer pipe. Sergeant Stone tramps up, hunkers down, and puts a weed in his mouth. "Got damn, I'm still galled from yesterday," he says, scratching his crotch. Without expression, Lieutenant Dobbins looks at Sergeant Stone, who keeps scratching his crotch.

"We are pulling out," Lieutenant Dobbins says, turning to the rest of us. "The First Battalion will move to high ground facing Biscari. We are to protect the left flank of the regiment. The Second and Third Battalion will attack Comiso Airport, now held by the Germans. Check the men and equipment . . . and prepare to move."

"You feeling all right, Lieutenant?" inquires Last Arrow.

"Yes, Sergeant. Thank you. You men feel all right?"

"Yes," we all nod. "Thank you, Sir." We turn and leave for our squad areas. I fill the squad in on the situation. Then we saddle up and wait.

Medicine Man comes up and sounds off. "Second Platoon, how do you feel?"

The men sing out: "Fine! Great!"

"'Atta way to go!" Medicine Man answers. He lights a cigar, then comes to me. "Hey, Echo, where in the world is Biscari?"

"I don't know. Heck, we haven't seen Scoglitti either."

"Say, Echo, you're right. Forgot about Scoglitti . . . bet we don't see any towns in this barren country either."

Shield Chief: "Second Platoon! Let's go!"

Stone: "Second Platoon! Let's go!"

Medicine Man adjusts his pack and medical bags. "Well, another day at the office." I take the Musette bag, then give Cheyenne and Corporal Ingalls each a grenade, for they gave me theirs back at the pillbox. B Company moves out.

We follow a road and pass D Company, which is dispersed with heavy machine guns and 81mm mortars; they wait for the battalion to form. C Company approaches from another direction, while A Company sits along the road, waiting. Sergeant Benning of C Company shouts, "There's A Company a-settin' on their asses as usual!" There's a burst of laughter from C Company. "C for cow shit!" he continues. A Company laughter follows. Then both sides hoot and barb each other.

Back in Oklahoma, as National Guard units, the two companies were always feuding. Both were from Oklahoma City. A Company was from uptown Oklahoma City, while C Company was from across the railroad tracks and stockyard district. The uptown boys and the cowboys from the stockyards would go to fist city at the drop of a hat. While both companies are built to wartime strength with men from other states, a little feuding still goes on.

B Company approaches where the battalion commander and two officers stand just off the side of a road. Lieutenant Colonel Stevens, the battalion commander, eyeballs A and C Companies: "Damn, if we ever get these two outfits pointed in the same direction, there will be hell to pay."

Major Jonathan, the battalion executive officer, sees B Company: "Here come my Indians now."

"Let's get the cowboys and Indians together and get the show on the road."

The major, who was our company commander back at Fort Sill in 1940, asks, "How's it going, Sergeant Shield Chief?"

"Good, Sir," Shield Chief answers.

Major Jonathan smiles and nods. "Good Buffalo, Echohawk, Last Arrow."

"Sir," we nod. The major's pistol belt appears to wrap around him twice, as he is tall and slim. Near is another battalion officer, Captain Godfrey. He is known by the officers as "Pancho." White dust on his shirt, soaked with perspiration, is now ashen gray. The captain has a cord that passes between his legs, and the cord is tied to the front and back of his waist belt. I figure this to be a remedy to ease chafing from woolen trousers in this hot weather. Jeeps with radios squawking roll through the column, raising white dust. B Company leads the battalion. We cross a big highway and spot a sign on the highway that had been shot away. It reads Vittoria, but we can't tell which way it points. We strike out across the barren countryside, crossing donkey trails and farm roads. Ahead is an improved road that we follow. Straddling the road, First and Second Platoons lead—First on the right, Second on the left. The Third and Weapons Platoons follow. Judging by the sun, the company is heading north and west. Now the road is walled with tall cactus. We lose sight of First Platoon. I glance back to check interval. Due to our wide interval, there is no conversation among the men. The morning grows hot with no breeze.

Abruptly, a motorcycle roars from the wall of cactus and onto the road. The driver burns rubber and gets away. Startled, we stop. "Shoot him! Shoot him!" Last Arrow yells from the left. I take aim, but the speeding motorcycle is lost in a cloud of dust.

About two hundred and fifty yards ahead, the road turns left. "Wait till he turns!" Shield Chief hollers on the run with tommy-gun ready. Our guys react, come up, and kneel with M1s leveled. The motorcycle skids and then breaks left. The man guns the motorcycle and streaks across the front, raising a curtain of white dust. We take aim. The man is bent low over the handlebars. "Now!" Shield Chief shouts. We open fire. The motorcycle careens, hits the ditch, and flies end over end as the driver cartwheels through the air. There's Browning Automatic Rifle fire from First Platoon. It kicks up cotton balls of dust beyond the road. White dust fogs up the area as everybody hurries forward for a look.

Thrown from the road, the man lies facedown. He wears grayish-green coveralls and has blond hair. His hands are covered with blood, and he shows no sign of life. The motorcycle is banged up too. Gasoline leaks, and the fumes are strong. Lieutenant Dobbins and Shield Chief approach. "Don't bunch up!" Shield Chief barks. "Keep moving!" Second Platoon moves again. I wipe sweat from my face. That man was checking on us. Only seeing foot soldiers, he figured he could get away quickly on a motorcycle. First Platoon turns right and leaves the road. Shield Chief signals: "turn right." Now B Company heads due north cross-country. We come across a few stone houses at the immediate front and right front. There are lots of mesquite trees and cactus too.

Someone calls: "Pass the word back. Where's Cindy?" Word echoes back and is picked up by Sergeant Stone, who brings up the rear.

Stone bursts out singing: "I wish I was an apple a-hangin' on a tree. Every time Cindy would pass, she'd take a bite of me. Git along home, Cindy. Git along home, I say."

On Louisiana maneuvers, Stone would sing this, then shout, "When it gets too hot for the rest of you, it's just right for me!" On a twenty-mile hike, weighed down by a full field pack, the men would be dragging with exhaustion. They could say nothing to a sergeant as strong as a Mississippi mule. Now Sergeant Stone strides up singing—and enjoying the attention. Some join in. Stone couldn't carry a tune in a horse trough, but who cares? His singing is relief and fun.

Gunfire comes before we can hit the ground. The fire came from the immediate front in the stone houses. Now heavy fire follows from the right, where First Platoon returns fire. I look to Shield Chief as he and Lieutenant Dobbins confer. Then Shield Chief signals "forward." I get up and move forward. The squad follows. Last Arrow is on my left. As we move, carbines pop at us; the shots are wild. I check to make sure we have interval. The ground has gullies, islands of tall cactus, and the ever-present mesquite trees. Near the houses are sheds and stone enclosures with low walls and sheep pens. A machine gun rakes First Platoon on the right. M1 and Browning Automatic Rifles hit back. At the sheep pen, I motion *hold*; ahead and to the right is a house seventy-five yards away. Between the house and this sheep pen is a shed. I crawl as fast as I can to the shed for a better look.

The shed is filled with dry manure. A soldier waving a pistol appears at the side of the house, and four more with carbines show. The soldiers take M1 fire from Last Arrow's men on the left. Lead strikes the wall and roof of the house. The soldiers duck. At the right is steady fire with the sound of a grenade. The enemy machine gun is silenced. The soldier with the pistol rises and looks in Last Arrow's direction. I aim for his head. Then the man raises a white handkerchief to his left ear. The hanky is bloodstained. I pause, aim high, and fire. Dust explodes off the wall above his head. He sees me and throws up his hands, dropping the pistol. I empty my clip over the soldiers who are lying down. "Hands up!" I shout. "Hands up!" The soldiers get up, drop weapons, and raise hands. I reload quickly, as more could be around. A hail of lead from Last Arrow's men whangs into the wall and roof. The enemy soldiers stiffen and jabber. I glance right and kneel, as there is still carbine fire.

Last Arrow's men emerge from the gullies and groves of cactus with bayonets leveled. The enemy soldiers huddle together with arms straight up and eyes bugged out.

"Move the prisoners back!" Lieutenant Dobbins shouts.

He and Shield Chief come up. "Don't bunch up!" Shield Chief yells. "Last Arrow, watch your flank!" At the right, enemy soldiers surrender to First Platoon. There are scattered M1 shots. The word goes up: "Cease fire!" Looks like thirty or forty prisoners.

Captain Lee appears and orders two of our guys to move the prisoners back. First and Second Platoons reorganize and move forward again. We send out scouts this time. Sergeant Stone bellows from the rear: "All right! Second Platoon! Got dammit, let's keep your eyes open!"

I check interval. Last Arrow is at my right. Good Buffalo is in reserve. We move slower since that shootout back there. *Wonder how the Second and Third Battalion are doing at Comiso? Wonder if we'll get to see Comiso?* We see hills. I think to myself that we should be coming to the high ground near Biscari. I adjust the Musette bag . . . those hand grenades are getting heavy.

The day is hot, real hot. Someone sounds off: "Hey, where's Cindy?" Word is passed back.

"When it gets too hot for the rest of you, it's just right for me" returns the voice of Sergeant Stone.

Oh, boy, before Stone can sing "Cindy" Lieutenant Dobbins yells, "Hold it!" Shield Chief looks at us and chops the air in sign language: "cut, stop." A B Company runner has come up to Dobbins. They talk and then leave. Second Platoon halts. At the right, First Platoon stops too; we get off our feet and drink water.

Medicine Man, who has come up to check the men's feet for blisters, stops by. "Say, you Indi'ns win another battle." The Choctaw medic smiles and lights a cigar. "In movies, heck, one white guy would drop one Indi'n and his horse with the same bullet. There'd be a skinny white girl cuddling up to him while he shot more Redskins without reloading."

"There you go," I answer, amused. Medicine Man makes his rounds, then goes to visit Shield Chief. I put down the Musette bag with the grenades, slide out of my pack, and take out drawing paper. The men of the platoon are dispersed. A few sit and smoke, while the rest are lying down with arms crossed over their faces as protection from the sun.

I look around to see if there is anything interesting to draw in this hot dry land. Then I hear the voice of Shield Chief: "Second Platoon! On your feet! Let's go!"

From the rear comes the voice of Sergeant Stone: "Second Platoon! On your feet! Let's go!"

We move out and veer off to a hill with a few trees. The hill is shelved with strata of white rock. At the top of the rise we can see trees and vegetation. Beyond are two-story stone houses with red-tile roofs. Near the houses are sheep pens and sheds.

Lieutenant Dobbins yells, "Hold!" Second Platoon stops.

Shield Chief: "All squad leaders! Over here!"

Sergeant Stone: "All squad leaders! Over here!" The men get off their feet. Squad leaders meet with Lieutenant Dobbins and Shield Chief. Sergeant Stone approaches. He plucks a weed, puts it in his mouth, and scratches his crotch.

"We dig in here," Lieutenant Dobbins says. "We are to occupy this high ground as it faces Biscari. We will protect the left flank of the 179th as it attacks Comiso Airport. A Company will be on the right, C in reserve, D with heavy weapons will be ready to support."

Lieutenant Dobbins drinks water. The metal canteen cap clinks as water trickles down the corner of his mouth.

"This ridge," the lieutenant continues, "with the line of trees is the Second Platoon area. The Third Platoon will be on our right. First Platoon in reserve with the Weapons Platoon ready to support. Sergeant Shield Chief, deploy the platoon."

Shield Chief stands with his tommy-gun at sling. His ODs are covered with white dust, and his shirt is soaked with sweat. "Bill, take this area here. Ecky, you take the middle where the nose of the hill slants. Flop, take the area beyond Ecky. Have the men dig away from the line of trees . . . those trees make good aiming stakes for the enemy when zeroing in. I don't want anybody skylined. Okay, move out."

"*Aho!*" we chorus.

We fill the men in on the situation and dig in. In a staggered line on the slope of the hill, our vision is good. We link with Last Arrow and Good Buffalo's squad. We set up interlocking fields of fire so that the front is well covered. We eat a K-ration dinner and keep watch on the horizon. *Dang, it's hot.* It must be 120 degrees in the shade, and the only shade was back there in those trees.

The air is still. I doze off.

"Your feet okay, Echo?" It's Medicine Man. He has a cigar in his mouth and a smile on his round face. He never looks tired.

"Y'ah, my feet are okay."

"This Sicilian ground is hard on moccasins. Jus' checkin'."

"*Aho*, thanks." I yawn and realize I must have been asleep for a couple of hours. Puffing the cigar, Medicine Man ambles off like a gunfighter in the movies. He talks to the men in the foxholes and seems to cheer them up. It's past midafternoon. Funny, there are no birds here. No cattle or horses either. I saw sheep pens, but no sheep. No farm dogs barking—nothing. If we are facing Biscari, it must be a one-horse town. Got to stay in our slit trenches and not be seen by the enemy. I roll over on my back and fall asleep.

Evening comes, and I check the squad. They are stirring in their slit trenches. Some eat supper K-rations. Others stand, stretch, and smoke. I eat a K-ration and drink water before going to see Shield Chief.

I meet Sergeant Stone, who is sounding off: "Second Platoon: be on the lookout for paratroops!"

"Hey, Stone, what's up?" I ask.

"Lieutenant says for us to be on the lookout for paratroops."

"Paratroops?"

"Yeah, German paratroops. They think there might be some around here."

Stone moves from Second Squad's area to Third Squad's area. "*Second Platoon: be-on-the-lookout-for-paratroops.*" He sounds like those police calls on the *Gang Busters* radio show.

"That-is-all," someone adds with a snicker.

I find Shield Chief sitting on the edge of his slit trench cleaning the dust off his tommy-gun with a GI hanky. "Phil, what's this about paratroops?"

"*Ka-ka-ti-ra-ita*" (I don't know), he answers, laying aside his tommy-gun and picking up his hatchet and whetstone. "Lieutenant Dobbins got the message

Comiso Air Field Hangar, Comiso, Italy. Image courtesy of the 45th Infantry Division Museum.

from a company runner, then told Stone to pass the word. The lieutenant's gone to the company CP [command post] to find out more."

"What do you think, Phil?"

"Well, could be American paratroops. Maybe they're going to drop at Gela where the 1st Division is, and the Brass don't want us to fire on their planes. Could be the 1st Division has its hands full trying to take Gela. There wouldn't be reason for our paratroops to drop here. As for German paratroops, it wouldn't make sense for them to jump here either. We're one battalion in a holding position, protecting the left flank of the 179th while it attacks Comiso Airport. All the fighting is there."

Phillip Shield Chief is a descendant of a Pawnee war chief, Whetstones His Hatchet. He pauses, blows his breath on the hatchet blade, and runs a thumb over the razor-sharp edge. "But if the German paratroops drop on this Indi'n camp, they'll get a hair-raising reception, literally."

"*Aho,* Chief. I read you loud and clear."

Good Buffalo comes up. "*Nawa, tiwat.*" (Hello, cousin). Last Arrow and Leading Fox are a few paces behind. Shield Chief tells them what he told me. Good Buffalo takes a small coil of spring to his chin, holding it in the thumb and forefinger, compressing it to pluck whiskers from the chin. Old-time Pawnees used this method of shaving. Sergeant Floyd Good Buffalo manipulates the spring deftly, then speaks: "German paratroopers are the cream of the crop. They jumped in France, Holland, and Crete, then handily defeated the opposition. Let's get ready to fight them. *Tus chaticks-si-chaticks*" (We are men of men).

Last Arrow, a former boxer, speaks: "We ought to come out of our corner and land a haymaker before the bell sounds. We're not playing games. Matlock could send out Ruling His Son to find the Germans. If anyone can find them, he can. Then we and Matlock could—"

"Good idea," Shield Chief interrupts, "but we got to wait and see what Battalion does. I'm sure they have plans. If this paratroop thing is any real threat, they'll inform us."

Last Arrow replies: "Well, don't like this waiting. Landing on the beach back there in the wrong place didn't seem like good planning. I'm sure other units waited on Battalion. Waiting on the beach is real bad—the Luftwaffe didn't wait."

Leading Fox speaks: "Bureau of Indian Affairs . . . Bureau of Indian Affairs."

We ponder the situation and look to the front. The Sicilian countryside is dark. A moon, just under a quarter, is faintly showing. "A hunter's moon," Last Arrow notes. "When the moon is like this, the old Indi'ns call it the hunter's moon. Deer feed then . . . making the hunting good. Good when looking for the enemy too. A full moon is too bright . . . it throws a lot of shadows and causes the enemy's imagination to be high, making him more aware of sounds and movement. The time is right with a hunter's moon."

"What you Indi'ns doing? Making medicine for tomorrow's massacre?" It's Medicine Man.

Shield Chief greets him warmly. "*Aho,* make yourself to home." It's always good to see Medicine Man. It makes you feel good to know that if any of us get hit, he'll take care of us.

The stocky Choctaw adjusts his paunch, then sits down in Indian fashion. "Phillip, what's this about paratroops?"

"Don't know. It was word, probably from Battalion. They just said paratroops. Don't know if they are ours or Germans. We were just talking about what to do in case they were German paratroops. Bill, here, thinks we ought to land the first punch before the bell sounds."

"Tonight," Last Arrow comes on. "Tonight, while there is a hunter's moon. We could go out and slip up on them with bayonets."

"At night!" Medicine Man explodes. "Don't you guys know that Indians never fight at night?! Why, in the picture show when Indians attack covered wagons?! In the circle of wagons, the hero tells the desperate settlers to hold out until dark—for Indi'ns never fight at night!"

We muffle laughter with our hands. Medicine Man continues: "Then the Indian Chief who needs a shave, and wearing a Sioux war bonnet, Kiowa war shirt, Cheyenne leggings, Cherokee moccasins, and Navajo jewelry . . . waves a chicken feather lance. The Indians knock off for the day." We shake with muffled laughter. "But you 'skins did all right!" Medicine Man says, composing himself. "I met other medics in the rear. Heard there were sixty enemy dead where you guys went through." We sit quietly and reflect.

Shield Chief stands and yawns. "You guys better get back to your squads. Check your men and their fields of fire. Same password. Ecky: put two men out as outposts for the platoon."

"*Aho*." We break up and leave.

I attend to details as instructed, setting the night watch before I retire to my slit trench. Then Cheyenne calls from his trench.

"Hey, Ecky. What they mean, 'look out for paratroops'?"

"Don't know, Chey'. I asked Phil about it and he didn't know. It was something that came down from Battalion. Lieutenant Dobbins went to the CP to find out more. He's not back yet."

"Might be the message came from higher up, and by the time it got to company level it was all mixed up," Cheyenne speculates.

"Could be," I say, laying out a couple of hand grenades just in case. "Where we are now, I can't see anything happening." I drive my Pawnee knife into the wall of the slit trench for quick grabbing and settle in my foxhole.

I hear voices as footsteps approach. It's Shield Chief and Good Buffalo.

"Ecky," Shield Chief calls.

"*H'yo*."

"Lieutenant Dobbins is back from the CP—the Second and Third Battalions captured Comiso Airport late this afternoon."

"Gollee! That's good!"

"Thought you'd like to know since our brothers, Oohs Riding Up and Lynn Good Buffalo, are in the Third Battalion." Cheyenne again calls from the darkness.

"Did we take Comiso?"

"Y'ah!" Shield Chief answers in good spirits.

"Wish we knew more," Good Buffalo adds.

"My cousin Two Hatchets—he's in E Company. Hope he's okay." Cheyenne calls.

"Second squad!" Shield Chief sounds off. "The Second and Third Battalions have taken Comiso Airport!" A cheer goes up from the darkness. "We're going to tell the rest of the platoon the good news." Shield Chief and Good Buffalo move off into the darkness.

"Hey, Ecky. That's sure good news!" Cheyenne calls.

"Y'ah, Chey'. Real good news. We'll learn more in the morning." The dark front of B Company, 179th Regimental Combat Team, falls quiet. I shift my back and shoulders. I pull up my shirt collar and let the clods of dirt settle in my slit trench and drift off to sleep.

A hand touches my shoulder: "*Ecky. . . .*" It's Cheyenne. I sit up quickly. "*I heard planes,*" he whispers. I listen. The night is quiet—graveyard quiet. Millions of stars with a hunter's moon. We hear hurried footsteps on the forward slope.

It's Sam Bear. "Ecky!" he calls, looking in all directions. "Hey, you heard planes?" He has been on the outpost.

"Alert your men, Ecky!" Shield Chief says as he comes out of the dark with his tommy-gun ready. In his belt is his hatchet. "Nobody moves about. Stay in your holes. Fix bayonets. Keep alert!"

"Bear, get back to the outpost," I say, grabbing my M1.

"*Aho!*"

"Let's go, Chey'. Help me get everybody up."

"*Aho!*"

Shield Chief hurries to the rear to alert Stone and check with Lieutenant Dobbins.

Within a few minutes Second Platoon is ready. No one talks. We listen and watch. We continue to hear planes as they seem to circle Biscari, then head west, probably to Gela. They are German bombers attacking the beaches and shipping facilities at Gela. They circle inland, then go back. After a while the planes go away and all is quiet again. We stay alert. Struggling to stay awake, I doze.

More planes shake me awake. The voice of Shield Chief comes over the roar of the distant engines: "Everybody up!"

"My God, look back there!" someone exclaims. Far to the rear is antiaircraft fire but no sound—we're too far away. I'm thinking the planes this time could be paratroops. However, they're coming from the direction of Gela and seem to be flying in a state of confusion. One of the plane's motors is choking and popping. The antiaircraft fire spreads. Fountains of red tracers rise in the night sky as we stand and watch. In the distance there is a flash in the sky before a plane falls from the flames.

After a while the night spectacle is over. No more planes and all is quiet again. I hold my watch close to my face. It's about 11:30 . . . almost midnight. I watch the front a while, then lie down in my slit trench. I keep my steel helmet on. Shift my shoulders and back. Pull my shirt collar up and let the clods of dirt settle.

Tirawa, bless our soldiers.

I hear a yipping, then a prolonged howl of a wolf. A Pawnee is signaling: "no paratroops." I look up at the Mediterranean sky. It is diamond-studded with stars and a hunter's moon. I drift off to sleep.

6

Counterattack Time

Born at sea, baptized in blood, your fame shall never die.
The 45th Infantry Division is one of the best, if not actually the best division
in the history of American arms.
—General George S. Patton

Hupiri-Kucu—the Morning Star—looks down from the eastern sky. It's *Ti-rawa*'s messenger, signaling the coming of a new day. The Morning Star reflects many colors. I hear Shield Chief singing a morning song as the old-time Pawnees did. With the palm of his hand, he drums the top of his steel helmet, which he holds in his lap. The drumbeats are soft and go well with the morning song. After a while his singing fades. The drumming continues, then it fades too. The countryside awakens: yawning valleys with columns of cactus that march to the horizon, thorn trees that stretch their limbs to the dawn sky, and rising from the night shadows are the ever-present mesquite trees.

"Second Platoon! Everybody up!" The voice of Shield Chief.

"Last Arrow, Echohawk, Good Buffalo! Get your men up!" It is the hour when we ready ourselves for a possible enemy counterattack.

We watch the front till sunup, but no counterattack comes. We chow down to a K-ration breakfast. Cheyenne and I eat together. Like everyone else in the squad we talk about last night's fireworks. After eating, we visit Shield Chief to see if he has any news. Good Buffalo and Last Arrow are with Shield Chief. They're drinking coffee and talking about last night. Shield Chief says that some of the planes were German bombers attacking the shipping at Gela, where the 1st Division is fighting. The planes that came in later had different-sounding motors. They drew heavy antiaircraft fire; some turned back, and some circled inland like they were mixed up, breaking formation. Shield Chief observes, "That's when one was hit and exploded and went down in a ball of fire."

Last Arrow joins in. "All of us saw that. If they were German paratroops, they picked a bad time to come in."

"Y'ah, after the German bombers." Good Buffalo adds. "That doesn't make sense. Especially when all radar and antiaircraft batteries had picked them up. The fire from the beachhead guns, fire from the ships in the harbor, and the fire from the Navy must have really been something!"

"And we're far inland too," Cheyenne says. "Our tanks, half-tracks, and antiaircraft units protecting the field artillery and all the weapons companies got into the act."

"Where's Medicine Man?" I ask.

"He's probably heard something at the Battalion Aid Station."

"He's at the Battalion Aid Station now," Shield Chief answers. "All right, it's broad daylight. Let's don't bunch up. You guys get back to your men. Should hear from Battalion soon. I got a feeling the Germans aren't going to roll over and play dead after Comiso."

"*Aho*," we reply.

A runner comes for Lieutenant Dobbins. Back at the squad, I tell the men to check weapons, ammo, and equipment. I instruct the men to take it easy on water, as the two canteens we have were to last three days. Same goes for K-rations, and this is the third day. I check my gear and take drawing paper from my pack. Using a handkerchief, I clean the paper and remove wrinkles, and then I lie down in my slit trench. The sun is warm. I doze off.

"All squad leaders!" The voice of Shield Chief.

"All squad leaders!" Stone echoes.

Lieutenant Dobbins is back. He informs us that the Germans have hit Second Battalion. Comiso is under a heavy counterattack, and the Germans are on the verge of retaking it. It is also relayed that the regiment has called First Battalion to help. First Battalion moves out for Comiso. We move with wide interval, as there are still pockets of resistance out there. We reach the far side of a valley where all the grass is burned. I recall what Ruling His Son said when scouting. He mentioned finding places where the Germans attempted to start grass fires. Maybe they set these fires. There have been skirmishes here and pockets of resistance. Maybe tracer bullets set the grass on fire. We stop when the scouts spot something and check it out. Moving again, I shift the Musette bag of hand grenades. It's getting heavy. We stop again. Lieutenant Dobbins is called. We flop and rest. The day is hot; all the men drink water during these short breaks. Shield Chief explodes: "Go easy on the water!" Canteens are put away and no one talks.

I take an empty canteen and place it in the pack. I remove the five grenades from the Musette bag and put them in the empty canteen carrier on my cartridge belt. The pack of grenades hangs heavily. I decide to remove one grenade and put it in my pocket. I discard the Musette bag with barber clippers and other things still in it. Lieutenant Dobbins returns and relates that there are Germans ahead. Second and Third Platoons will attack. First Platoon will swing left and flank them. We move out.

Second and Third Squads lead. First Squad is in reserve. We advance over a long stretch of burned prairie. I check my squad to make sure we have interval. About five hundred yards ahead are blackened hills lined with cactus groves. This is where they will be. Advancing, all eyes are on the front. Reaching the blackened hills and cactus groves, we find vehicle tracks and tracks from a half-track or tank. Here there are oily rags, cigarette stubs, and empty ration cans. The Germans hightailed it out of here by the looks of it. We stop and get off our feet. The heat is stifling.

A runner comes for Lieutenant Dobbins before they both leave in a hurry. Grant Shield Chief comes from the right. Grant talks with his brother, Phillip, and then comes to visit Good Buffalo. Last Arrow and I join them. But we do not bunch up. Grant asks if Medicine Man had any news. None, we reply. Then Grant says, "Just a minute, I see something." He walks out a few paces and extends his right arm forward with the palm of the hand open like a traffic cop signaling "stop." Grant moves the outstretched arm from side to side slowly, looking through the fingers of his hand. Then he walks back. "There's a guy out there watching us. Just over four hundred yards, between two hills. Ecky, step out and look down your arm to your hand. He's two fingers left of the saddle of the two hills." I step out, sighting down my arm and hand. Sure enough, there he is: a white speck. The white face stands out from the black background.

"Hey, Ecky!" Cheyenne calls from several yards away. "There's someone way out there spying on us. Direct front, four hundred and fifty yards. He's wearing eyeglasses."

"Y'ah. We've spotted him," I answer. I set my sights to four hundred yards. Kneeling, I draw a bead on the white speck and fire. It vanishes. The men in the squad flatten out and come up with M1s ready.

"'Atta way to go, Ecky!" Grant says.

"A long shot!" Last Arrow adds.

Good Buffalo stands for a better look. "Hope you got him! That guy could be spotting for artillery or he might be with a reconnaissance outfit."

Shield Chief appears, tommy-gun ready. "What's up?"

"Grant spotted a man out there spying on us. Ecky took a shot at him. About four hundred yards away," Last Arrow replies. Shield Chief eyes the blackened hills. "That's a long way. Hit him?"

"Couldn't tell," I answer. "He was lying down, looking toward us, we saw a white speck, his face. All I could see."

"All right. Let's don't bunch up," Shield Chief says, lowering his tommy-gun.

"There he goes!" Cheyenne shouts. The man runs from a gully at the left. At this distance, the man is a tiny figure.

"He's getting away! He's getting away!" Last Arrow exclaims. Grant steps forward with his M1, sets the sights, then takes aim. The man scrambles up a hill. At the top of the hill is a low wall. Grant fires. The man jumps to the top of the wall, then falls backward.

The squad cheers: "Yah!" A small car sputters over a hill from the extreme left. It motors to the wall where the man went down. The jeeplike car stops for a few seconds, turns around, and speeds away.

Shield Chief shouts, "Let him have it!" We open fire. The small car jitterbugs cross-country, leaving a cloud of ashen dust.

Lieutenant Dobbins returns at a fast walk. Wide-eyed, he asks what is happening. Shield Chief tells him. The lieutenant takes his binoculars and studies the burned hills. "Sergeant Shield Chief, we are to keep pressing forward. We've hit pockets of resistance." Lieutenant Dobbins puts away the binoculars but still eyes the front. "Could be the Germans have a force out to protect their right flank while they attack Comiso, like we did when the 179th attacked Comiso. Okay, Sergeant Shield Chief, move the platoon out."

"Second Platoon! Let's go!" Shield Chief shouts.

"Second Platoon! Let's go!" Stone follows.

"Scouts out!" Shield Chief calls. I send Cheyenne out. Moving forward, we see the man Grant shot. He is a German, lying facedown. His uniform and field cap are covered with ashes and burned straw. Around his neck are binoculars. They are the eyeglasses Cheyenne spotted. The sun reflected off the lenses, allowing Cheyenne and Grant to pick it up. The soldier has been hit in the ribs, just behind the left armpit. Sandy-haired, he looks to be about twenty-five years old. We keep moving.

We cross a burned flat as stubs of burned grass crunch underfoot. We pick our way through walls of cactus. Beyond are ravines and knolls. Untouched by fire are rivulets of flaxen grass. Enemy fire comes suddenly from the immediate front. We hit the ground; however, there is no cover here. Shield Chief dashes forward, zigzags, then hits the ground. The platoon follows.

I run as fast as I can. Cheyenne, who is down ahead of me, hollers, "Watch it, Ecky! Watch it!"

I drop to the ground a few yards from him. "You okay, Chey'?"

"Y'ah, I'm okay. Didn't see anything, but they are up there, and they are well hidden!" The squad comes up and hits the ground. They don't bunch up.

"Wees! Wees!" (Hurry! Hurry!) The voice of Shield Chief. I get up and take off. Cheyenne takes his place in the squad.

Rushing forward, we look left and see no one. Looking right, I see part of Good Buffalo's squad running forward. Bullets kick up dust around us, sending the squad to the ground. Fire is coming from a knoll dead ahead. M1 fire at the right is returning fire to the German position. I get up and run left in an effort to flank that knoll. None of the enemy fires at me, as they are engaging the M1s at the right. Cheyenne and Bear follow close behind. I dive into a shallow wash that resembles a buffalo wallow. I catch my breath before taking off again. I break right to the front and come to a ravine. Enemy fire hits the ravine, and to the back of me they're shooting at Cheyenne and Bear.

Guns blaze all along front.

"Cheyenne!" I call.

No answer.

"Bear!"

No answer.

I'm pinned down. A Messerschmitt flashes over, heading south. I wipe the sweat off my face and wonder where our air cover is. Automatic fire erupts from the left front before M1s return fire. I study the knoll at the front and realize it is too bare to get to. I decide to move left, thinking maybe there's another shallow wash running into this ravine. If there is, it can offer cover, and if I find it, I can backtrack, then bring the squad up. Automatic fire: left front again. M1s hit back. I move to the left.

The ravine is filled with cactus and thorn bushes that didn't burn. A goat path, on the right, joins the ravine. Nearby is a pen constructed with rotten poles. I come to a makeshift dam of dirt and piles of stones. On the other side of the dam I hear voices. I bring my M1 to ready and listen. I catch the words "For Christ's sake." Our men. Guys from Boston, replacements who now fill our ranks.

"Hey, who's that?"

"Private Pell and Sarkus! First Platoon!"

"This is Sergeant Echohawk. Second Platoon."

"Come over, Sergeant. Watch out, there's a machine gun up there."

I roll over the makeshift dam. "Where's the rest of your squad?" Pell and Sarkus are flattened against the bank of the ravine. Their faces are streaked with charcoaled sweat.

"Sergeant Sheen and the squad are pinned down. We are his two scouts. The platoon can't move; that gun caught us out in the open. Hell, they can see us easily on this bare-ass burned place for Christ's sake." The machine gun fires a long burst. We hug the ground. I glance to the rear and think, *Maybe I can go back and contact my squad.* I ease backward. Pell and Sarkus look at me like I am about to desert them and run. They are from Massachusetts, and I don't want them to think we Indians are scared. We eyeball each other.

"Let's go. Follow me."

I roll back over the dam. Pell and Sarkus follow. We pass the pen constructed of rotten poles and come to the goat path. "Maybe this path will take us near that gun. Stay low; we can be seen from the knoll on the right. It has Second Platoon pinned down." We belly up the path, which is barely a foot deep. Twenty yards ahead is a thin shelf of rocks that crosses this goat path. Beyond is another shelf of rock, then some cactus. Scattered M1 fire continues at the right. The machine gun at the left front fires back; our M1s continue firing.

We reach the first shelf of rocks, which is two feet high. I take a look. The second shelf is not cover enough. We crawl left and hear water in canteens jiggle and equipment rustle as Pell and Sarkus follow. The machine gun fires a burst; he's just above us. We freeze. I turn my helmet around backward and take a quick prairie-dog look. Up there are a few trees around what looks like a rock quarry. I turn to Pell and Sarkus. They are wide-eyed. "We're not close enough for grenades. We have to reach the second rim of rocks."

I dash for the second shelf and feel something drop from my belt. Reaching this shelf, Pell and Sarkus huddle near me. "Don't bunch up!" They slide away. I take a grenade from my pants pocket and yank the safety ring before I raise and throw it. The grenade bounces off a pile of rocks and rolls back.

"Duck!" The grenade explodes. Pell, a few yards left, throws his grenade and ducks. The grenade explodes on an embankment. He advances, firing his M1. A stick grenade flies end over end, lands in front of him, and goes off. Pell tumbles, rolling on the ground. He covers his face with his hands and screams.

"The sons of bitches!" Sarkus cries. He steps over the shelf and pitches a grenade and gets down. The grenade explodes on a pile of rocks. He stands and fires as fast as he can. A stick grenade hits him in the chest, drops at his feet, and goes off. He falls, then bounces up in a mushroom of dust, shrieking, "Got damn! Got damn!" I pull him to the shelf. His leggings and pant legs are shredded. Looks like the calves of his legs are torn off. Sarkus grips his legs in pain. "Got damn! Got damn!" Another grenade explodes; the concussion hits us. Pieces of metal hum as dust flies about. The whole platoon is firing; they heard our grenades. I reach for the canteen carrier with the grenades—it's gone. I remember something dropped from my cartridge belt. I run back and find the canteen carrier. Taking two grenades, I leave the carrier and my pack.

I dash for the goat path and crawl forward. The cactus runs in a broken row over the rise and can be seen from the knoll on the right. I duck in the cactus. Crawling forward, I take bad cuts and scratches. Reaching the top of the rise, I leave the cactus and move left. Fire from our guys keeps up. At the quarry, I can see a hand pitch a stick grenade over the rim of stones. It explodes. The machine gun fires. M1s hit the quarry as cracks and zings surround me. I jerk the safety ring and let the safety lever pop, then, holding the smoking grenade, I count to three and throw. Trailing smoke, the grenade arcs into the quarry and explodes. I scramble forward.

I see three men are down before suddenly one springs up and tries to grab my rifle. I slash his face. Hearing clods of dirt slide behind me, I whirl and fire. Dust flies on the other side of a man with a pistol. I hit him with my bayonet. The man falls back and slides down the embankment to a sitting position. He draws up his knees and grabs his stomach. I turn as the gunner attempts to get up, but he drops. I reach for the machine gun to hit him on the head, but the barrel burns my hands. I step back. The assistant gunner who tried to grab my M1 has his left ear cut off. The ear lies on his cheekbone. I notice he has a fresh haircut with sideburns shaved. I turn quickly in case another man appears. As for the man in the sitting position, his stomach and pants are red with blood. Bullets continue to whang off the rim of the quarry. I yell: "Cease fire! Cease fire!" My heart beats like a drum.

I hear men of the First Platoon shout: "Cease fire!" A few reach the quarry. There are wild shots. Squad leaders shout and try to reorganize.

I make my way to Sarkus. He's in a bad way. "Sarkus, the medic will be here to take care of you," I say, placing my hand on his shoulder.

With both legs bleeding, and in pain, he asks, "You all right, Sarge?"

"I'm okay." Sarkus puts a blood-smeared hand on my wrist.

I check Pell. Sergeant Sheen is with him. "How's he doing, Sheen?"

"Echohawk," he says. "He's doing all right, but. . . ." He stops short, then looks at Pell.

Pell perks up. "Sergeant Echohawk, you okay? Did you get hit?" Pell lies on his back, arms covering his eyes.

"I'm okay. Didn't get hit."

"Did we get that gun?"

"We got it."

"Good." Pell attempts to sit up.

"Pell," Sheen says gently. "Take it easy. A medic will be here shortly. Everything will be okay." Grenade splinters have struck him in the chest and face.

"Pell, Sheen, I'm going to join my platoon. Everybody is moving." Sergeant Sheen, who is kneeling beside Pell, reaches up and shakes my hand. First Platoon men mill around the quarry. A medic approaches, unhooking his medical aid bags.

Moving on, I retrieve my canteen carrier and pack, then drop back to the ravine and move right. I meet Sergeant Last Arrow with a few of his men. With him too are Cheyenne and Bear.

"Hey, you're all bloody. What happened?" Last Arrow says.

"Ended up with the First Platoon. Got into a fight with a machine gun. Two guys got hit, Pell and Sarkus. Sarkus got it in both legs. I helped move him. Pell was hit by a potato masher [grenade]. A medic is there taking care of them."

"Glad you didn't get hit, Ecky," Last Arrow says, looking toward the high ground and in the direction of the quarry.

"Looks like you been butchering hogs for a Creek Indian hog-fry," Bear remarks.

Cheyenne grins, then looks at my bloody uniform. "Glad you made it, Ecky."

Last Arrow puts a full clip in his M1 and checks the sights. "Heard all that shooting. Tried to get mortar fire up there, but the platoons are all mixed up. Might hit our own men. Shield Chief has been wondering about what happened to you. When we finally got organized, the enemy pulled back."

I turn to Cheyenne: "Did anyone in the squad get hit?"

"No. But on that flat ground, we were pinned down. Lucky we made it."

Glancing right, Last Arrow says, "We're moving. Let's go."

I see my squad advancing up the knoll. Corporal Ingalls leads. He has the second scout out. On the right and strung out is Good Buffalo's squad. I rejoin the squad. On the move, Shield Chief checks on me. I tell him everything's okay. Flies buzz around me. In this heat, they are attracted to the blood from Sarkus and the enemy soldiers at the quarry. I rub dirt on my shirt and thighs in an effort to get rid of the blood. Ahead are stretches of dry, wheatlike grass. The grass appears golden after leaving the burned countryside. We move past the bodies of German soldiers. American artillery killed them. The ground is so hard that the shells have not made craters. We keep moving.

The afternoon sun is hot. We come to a grove of trees and halt. Tired, we get off our feet. Men take off their shirts and pick burned weeds from their shirts and undershirts. Cheyenne calls: "Hey, Ecky, look!" Twenty-five yards ahead is a long row of bombs camouflaged with nets and straw.

We call Shield Chief. He jogs up. "German," he says. "Five-hundred-pound bombs. We must be near Comiso Airport."

Other men come and look. "Hey!" someone calls from Good Buffalo's squad. "Bombs! Whole row of them!"

"You guys stay down. Don't move around!" Shield Chief orders. "I'm going back to tell the Lieutenant."

More men come to look. Then, one hundred and fifty yards to the front, a shell explodes on a rise. We freeze. Then another shell comes in. Then another, and another. The front flashes and rumbles. A mass of billowing dust and lightning thunders toward us. A rolling barrage!

"The bombs!" someone shouts. We turn and run for it. Tearing through the grove of trees, we sound like a wild horse stampede. Spotting a small wash at the base of a tree, I dive for it. Two other men dive for it too. The barrage is deafening as the concussion blasts rocks us. The ground shakes as trees crack and shrapnel flies, humming at bullet speed. The storm of steel passes over. Our ears ring from the concussion. We all choke and cough in a heavy curtain of dust. The grove is gone. A few trees stand, leaning with broken limbs. Leaves float to the ground. The dust hangs for several minutes. There is a smell of cordite. My ears ring.

"Everybody fall back! Everybody fall back!" comes a voice from the rear. I wipe the dust and sweat from my eyes and shake from fear. Beside me are two men. One is Ralph Patrick, a BAR man from the First Platoon. The other is Sergeant Stone. Both show great fear.

"Everybody fall back!" the call is repeated. We pull back.

Checking the men, no one has been hit. We were lucky. It was a miracle that the stack of bombs wasn't hit. If they had been, none of us would be here. Medicine Man comes to check the platoon. He talks to Shield Chief and Good Buffalo. "Boy, that German barrage was something! I thought it was goodbye world, good morning Great Spirit."

Shield Chief wipes the dust off his tommy-gun. "Yeah, them Germans play rough. And this is just the third day."

"We're Men of Men. We'll take what they dish out," Good Buffalo says. "We'll get 'em. We'll get 'em." B Company takes up another position and digs in. Shovels and pick mattocks scrape and clang without letup. We won't get caught out in the open in a barrage again.

Late in the afternoon Shield Chief and I decide to go back to the Battalion Aid Station for drinking water. We move through mesquite trees and cactus groves. Parked among the trees a hundred yards away are three American trucks. Men in coveralls unload the truck beds. Looks like rolls of camouflage nets. As we draw near, we find that they are unloading the bodies of German soldiers. We watch as the grave registration men go about their work without talking. They lay the bodies in a row where shallow graves have been dug. Two men take a body by the arms and drag it to a grave. Twisted and stiff with rigor mortis, it lies awkwardly in the shallow grave. They move another with arms up. The fingers are spread with one hand in front of the face. The other is above the head. Like a basketball player that has just made a basket. The faded eyes are open, as is the mouth. Dirt is shoveled on the face and chest. One arm sticks up. "Help me with this arm," one says to the other. Both men put a foot on the arm and press down. They continue shoveling dirt over the body. For a brief moment, only the German soldier's belt buckle is visible. On the buckle are the words "Gott Mit Uns"—God is with us. We leave.

We never find the aid station. Upon returning, we walk to the high ground to see if Comiso Airport is near. Here, we come upon more German dead. Some have an arm up and curved over the head. They lie in a grove of cactus.

In places, the grass is burned. One body is in a running position, most of his uniform burned. Stuffed in a tunic of one of the Germans are American cigarettes. Though the cactus is green, it has burned. The odor of burned cactus and burned flesh is bitter and sickeningly sweet. No sign of Comiso. We start back as evening comes.

We are out of K-rations, and our water is almost gone. Squad leaders are called. Shield Chief is with Lieutenant Dobbins. He says that C Company, leading the First Battalion, jumped into the fight to support the Second Battalion at Comiso. The Germans used crack troops and Panzers against the 179th. The Germans were beaten back and failed to retake Comiso Airport. C Company had a lot of casualties. The lieutenant says we are to hold current positions. We will be given light machine guns from Fourth Platoon to strengthen our defenses: the Germans could counterattack again. He says that the kitchen truck will be up at dark with water and rations. We squad leaders return to our squads and tell them what the lieutenant told us.

Sundown arrives, but the heat of the day lingers. Weapons and ammo are checked. We stay in our slit trenches in fear of another barrage. Night falls as the guard is set. The Sicilian countryside is quiet. I think of Pell and Sarkus, about the quarry and the enemy soldiers killed there. That terrifying German barrage—and how lucky we were to come out alive. Best get this off my mind; tomorrow will be another day. And we'll get it on again.

My stomach growls with hunger, and my mouth is dry with thirst. "Second Platoon! One squad at a time go back for water and rations!" the voice of Sergeant Stone orders. "Last Arrow first. Echohawk second. Good Buffalo last!" One of the kitchen crew guides us through the dark to the B Company kitchen truck. We are resupplied with water and rations. This time we get C-rations: canned food. The kitchen crew waits on us with blue flashlights. They know we've had a rough day. We are all tired, hungry, and thirsty, so there's little conversation. And other platoons are waiting. Back in our slit trenches, we wolf down a can of cold hash and drink water. "See you in the morning, *Chibonni*" (American Indian slang for "boy"). He's pulling my leg. I leave, scratching.

I check on Cheyenne before heading for my trench. He's asleep, lying in his slit trench with his steel helmet on. Back at my hole, I place my M1 with bayonet where it's handy. I also stick my Pawnee knife into the wall of the slit trench where it can be grabbed quickly. I lie down and shift my back, letting the clods of dirt settle. I smell my shirt, crusted with dried blood and charcoal dirt: *Man, it stinks.* I take it off and spread it on the ground. I take the raincoat from my pack and put it on. I have cuts and scratches from the cactus I crawled through at the quarry. The cuts on my hands are swollen. The Sicilian night is clear. It twinkles with millions of stars. *God, I'm tired.* I fall asleep.

It's late; I check the squad. The men are exhausted. Some are asleep. Santana says he doesn't want to sleep where I told him to dig in. A few feet away from his hole is a dead German. I tell him it's okay. Lying in his slit trench, his legs prop over the edge like a tall man in a bathtub.

"*Hesci*" (Hello, in Creek).

"*Hesci*," Bear answers. "How you doing?"

"Rough. I get the feeling somebody's trying to kill me." Bear replies, sitting up and scratching. He brushes threads of grass from his short-cropped hair. "What do you hear from the Bureau of Indian Affairs?"

"Nothing."

"Nothing?"

"Nothing."

"Where are we?"

"Don't know. I'm just an FBI like you, ya know, a full blood Indi'n under the Bureau of Indian Affairs. Maybe Patton's making good medicine," I say, scratching.

"Who's Patton?" he asks, scratching.

"You know. The great white war chief with shiny stars on his helmet, cowboy guns, rabbit teeth, and necktie."

"What's a necktie?" he asks, scratching.

A hand touches my shoulder. "*H'yo*," I react, sitting up in the darkness.

It's Sergeant Stone. "The company's sending out a patrol. Alert your men and let them know."

"Who's going out?" I ask.

"Corporal Sun Chief. He's just going to try to feel them out. The captain wants to know where they are at all times since they tried to retake Comiso."

"Okay, will do," I say, standing and stretching.

The night air is cool; all is quiet. "I got to alert Last Arrow, then get to the outpost and make sure they know Sun Chief is going out," Stone says, turning to leave.

I move to Cheyenne. "What's up, Ecky?" he asks from a well-camouflaged slit trench. He's a light sleeper.

"Stone just told me we got a patrol out. It's Sun Chief. Wants the platoon to know."

"Good."

Footsteps are heard coming from the front. "Who's there?" I sound off.

"Ingalls."

"What you doing tomcatting around? Thought you had an early shift."

"Did. But us ol' country boys are used to hitting the hay early. So traded shifts. Me and ol' Flowers have been on outpost. Told him if he wants to be in the platoon he better get in the harness and pull the wagon like the rest of us."

I tell Ingalls about Sun Chief's patrol, then ask him to alert the squad. "Okay," Ingalls yawns. "We'll start with San Antone here. I was just coming back to wake him for the next outpost shift." His slit trench is close by. Ingalls gropes in the dark to Santana's foxhole. "It's empty." Then he ambles to a dark figure curled up on the ground. "San Antone. He's a hard sleeper," Ingalls says, glancing back at me. He kneels and takes the wrist. "Hey, San Antone—eeek!" Ingalls jumps back like he was shot out of a cannon. "Got *damn*—that's a dead German!" he says, quickly wiping his hand on his pants.

"What's all the racket?" San Antone calls, a few paces beyond in the darkness.

"Got damn you, San Antone!"

"What did I do?"

"Aw . . . nothing," Corporal Ingalls replies. "O-o-oh, I can't stand dead people. Back home, I couldn't stand funerals."

"What's all the commotion?" Cheyenne asks, stepping from the dark.

Ingalls, still wiping his hands on his pants, answers, "It's this got damn dead German. Thought it was San Antone layin' there." Cheyenne looks at the dead German, then we look at each other and laugh.

Daybreak comes. B Company gets set for "counterattack time." Weapons ready, we watch the front. The morning light expands, and no counterattack comes. We uncoil and eat a C-ration breakfast.

Medicine Man: "Just your ol' country doctor! First call! Sick, lame, and lazy!" Since Cheyenne has a cousin in E Company, he asks Medicine Man if he heard anything about Second Battalion. He says no. Then Medicine Man says that C Company had a lot of casualties when they went to help Second Battalion at Comiso.

The day grows warm, and we start to smell the German dead. And—none too soon—B Company moves. First Battalion marches north. The column moves like an accordion: it stretches and contracts, causing men to straggle and then jog to catch up. The heat is fierce. Sweat streaks our faces, and we drink a lot of water. The battalion stops before each company moves in a different direction and halts. Word comes: we are to dig in.

Lieutenant Dobbins, his face red and sweaty with heat, briefs us. Second Battalion is on the left. We're in the middle. Third Battalion is on the right. Patrols will be sent out to keep contact with the Germans. There is air activity about; we assume the planes are ours because we have Comiso Airport under control. I take pencil and paper from my pack and make drawings. However, a bright sun on the paper gives me "snow blindness." I discard most of the drawings. We stay put the whole day. When evening comes we have a C-ration supper—a can of hash. I arrange the guard and put out an outpost. Cheyenne and I visit Shield Chief. Medicine Man and Good Buffalo are with him. We ask Shield Chief what he thinks is happening. He guesses that the 179th is tightening the line until the 180th and the 157th pull even with us. If the three Regimental Combat Teams can come abreast, then the 45th Division can drive deeper into Sicily. He pauses, then adds: "If the Germans don't counterattack again."

"We'll be ready for them," Good Buffalo says.

"For sure," Cheyenne pipes up.

"By the way, Echo," Medicine Man says, turning to me. "Forgot to tell you. At the Battalion Aid Station, they said Pell was blinded by an enemy grenade, but they think it's temporary. Sarkus lost a lot of blood and will need attention. Both have been evacuated. Sarkus left word for you; he wishes you good luck."

Night falls as I make my rounds to check the men before visiting Corporal Sun Chief to see how his patrol went last night. He tells me everything went okay. "We slipped up on them. Most were asleep. Some were up talking. When the Germans move around, they're noisy. It's those hobnail boots they wear. The Girl Scouts could trail them." We sit in the dark and chat for a while. Now and then Sun Chief speaks in Pawnee.

I stand and stretch. "*Tiwat, ti-ku-skipi*" (Cousin, I'm sleepy).

"*Aho*," he says. I return to my slit trench and lie down, shifting my back and shoulders over clods of dirt. The days are now blurring into one as we advance, dig in, and repeat under the hot Mediterranean sun. Hearing American artillery thumping in the distance, I drift off to sleep.

Dawn comes. I gaze at *Hupiri-Kucu*—the Morning Star. I think of the Pawnee morning star song:

Day is here.
Daylight has come.
Tell the children that all animals are awake.
They come from places they have been sleeping.
The deer leads them.
She comes from her cover, bringing her young into the light of day.
Our hearts are glad.
Daylight has come.
The light of day is here.
Yes, daylight is here.
But there are no animals, nor deer with her young.
Our hearts are glad . . . glad that we've lived to see another day.

The men begin to stir with their machine guns, tommy-guns, Browning Automatic Rifles, and M1s with bayonets at the ready. We watch for a possible German counterattack. None comes this day.

We build small fires with twigs to heat canteen cups of water for coffee. I join Cheyenne for hot coffee, and we share a can of cold meat and beans. We comment on not seeing any livestock, especially horses. "My people, the Cheyenne, raised fine horses," Short Nose says with a nostalgic and faraway look. "They had many herds. The herd boy was told to watch the horse's ears. Horses can hear a long ways. When hearing something, ears go up. It'll turn the head that way too. Then you know that someone is coming and the direction he's coming. 'Watch the ears,' they always say."

"The Pawnees had good horses too." I perk up. "The old-timers had war ponies, buffalo ponies, and kept horses for work, too. The war ponies had stamina. Buffalo ponies had speed. The workhorse was used as a packhorse. Gentle, it was called a 'woman's horse.'" I pause and smile. "But the young women liked fast horses."

"There you go . . . Pawnees and Cheyennes are always talking about fast horses and fast women," Medicine Man says as he walks up behind us.

"*A-ay,* my fren'," Cheyenne says.

"Sit: for you this pipe is always lit and the robe spread." Medicine Man smiles.

"Thank you, my friend." He has a cup of coffee and sips on it. "Say, Medicine Man," Cheyenne says. "Hear anything new?"

"Nope, nothing. Both sides are eyeing each other like a couple of game roosters with their neck feathers up." We hear American artillery begin to fire. The fire increases before American fighters pass over heading north. We look at each other before Medicine Man gulps the last of his coffee and Cheyenne puts on his steel helmet. I get back to my slit trench and stay put.

After a while Shield Chief calls me. "*Wees!*" (Hurry!), he says. I grab my M1 and hurry to Shield Chief. Lieutenant Dobbins is with him. Showing fear, the lieutenant says the Germans have counterattacked near the position held by Third Battalion. Captain Lee wants some men to guard a bridge on the left front. I am told to take six men and leave the rest of the squad so there won't be a platoon gap. He shows me where to find the bridge on his map. I look to Shield Chief. He nods with a low voice, "*Wees.*" I hustle and take the first six men in the squad and leave the rest with Corporal Ingalls. I fill them in on the situation and then take the canteen of water from my pack before putting it in the canteen carrier that Medicine Man brought. We take interval and dogtrot to our left.

Finding a road, we turn right. Here the road is lined with tall cactus and mesquite trees. A layer of dust on the cactus indicates recent traffic. The road dips and is intersected by small farm roads and donkey trails. We stop. The men watch me. If I stop, they stop. I move, they move. I study the immediate ground and everything ahead. We move again. This time we stay off the road. Movement is spotted ahead; we get down. There are men coming this way a hundred and fifty yards from our front. They stay off the road as they advance toward us.

I click the safety lock off as I raise my M1. "Get ready!" I take aim. My heart pounds as the men inch closer with every step. As they come closer I realize it is our guys. I lock my M1, stand, and walk out into the open.

"Hey!" the leader calls. "Sergeant Benning here. C Company!"

"Sergeant Echohawk! B Company!" I respond.

Sergeant Benning approaches, his face sunburned and streaked with sweat. Without looking back, he signals: "halt." His men get down. "Ecky Hawk, glad to see you. We been running our asses off out there." Benning hunkers down and removes his helmet. "Son of a bitch! It's hotter 'n a depot stove."

"Did you guys run into anything out there?" I ask.

"Oh, hell, yes." Benning answers, wiping the sweat from his face with a sleeve. "Our company commander wanted a patrol out to keep contact with the Germans. There's a bunch of them up the road and across the bridge. About a hundred or more. They got a half-track with them, either that or a tank."

"Tank?"

"Y'ah. Hell, don't know for sure," Benning replies nervously. "Heard a heavy motor. Got to be a tank. But we did see Germans. They were thick as dog-dick gnats. We got our asses away from there fast." He takes a stone and slings it forward. "Got damn, them bastards kicked the piss out of us, day before yesterday. That's when C Company pitched in to help the Second Battalion. Got damn it was awful! Awful! Still shaking yet . . . can't get over it!"

I look at this cowboy from the Oklahoma City stockyards and say nothing.

Cheyenne, overhearing Benning, crawls closer: "They caught us out in the bare-ass open, on a long stretch of burned ground. They hit us with the got-damndest mortar barrage a man will ever see. They blew Big Bill Orland in two. I saw Johnny Trotter's guts spill out of his damn shirt. The wounded were screaming. I cried, then I remembered I was always mouthing off, 'First off, I'm the toughest son of a bitch in C Company.' So I got up and hollered that and yelled, 'Come on, let's go!' We started forward. I don't know how we did, but we did."

Benning bows his head. Wipes his eyes with a big fist. His knuckles show cactus cuts. "Big Bill . . . he was a good ol' boy. Sho' was rough. He and I used to rodeo together at Guthrie during the '89er Celebration."* Sergeant

★Oklahoma's '89er Day Celebration, held in the territorial capital of Guthrie, commemorates the state's first land run held on April 22, 1889.

Benning stands and drinks water. "Somebody said that tracer bullets set the grass on fire. Could be. The Second Battalion locked horns with them son of a bitches before we got there. About burned the country up. After we got out of that mortar barrage, we flat took them Germans to knuckle junction." Benning adjusts the crotch of his pants. "These got damn OD britches sure gall a man in hot weather."

He glances back to his men and gives a sharp whistle. "Let's go! Let's haul ass!" Benning adjusts his pants again. "Watch it, Ecky Hawk, them son of a bitches are at that bridge."

"Thanks, Benning, I'll see ya."

Sergeant Benning moves off with a rolling gait, chest out, like a bronc rider ambling to the chute to mount up. As his patrol passes I hear him bellow: "All right! Got damn it! Ain't out of the woods yet. Let's get interval!"

We move forward and I check interval. We carry our M1s at the ready. We spot a row of dense trees crossing our front, indicating a river. I spot the bridge and signal "hold," then slip forward for a closer look. All is clear as we set up positions. I place the BAR man where he can cover the bridge. The wooden bridge is seventy-five yards long and passes over a dry riverbed. The trees that line the banks throw heavy shadows. We hear motors nearby but nothing heavy. I look at the far end of the bridge for movement. Flies drone about my shirt, which is still crusted with dried blood. Near the end of the bridge, grasshoppers flitter from the shadows and into the sunlight. Something spooked them. I clear the sweat from my eyes and watch for any movement.

Way behind us comes the sound of vehicles. They are American. Maybe that's our antitank guys. Would be glad to see them wheel antitank guns up. We can't stand up now that the Germans know that someone is here with all those vehicles grinding around back of us.

"Soldier!" comes a sharp voice from behind. One of my men answers. I hear questions fired. One of my men answers again.

A neatly dressed officer approaches me. "Who's in charge here?" he asks sharply.

"Here, Sir," I reply, staying down.

"Report!" he snaps. He is a major.

"Sergeant Echohawk. B Company, 179th, Sir," I answer, with no intention of standing. The major walks to me and frowns at my uniform. It is rumpled from the seawater of the first day. My shirt is shredded from the cactus and covered with charcoaled ash. My pants are grimed with sweat and crusted with dried blood.

The major explodes: "Who's your commanding officer, Sergeant? What's your situation? And stand!"

Portrait, soldier of the 4th Indian Division, British Eighth Army. Naples, Italy, May 16, 1944.

Portrait, Corporal Nkemelan Motsedsele, Company Bechuana, African Auxiliary Pioneer Corps, British Eighth Army. Naples, Italy, March 1944.

Portrait, Private John Grieve, 6th Battalion, Black Watch Regiment, British Eighth Army.

Portrait, British infantryman, Private W. O. Sellers, 1st Battalion, Green Howards, 5th Division. Sellers was wounded on the Anzio Beachhead. British 92nd General Hospital, March 25, 1944.

Portrait, Ceylonese soldier S. Ossen of the Royal Army Service Corps, British Eighth Army, dressed in hospital robe. 92nd General Hospital, Naples, Italy, April 1, 1944.

JAPANESE-AMERICAN BATTALION
PVT. FREDDIE MOROHASHI
ITALY MAY 20, 1944
(ATTACHED TO 34ᵗʰ Div)

TERRITORY OF
HAWII

Portrait, Japanese American soldier, Private Freddie Morohashi, 100th Infantry Battalion, attached to the 34th Division. Later the 100th became the 1st Battalion of the 442nd Infantry Regiment. The 100th Battalion's high casualty rate earned the unit the nickname "Purple Heart Battalion."

Portrait, French Moroccan soldier attached to the US Fifth Army. Pozzuli, Italy, March 1944.

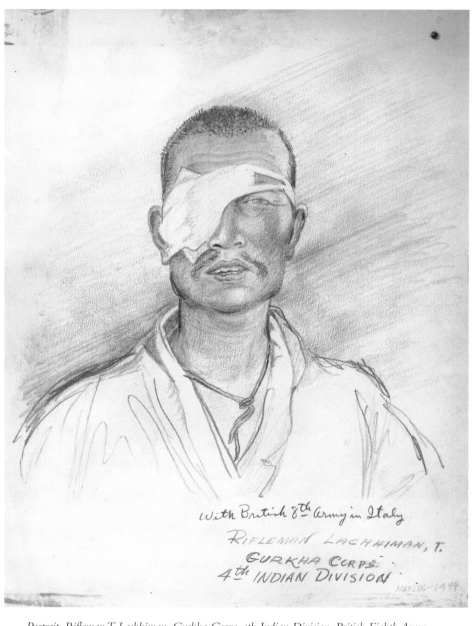

Portrait, Rifleman T. Lachhiman, Gurkha Corps, 4th Indian Division, British Eighth Army. 1944.

Portrait, veteran of Tunisia and Italy. Sergeant J. Prytherack, 1st Battalion, Irish Guards. 2nd Evacuation Hospital, March 25, 1944.

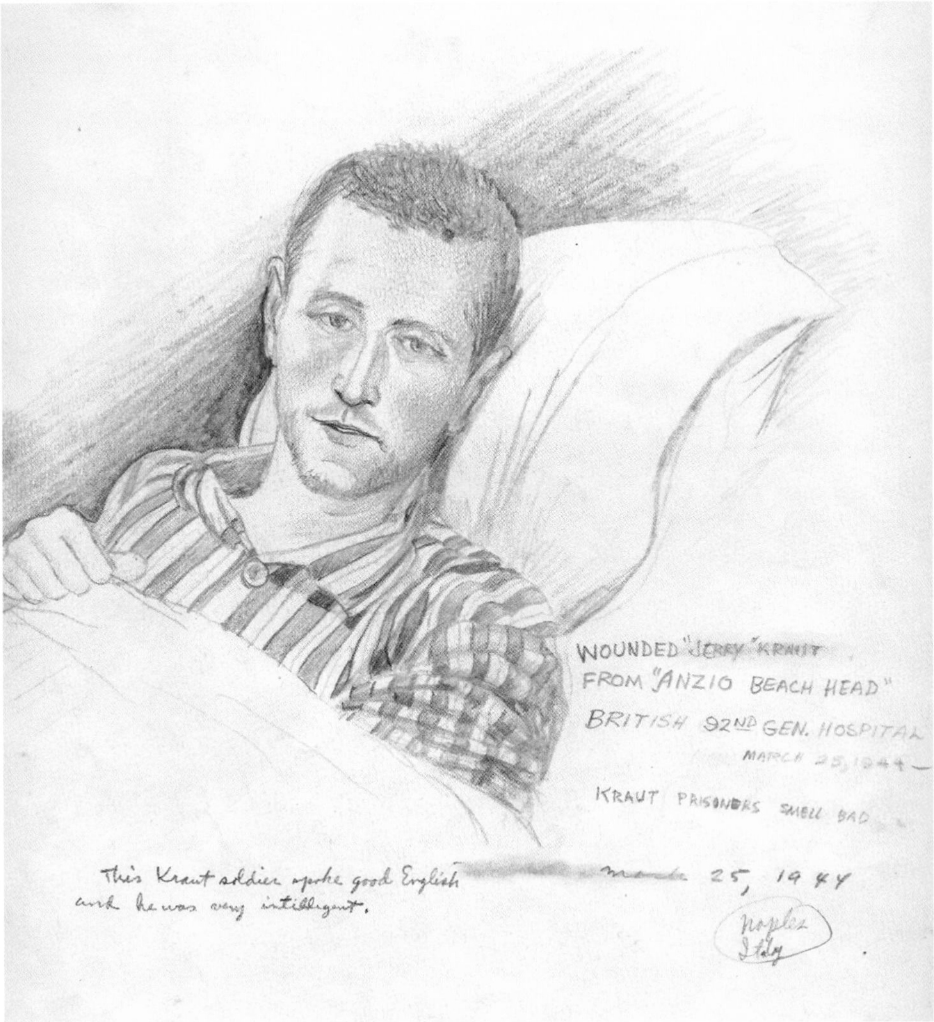
WOUNDED "JERRY" KRAUT
FROM "ANZIO BEACH HEAD"
BRITISH 92ND GEN. HOSPITAL
MARCH 25, 1944
KRAUT PRISONERS SMELL BAD
This Kraut soldier spoke good English
and he was very intelligent.
25, 1944
Naples
Italy

"Wounded Jerry Kraut from Anzio Beach Head. This kraut spoke good English." British 92nd General Hospital, near Naples, Italy, March 25, 1944.

Portrait, Private Joseph R. Clark, 6th Sea Force, Highlanders 5th Division, 10th Corps. Wounded at Anzio, Clark was nineteen years old.

Within the drawing:

GERMAN PRISONER

PANZER
GERMAN DIVISION
"ANZIO BEACH HEAD"

93 EVAC

MAR. 4 '44

real sharp Kraut

Panzer Grenadier Wilham Sieghardt, captured near Anzio Beachhead, 93rd Evacuation Hospital, Anzio, March 1944.

OPPOSITE: *Portrait, Private First Class Wallace W. Friend, Company G, 504th Parachute Infantry Regiment. Friend was from Cleveland, Oklahoma, near Pawnee. Anzio Beachhead, March 1, 1944.*

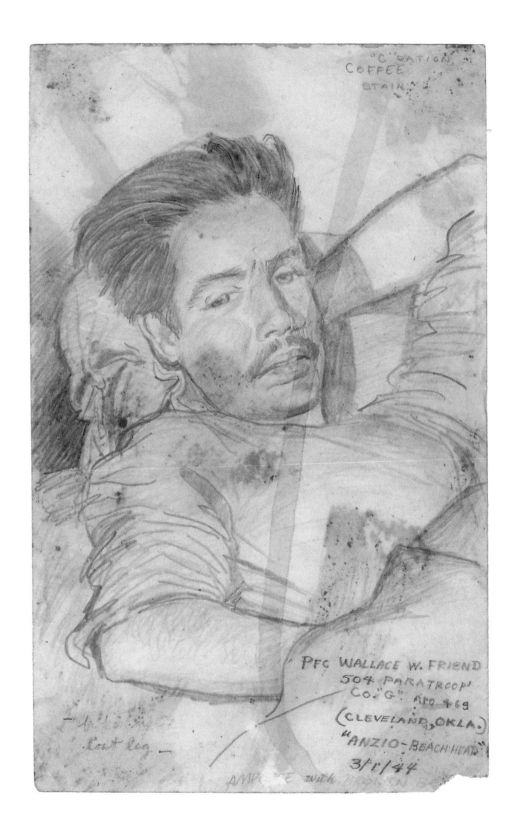

"C" RATION
COFFEE
STAIN

PFC WALLACE W. FRIEND
504 PARATROOP
CO. "G" APO 469
(CLEVELAND, OKLA.)
"ANZIO·BEACH·HEAD"
3/1/44

lost leg

Portrait of G. Rawes of the Scots Guard. Anzio Beachhead, 1944.

OPPOSITE: *"Jerries captured on Anzio Beach head" on March 3, 1944. These were nineteen- to twenty-one-year-old Panzer grenadiers. Drawn on Red Cross stationery at 93rd Evacuation Hospital, 1944.*

Supermen? AMERICAN RED CROSS

"Jerries" captured on "Anzio Beach Head" March 3rd, near Carroceto, Italy. 19-21 year old Panzer Grenadiers (Drawn at the 93rd Evac. Hosp.) 1944

FORM 559 A

Portrait, Private Thomas Henderson, 23rd Armored Brigade, British Eighth Army. Henderson was a veteran of El Alamein, Tunis, Sicily, and Italy. Anzio Beachhead, 1944.

"Sir, across this bridge are one hundred Germans and one tank . . . and—" The officer drops like he was poleaxed. He wiggles for the ditch in record time. I continue, ". . . and my commanding officer is Captain—"

"Never mind," the major interrupts nervously. "How many men do you have, Sergeant?"

"Six, Sir."

"Six!" he gasps. The officer pivots on his hands and knees, then scurries down the ditch.

Bear, who is a few yards behind, growls: "White man." We hear the American vehicles grind, bump, bang, and drive away, leaving the six of us to face a hundred Germans and a tank.

At sundown, we are relieved by Last Arrow and six men. I fill him in on the situation, then head back to the platoon. I report to Lieutenant Dobbins and Shield Chief. I tell them what happened, then add: "One of my men, Mac Lindsay, was in the rear when American vehicles drove up. He said an officer stood in a jeep with newsmen around him. The vehicles were just off the road and hidden by groves of cactus. Mac couldn't see much and wasn't about to stand and look. That's when a major walked up, then crawled back, as Mac said, like a turpentine cat." Lieutenant Dobbins was pleased about guarding the bridge and so many Germans there. He said the Third Battalion stopped that counterattack this morning and drove them back two miles. The Germans reportedly lost seven tanks and fifty infantrymen.

Twilight comes and that means supper. A can of cold hash and water are in order. I check with Ingalls about the outpost, then see if the men's feet and weapons are okay. Night falls as the kitchen truck arrives. One squad at a time goes back for water and rations. We get three days' supply of K-rations, which means we're expecting to move and fight. Shield Chief instructs Stone to draw rations for Last Arrow and his men, who are guarding the bridge. It's a clear night, with a peaceful canopy of stars. A wolf call is heard before echoes follow. It's a Pawnee, and no Germans are near. Tired, I fall asleep.

Dawn comes, signaling counterattack time. B Company is ready with weapons bristling. When none comes, we buddy up and eat a K-ration breakfast. We prolong a canteen cup of coffee and visit. "First call! Sick, lame, and lazy!" Medicine Man says as he walks from our rear. We ask if he heard anything. He tells us what Lieutenant Dobbins already told us.

Medicine Man chats with the men, then calls on Shield Chief. Approaching Shield Chief too is Lieutenant Dobbins. He greets Medicine Man, then talks to Shield Chief. Shield Chief calls: "Second Platoon! Let's go!"

"Second Platoon! Let's go!" the voice of Stone follows. B Company joins A, C, and D Companies as they move out. Judging by the sun, the First

Battalion marches north. As we advance we move along roads, passing a few houses. Here there is no burned field nor stench of the dead. A jeep with the battalion commander and a radio man drives up the column. Following close behind is another jeep with two officers.

The morning is hot. Someone in the first squad calls back: "Where's Cindy? Pass it on!" The word passes.

Sergeant Stone, bringing up the rear, sounds off: "When it gets too hot for the rest of you, it's just right for me!" Then he starts to sing "Cindy."

The column stops. Saved by the bell. The battalion commander and other officers in the jeep return. Companies separate and take up positions before the word comes to dig in. At the front is a highway. Squad leaders are called by Lieutenant Dobbins, who checks his map. He says ahead is Highway 124, the Grammichele-Caltagirone road. The 179th Regimental Combat Team's front line runs parallel to Highway 124. Second Battalion is on the left. First, Middle, and Third are on the right. We are approximately twenty-five miles inland. The lieutenant studies the map, then looks up at the highway. He figures the 45th Division is ready to attack. We'll use Highway 124, since it runs to the center of Sicily.

Lieutenant Dobbins puts the map away and grins. "Thought you'd like to hear something amusing. Colonel Stevens was called to Regiment for a battalion commanders' meeting the other day. While there he heard that when Second Battalion took Comiso some of our guys pushed ahead and captured the mayor, the chief of police, and the telephone building of Ragusa." He continues: "The GIs who captured the telephone building were Italian Americans from New York and Boston. At the switchboards they had fun answering frantic calls from Italian units wanting to know the situation. This fouled up the Germans attempting to coordinate operations with their Italian allies. Our guys had them running around like Keystone Kops.* This happened just outside our boundary in the British sector." We return to our squads and fill them in on things up to now. Expecting to advance, we check weapons, ammo, and equipment. We stay in our slit trenches. I think about doing some drawings, but just as I get my pencil and paper out we move and wait the whole day.

A little after sundown, we see vehicles on Highway 124. Coming from the right, they cross in front of us. On high ground, we have a good view of the land ahead. I look to Shield Chief, noticing that Lieutenant Dobbins and Sergeant Stone are with him. I join them. The lieutenant watches with binoculars. "They are British," he says. Puzzled, Shield Chief looks at Lieutenant Dobbins, then at the traffic on the highway. The lieutenant puts the binoculars away.

*Keystone Kops were policemen in silent film comedies usually portrayed as incompetent or stupid.

"*They wore funny knee pants in Sicily and flat steel helmets. They had more discipline than we did but we fought as hard as they did. They had English rifles and wore a gas mask on their chest, like [in] World War I. They drank a lot of tea instead of coffee like us.*"

"Each Army has boundaries with its own objectives. It's crucial in combat. One Army could accidentally fire on the other. Can't understand why the British are in our sector."

"Doesn't appear right, Sir," Shield Chief says.

"Why, that's coon shit in the horse barn," Stone blurts out.

The lieutenant looks at Stone. "Well. Yes," he says. Then the lieutenant turns to Shield Chief. "Sergeant Shield Chief, there's nothing we can do. I'm going back to check with Captain Lee."

"What do you think, Phil?" I ask Shield Chief.

"*Ka-ka-ti-ra-ita*" (I don't know), he answers. "The British got no right bustin' through like them wagon trains a-comin' through Indi'n country."

Stone joins in. "Got damn, it looks like somebody left the gate open in the north forty." We eat a K-ration supper and drink water.

Nightfall. I call on Shield Chief to see if Lieutenant Dobbins found out anything. All he had to report was that Battalion was ordered to hold. Everybody's upset. I ask Shield Chief about the outpost and guard for the night. "Same as usual," he says. "Let's don't take chances." I visit Cheyenne and Bear for some time, then return to my slit trench. It's another starry night. I hear a wolf call near Highway 124, then drop off to sleep.

Counterattack time arrives. Our hearts are not in it, for the British have squeezed us out. We eat a K-ration breakfast. Later in the morning heavy traffic rolls on Highway 124. Lieutenant Dobbins says they are Canadians. It is a long, hot day, but I manage to make a few drawings. When getting snow blindness, I visit Shield Chief, who is cleaning his tommy-gun. Sergeant Ruling His Son is there too. He tells us about scouting yesterday evening for bread and wine. He says he came to a village where the doors were boarded up and there were no people. When returning, he explains they were surprised to see the British. They didn't see him. Ruling His Son wondered what the British were doing square in front of us. I return to my trench and rest as the day comes and goes. In the evening we eat our K-ration supper before going through the motions of putting out the guard for watch.

As the sun dips below the horizon, B Company is pulled back from the line. The First Battalion loads onto two-and-a-half-ton trucks. They have blue lights on and roll at a speed to ensure orderly movement. A motor officer, standing in a jeep, moves along the column to check speed and interval. Crowded, we sit shoulder to shoulder with M1s between our knees. Some men sit in the aisles. Often the trucks turn off the road, bang, bounce, and tip side to side to get around blown-out bridges. Military police with blue flashlights signal the trucks safely past. On the highway again, we resume speed. The motor officer passes, standing in the jeep. Peering through the dust, I see it is a starry night. Spotting the North Star, I figure out we're heading west. The convoy reduces speed to cross a bridge erected by engineers. The heavy equipment and vehicles are dispersed in the dark. Still working on part of the bridge, they yell out: "Good luck!"

Riding herd on the convoy, the motor officer moves us along. We slow, resume speed, and then repeat. We bounce, rattle, eat dust, and cough as the convoy advances. It beats walking, we joke. To avoid shell holes, the trucks move at a snail's pace. We spot a sign riddled with bullet holes; it leans in a ditch and reads Biscari. We come to a junction where an MP signals us to the right with a blue flashlight. Rolling north, the trucks slow to avoid bomb craters. On the road and in the ditches are burned vehicles and demolished tanks; they're German. We see a sign pointing south that reads Gela.

After a while the convoy stops for a ten-minute rest stop. We stretch and relieve ourselves. Nearby is another sign that reads 117. The convoy rolls again. The farther north we go, the smoother the road gets. The wagon master standing in the jeep passes by. With the humming of motors, I doze off.

The truck's sudden stop shakes me awake. The tailgate bangs open. "Everybody out!" We unload. Someone asks the man at the tailgate for the time.

The soldier takes a blue flashlight and looks at his wristwatch. "It's one forty-five in the morning."

The voice of Shield Chief is heard over the commotion of off-loading: "All right! Second Platoon! Over here!"

The voice of Stone follows: "All right! Second Platoon! Over here!" A few yards away in the darkness are an armored scout car and jeeps with machine guns mounted on them. It is the 45th Reconnaissance; they've been scouting the roads ahead. One of their men talks to two battalion officers before the battalion moves out on foot.

Our legs are stiff from the long ride. The night is cool, and the North Star is dead ahead. Weary and sleepy, B Company plods forward through darkness, sounding like a long string of packhorses moving through the night. We stumble in and out of rocky gulches and skirt groves of cactus as we advance. We wade through knee-deep grass where every now and then someone trips, sending their steel helmet clunking to the ground. We maintain interval as we move. Finally we stop to rest when word comes down to dig in; the men drop to the ground. Shovels scrape and pick mattocks clang on the hard ground as men dig their trenches.

Lieutenant Dobbins calls the squad leaders. He says the 157th will attack Caltanissetta with the 179th in support. The Second Battalion was left behind to support the 180th. Only two battalions will be on hand to help the 157th. Our current position is southwest of Mazzarino. Ahead is a pocket of Germans bypassed by the 157th. We will attack them at 0600. We return and tell our squads what the Lieutenant said. With only a few hours before daylight, we try to sleep.

Day breaks when Shield Chief yells: "Second Platoon! Everybody up!"

Stone follows: "Second Platoon! Everybody up!" Breakfast for the day is a cold K-ration with a canteen cup of hot coffee made over a tiny fire of ration box tops. Gulping coffee, we check weapons, ammo, and grenades.

"Last Arrow, you and Echohawk lead. Good Buffalo, you're in reserve!" Shield Chief calls. He approaches with tommy-gun ready: "You men ready?"

"Ready!" the men sing out.

"Good!" Shield Chief says, adjusting the hatchet tucked in his belt. He looks at me, puts his right hand to his mouth, and points forward with the forefinger: "talk." He makes the same sign to Last Arrow. Shield Chief returns to his position.

"Men!" I address the squad. "If it's hand to hand, help each other. Shoot first, then use bayonets. Slash the hands, then go for the throat. Roll up your sleeves and mean business. I'll go first!"

We kneel and wait. A red ball of a sun peeks over the eastern horizon. "Fix bayonets!" Shield Chief shouts. Men stir about as bayonets click. Last Arrow steps out in front of his squad before I follow and do the same. Shield Chief motions: "forward." "Second Platoon! Let's go!" Lieutenant Dobbins and Shield Chief position themselves between the two lead squads before B Company advances.

As we move, American bombers roar over heading north. From the left rear comes a thunderous boom. It is the big 155mm "Long Toms" that are shelling at long range, supporting the drive on Caltanissetta. The sun is above the horizon, making our long morning shadows shorten. Ahead is a line of stone houses surrounded by trees, shrubbery, a goat pen, and haystacks. In a nearby field is a pitchfork driven into the ground with a white shirt draped over the handle. Someone left in a hurry, or maybe the shirt is a signal of some sort. Before we have time to discuss the situation ahead, gunfire erupts at the immediate front. We hit the ground. Shield Chief shouts: "Move! Move!" We move. At the right, Matlock's Third Platoon advances Indian-style: each man runs, zigzags, hits the ground, then pops up from a different place and dashes forward again. Some of his men fire on the run. We close on the houses from the rear. They face a single street. We keep moving between the houses on a dirt street and draw no enemy fire. *They seem to be deserted*, I think. Suddenly I hear a vehicle pulling away. Dashing forward between the houses, we see a German jeep speeding away with three trucks following close behind. We fire as they race across an open field to a road lined with cactus. The vehicles escape, leaving a cloud of dust.

"Hey, Ecky! Look!" San Antone calls from the next house over. "Way up the road! Looks like a tank parked at a road junction!" Cheyenne and Bear are with me. We look but can't see because of cactus and dust. The road the Germans took turns north to a road junction. From the right comes the sound of a motorcycle. A motor starts, then chokes. It's another German trying to make a getaway. Cheyenne, Bear, and I raise our M1s and make our way toward the motorcycle. Four houses down and across the street, a man straddling a motorcycle is seen. He is in the shadows of trees near a front-yard wall.

Raising my M1, I click off the lock and aim for the man's head. At that distance, our BAR man pops up from behind the wall and aims. "Don't shoot!" the motorcycle man cries. "Don't shoot!"

"Got *damn* you, Flowers!" the BAR man explodes in anger. I lock my M1 and walk forward. "Soldier! You almost got yourself killed!" Private Flowers turns with mouth agape. "Flowers, that's a dumb fool thing you're doing with the German motorcycle when we don't know if this place is clear or not!"

"Flowers, you ain't for shit! I ought to blow your butt off anyway!" Slade says, still pointing his Browning Automatic Rifle at the little paratrooper.

"Now, now. Just a minute. Let me explain. I found a booby trap on it. That's what I was looking for. Us paratroopers had booby-trap training. This thing has seen better days. The Germans left this motorcycle on purpose, knowing our guys would find it and try to start it. Then the booby trap would explode and kill somebody."

"All right! Don't bunch up!" Shield Chief yells from up the street.

"Okay. You're off the hook," I say to Flowers. "But don't get too anxious next time. Us Indi'ns shoot first, then ask questions. You just lucked out. Okay?"

"Okay," he responds.

B Company reorganizes. "Echohawk!" someone calls.

"*H'yo.*" It's Lieutenant John Heller. He's in a jeep with a driver and a soldier with an M1. They've just driven up. Two other jeeps follow. In those jeeps are soldiers with M1s.

"Battalion wants a couple of B Company Indians for a roving patrol. It's my patrol, and I want you to volunteer," Lieutenant Heller says, grinning.

I grin. "Come on, Chey', let's go with John."

"*Aho.*"

"Come on. We'll let you Indi'ns burn a wagon train. One of you ride on the hood and the other in the back." I tell Bear to tell Shield Chief that Cheyenne and I are going on a roving patrol with Lieutenant Heller. I turn to Cheyenne. "I'll ride shotgun, you ride in the back." We mount up and roll.

Lieutenant Heller is from Okmulgee, Oklahoma. He married a Creek Indian woman who was a classmate of Shield Chief's at Bacone Indian College. So we know each other personally. "How's Phil and the rest of the Pawnee guys?" Lieutenant Heller inquires.

"Fine. Had some shootouts. Everybody made it okay, though. How about yourself?"

"Can't complain. But it's been getting rougher than hell lately."

"John, we ought to take it easy. One of our guys thinks he saw a tank at the road junction ahead." At the mention of tank, the driver slows suddenly.

I almost slide off the hood. The jeeps behind have slowed too. "What did the tank look like? Or was it a half-track?"

"Don't know. I didn't see it. One of our guys said it looks like a tank parked at a road junction. I couldn't see anything, though. Too much dust and cactus." Our motor patrol turns north and eases up to the road junction, where we see nothing.

"Well, could have been a tank, part of a delaying force," Lieutenant Heller speculates. "It might have been lying low, waiting for us to follow up their withdrawal," he adds. We come to a hill and stop. Lieutenant Heller peers through binoculars. "I think they flew the coop." We roll again through barren country and check intersecting farm roads and donkey trails.

Ahead of us is a rise. Beyond it is a wide valley with rocky knolls that look like small volcanoes. The roving patrol picks up speed. Riding on the hood, there's a breeze in my face. Air rips as an explosion hits. The driver brakes. We all dive for the ditch as Lieutenant Heller shouts: "Get those jeeps off the road!"

I scramble from the ditch and get away from the road. Air rips—and another explosion. It's the tank; he's still up there. "Cheyenne!"

"*H'yo!*" he answers a few yards behind.

"Let's go! See what's ahead!"

"*Aho!*" We crawl forward, eventually dashing from cactus to cactus and knoll to knoll. We make sure to stay away from the road. Up there, we spot a knoll of rocks on the right side of the road. This is where the tank was hiding, but it is now gone. On top of a rise, we see the tank in the distance, moving away from us in a cloud of dust. We get back to the road and wave to the men. They see us and mount up.

In a few minutes they arrive. Lieutenant Heller stands in the jeep.

"It was one tank, Sir!"

Holding binoculars in the left hand, Lieutenant Heller gives me the thumbs-up sign with the right hand. He uses the binoculars. "Yeah, he's out of sight now. When that tank fired, the shell passed over low and exploded behind us. Awful close. Sure scared the hell out of us." Some of the men walk up from the jeeps for a look. "Eck, we'll leave a couple of men with you. You guys watch this place. I don't think the Germans will try anything. It's all delaying action. Battalion will come up this road and you men can join your outfits. I'm going back and report to Colonel Stevens. Thank you for volunteering."

"Any time."

"All right! Revenuers, let's go!" The men mount up. The jeeps wheel around and head down the road. One man sits on the hood while the others are seated with rifles between their knees. It looks like they're off to bust some stills.★

The men Lieutenant Heller left me are from A Company. I tell them to take the right side of the road and watch while Cheyenne and I take the left. We get well away from the road. "Just a minute," Cheyenne says, looking at the ground. "Flies low on the ground. Somebody is near!" I check the ground and find a tiny morsel of meat; it seems to be bacon or sausage. When Indians dry meat, they put it on racks eight feet high. Flies never get that high, but they will find something that's fresh and low. It's happening here.

We read the ground; there are two people. One is eating as he moves. We follow impressions in the grass that show they ran to the forward slope of the hill. On the forward slope is a layer of rocks that form a shallow cave. Crouched there we find a civilian.

"Hey, there!"

The man is startled. Wide-eyed, he stands and bows a couple of times.

"You speak English?"

The man looks us over before answering, then says something in Sicilian. "Keep an eye on him," I tell Cheyenne. "There's another one near. Going to look."

"*Aho.*"

Out there is a shallow draw. It runs north. The right side is in the morning shadow. The left is in sunlight. When animals hide in the morning they blend into the east side of a north and south draw, the morning-shadow side. I take this side as I inspect the area. Walking quietly, I find a man hiding in the brush.

"Hey, there!"

The man throws up his hands in fear.

"You speak English?"

He starts to say something, hesitates, then rattles off in Sicilian.

Back at the cave, the two men talk to each other and glance at us. One reaches into a sack that is back in the cave and removes a skillet. The other speaks to us and points to a small circle of stones. They build a fire. Once their small fire is lit they take potatoes from the sack and peel them. I turn to Cheyenne. "They might be collaborating with the Germans." The two men register at the word "Germans." Cheyenne touches my sleeve and uses Indian sign language signaling that they understand our talk. I look at their hands and wrists and note they are not sunburned. I tell Cheyenne that they haven't been out in the sun and these aren't farmers: they don't have working man's hands.

★Revenuers were agents of the US Treasury Department tasked with enforcing laws related to the illegal manufacturing and transportation of alcohol during Prohibition.

I point my MI at them and click off the lock. "We know you understand English. Stand up."

"Don't shoot! Please!" They stand.

"What are you doing here?" I ask, lowering my MI and locking it.

"We own land here. When we heard the Germans were here, we came to see if our people were safe. My father and mother live here; they are old. The Germans took all the wine, pigs, and chickens. They took the young men to work. When the Germans wanted us to spy on the Americans, we ran away. My name is Roberto and this is Mario. We are actors from Palermo."

"I'm Sergeant Echohawk. This is Cheyenne. We are American Indians."

They look at us, eyes wide. They are nervous. "Have some potatoes. Very good potatoes," Roberto says.

Mario kneels, takes the skillet, and offers the fried potatoes. "Yes, very good potatoes. Eat: *multi, multi.*" We sit, take some with our fingers, and eat them hot. Roberto reaches in the sack and takes out two cloths, spreading them on our laps as napkins. "Sorry we have no wine. God bless President Roosevelt."

Mario adds: "God bless America."

"Buy more war bonds," I remark with a mouthful.

"Roberto, what kind of actors are you? I mean what do you do? Song and dance or act in pictures?"

"We do many things," he says, gaining his composure. "Mostly, as you say, song and dance. Would you like to see one of our acts?"

"Yes, Roberto," I reply. Roberto and Mario rise. They dust off their trousers before they adjust their shirt collars and lapels. The two stand side by side, raise their chins, and burst into song with arms outstretched. They dip left and right with a cross-legged step and raise dust, tap-dancing like something from Fred Astaire or Bill Robinson or Al Jolson's bended-knee "Mammy" routine. They slow to a ballroom glide, something Rudolph Valentino would do. They hit it again, pounding their feet and singing in Italian. We blink, then give them room. The duo stops in a fog of dust. Roberto and Mario step forward and bow.

Cheyenne and I don't know what to say. We're a couple of Indians who never saw anything but Indian powwow dancing and traveling medicine shows. We clap, rewarding them for their show with cigarettes, gum, hard candy, and K-ration biscuits. Overwhelmed, Roberto and Mario tear into them.

We hear jeeps. It's Battalion approaching from the rear. We tell Roberto and Mario we must go. I take more fried potatoes and wrap them in a hanky. I comment on the taste. Roberto says they have been fried in olive oil. As the battalion comes up, we rejoin B Company.

Moving up the road, I give my squad the fried potatoes. They eat them, smacking their lips. I look back. Roberto and Mario are standing side by side on the hill. They bow in unison and wave. I wave back. The potatoes fried in olive oil were still warm. It is our first hot meal since the night before hitting the beach at Scoglitti one week ago.

The 157th has stormed Caltanissetta. We of the 179th advance steadily, supporting the 157th. After a day's march under a broiling sun, First Battalion takes up positions at sundown. The heat lingers, and we are dog tired. Soaked with sweat, we all gulp down water. We dig in and set the guard for the night. I eat my K-ration supper, which is a dehydrated fruit bar. I also have a packet of bouillon soup powder, enough for one canteen cup. This requires fire to heat water. I have some precious drinking water, but I can't make a fire at night. So, no warm soup on this evening. Tired, I lie down in my slit trench, where I drift off to sleep to the sound of my stomach growling from hunger.

7

The Katy Line

Company Command relied on Brummett Echohawk and his squad for some of the most difficult scouting missions assigned to the regiment during the war. Echohawk insisted on conducting patrols in small, segregated units of Indians or alone when possible, believing that "to us a fight was personal. I wanted that guy out there and so did the Cheyenne and this is how we're going to do it. We're not going to go in a group like somebody going to a parade." This sentiment held by men like Echohawk was not unwarranted, as many of the warring and hunting techniques passed down by elders translated well into combat. Common hunting practices that worked well in combat situations included moving when the wind blew and to stay silent, as well as navigating without a compass at night using the wind and stars. Other skills included things like not walking on your tiptoes at night because the center of balance lies in the line of sight. It was this type of knowledge that led to successful scouting patrols by American Indians of the 45th Division. As Echohawk explained, "This is the way we did it. This is why so many American patrols were shot up, because they didn't know how to do it." The usage of skills such as these contributed to the prestige of American Indians in combat, earning them reputations as soldiers of the highest caliber.

Day breaks and B Company is up at the crack of dawn. Counterattack time comes and goes. I wolf down a K-ration breakfast—a delicious serving of dehydrated eggs, hard cracker biscuits, and powdered coffee. The 179th moves out.

We hear that Second Battalion has joined us. They were left behind to help the 180th, who had their hands full with Germans. This means that the 180th has passed through us. The vehicles roll again, raising dust on the road. We are covered by the white dust they stir up. By the time the convoy passes it looks like somebody hit us with a sack of flour. There is no conversation and a wide interval. We'd have to raise voices to talk, and that would take energy. There is only the sound of tramping feet, coupled with the sound of passing jeeps and weapons trucks.

We stop, move, repeat. The column strings out, then closes, then again strings out before closing. Weary men lugging machine guns, boxes of ammo, mortars, mortar shells, and heavy base plates lag, then struggle to catch up. Adjusting my pack, I feel sweat run down my back. The Sicilian sun burns down on us. The column stops as word comes: "Off your feet!" Men flop down to drink water and take off their packs. All around me men unbutton shirts and pull out shirttails. They remove steel helmets and wipe sweat from their faces.

A runner comes for Lieutenant Dobbins. Medicine Man comes up to check the men while they rest and smoke. After a while Lieutenant Dobbins returns and calls all squad leaders. The lieutenant tells us that Caltanissetta, Sicily's largest inland city, has been taken. He says the 179th will move and pass through the 157th. Lieutenant Dobbins's face is red with heat. He looks shaky, like he might be coming down with heatstroke. We're too beat to feel any joy about Caltanissetta being taken. Like Scoglitti, Comiso, and Biscari, we'll never see Caltanissetta either.

"On your feet! Second Platoon! Let's go!" the voice of Shield Chief comes.

"On your feet! Second Platoon! Let's go!" the voice of Stone repeats. We move out and so do the vehicles. An ambulance goes by; someone must have had a heatstroke. A sign appears ahead reading Caltanissetta. The ambulance returns, passing by at a rapid pace. A jeep with a driver, an officer, and a radio man passes. Then we see Caltanissetta at a distance: white buildings, cathedrals, walls, and cypress trees. Under a turquoise sky, it's a jewel in a barren land. Looks like Jerusalem—or what I picture it to be. This gives me a lift, and I wish there were time to sketch this.

But when entering Caltanissetta there is an awful stench. In the streets are dead Germans and dead horses harnessed to overturned wagons. All are bloated from the July sun and are swarming with flies. Blackened vehicles, broken water lines, split telephone poles, and downed trees speak to the ferocity of the battle for the city. Shell craters can be seen all around as we move deeper into the city. Many of the buildings are destroyed, while those spared have been riddled by machine gun fire and scarred by shrapnel. Caltanissetta is not Jerusalem. Not beautiful, not living. Caltanissetta is a city of the dead.

The 179th marches northwest from Caltanissetta. A highway sign reads 121. American fighters and bombers roar over to strafe and bomb the retreating Germans ahead. Traffic increases with tanks and half-tracks moving ahead. A sign appears: Vallelunga. There we turn left. Evening comes as the 179th relieves the 180th and gets set to attack the Germans in the morning. Tired, we have a K-ration supper.

Later in the evening, I'm called to the command post, where Captain Lee says that Battalion needs a patrol tonight. He explains that a German armored column is reported eight miles ahead, four miles right of Highway 121 near a road junction. The main road runs south and forks. One road goes southwest, the other east through rough country. The captain points it out on a map. Battalion wants to find the column and know the direction they are moving, for they could alter our plan of attack. He says that they won't use the main highway at night and that the German armor will use offbeat roads like this road junction to move. Captain Lee says to take all the men I need, then adds: "Be careful, Brummett."

Back in the platoon area, Major Carl McGee is there. The major is from Pawnee. We're glad to see him. Major McGee brings a copy of the Pawnee weekly newspaper. He gives us candy, chewing gum, and cigars. While chatting, the major begins to tell why the British side tracked us. In the quartermasters, he is close to Division Headquarters and hears the latest. Though I would like to hear, I explain that there is no time: my patrol must cover sixteen miles tonight.

Having heard I am going on a deep patrol, Shield Chief talks to me. "Walk flat-footed in creek beds so you won't trip. Sound travels in creek beds. Look down often, for the sense of balance lies in sight. Be *skiri* (wolf). Be alert. Turn and look behind often and try to smell things; scent tells a lot at night. Check the wind. Guide on the North Star, the one who does not move."

"*Tudahe*" (Good), I tell him.

I choose four men: Cheyenne, Bear, San Antone, and Pete Miller, a BAR man. I fill them in on the task at hand. I have them take tiny pebbles to check thirst, as we will run most of the way. I tell San Antone, the Comanche, that he is to check the wind, for we must know what direction the wind is coming from at all times in case it clouds up and we lose the North Star. I look at the dark horizon, fix a line of march in my mind, and concentrate on the arrival point. We leave our packs behind. I lead us off into the night. At first we run fifty yards and walk fifty yards to establish a rhythm of running and breathing. Then we increase the distance and adjust the pace. We make sure to stay off Highway 121 but run parallel to it; the Germans will be watching. I notice that the stars are out and look up to see the North Star, *Karariíwari*—the one who does not move; we are running northwest. After about four miles we rest. Then we turn right to avoid the Germans we know are deployed at the eight-mile point. We cover another four miles and rest. Moving again, we turn left. I concentrate on the fixed line of march. A right-handed man walking at night drifts to the right, while a left-handed man drifts left. We adjust to the North Star and keep running. Ahead I see foothills and mountains looming above. We stop for a breather. The captain said the road junction was in rough country; boy, was he right.

Off again, we start climbing big hills. After crossing a canyon we halt. Glancing back at the highest point, a rim rock juts out. On top are two sharp rocks that stand side by side. From this angle it resembles a wolf's head with ears up. This will be a landmark for the return trip. We take off, but now the going is rough. After a while we stop again. I look back to fix another landmark. The ridge back there is topped with trees and boulders. I picture the boulders as buffalo grazing among trees. I memorize it, then look ahead and concentrate now on the arrival point. We move.

Thirsty, I put a pebble in my mouth. I feel the wind change. "Ecky," San Antone says. "The wind has changed. I smell apples and freshly cut tree limbs. Somebody is close." We stand still. I smell apples too, or maybe grapes. "Come," San Antone says, moving quietly to the right with M1 at the ready; I follow. The rest of the men wait behind. In a wooded area, San Antone points forward and low to the ground. There is a faint glow about three inches in diameter at the base of some small trees. Someone has cut saplings here. When dew falls on a fresh-cut tree, the exposed inner wood and core will glow. We spot another and another, then come to a lean-to of cut saplings. A dark figure of a man is in the shelter, curled up. He sits up, startled. San Antone speaks to him in Spanish. Nervous, the man answers and offers a bottle of wine propped next to him. It has been opened and smells like apples.

The Sicilian pours his heart out talking and gesturing. "What's he saying?" I ask.

"He says he lives in a house by the roadside a short distance north of a road junction. When the Germans came, he sent his wife and two children to the mountains to stay with friends. He is hiding here to watch his house. He says there are Germans at his house and the road junction."

"Ask him how far the road junction is."

San Antone asks the man. Eager to help, the man answers and points right. "He says it in different figures. I take it to mean two hundred yards." San Antone turns: "Say, Ecky, you're a good navigator: you only missed the road junction by two hundred yards."

"Well, you know. Us Pawnees . . ." I quip. "Thank the man and let's go."

I tell the men about the man we found. We're two hundred yards from the road junction. The Germans are there. Turning right, we descend a rocky slope to a dry creek. We find a road that follows the creek. There we spot the man's house. A small car is there. On the road is a big vehicle. We can't see very well in this dark canyon. "I'm going to the road for a look," I tell the men. Moving quietly, I cross the creek bed flat-footed, then climb a bank to the road. Across the road is a mountainside. On this side of the road are trees and brush. At the right, the road is dark. On the left is a small car with a spare tire on the hood. The big vehicle on the road is a half-track. Several yards behind it is a tank—then blackness. I return and tell the men what I saw and that I'm going to find the road junction; the man said his home was a short distance north of the junction. I pull the pant legs out of my leggings and tell the men to do the same in case we're seen moving around. Our lace leggings would give us away. Germans wear jackboots without leggings. We're eight miles deep and right among them, so we've got to look like them in the dark. Our helmets, covered with netting, look German at night too. A big truck rumbles on the road toward us; we remain dead still. The truck passes by going south. I tell the men to stay put, leaving my M1 and web cartridge belt as I head toward the road.

I walk down the road with my head up so as not to seem suspicious if I'm spotted. A vehicle approaches from behind. I do not break stride as the vehicle passes. As it rolls down the road, men in the vehicle call to the right side of the road. Voices answer. I fade into the brush and move quietly. There is a small car that is parked off the road with the rear end in the brush. In the car are two men. I stand motionless in the dark. As one of the men gets out of the car I put my hand on my Pawnee knife. Facing me, the man removes his tunic and shakes it. He has a white body. He scratches his back and armpits while he picks things off his chest. This is like when I was a boy, hunting. Then I would hide near a spring with a bow and arrow and knife. Feeling safe, small animals drank water and played. Birds would ruffle feathers and pick mites with bills from under their wings: easy hunting.

A radio in the car hums and talks. The man in the car responds, turns, and calls out: "Gruber." The bare-chested one answers. Gruber puts on his tunic and gets in the car before the two German soldiers drive away. I think to myself that I could have put my Pawnee knife deep in Gruber's chest—but that's not the mission.

Ahead I spot a road junction in the direction the Germans are moving. I come to the junction and stop thirty yards from it to evaluate. One road runs southwest, the other east. The Germans are working on the east road as the sounds of hammering, banging steel, and humming motors can be heard. I walk closer to see if I can catch a peek. In the dark it looks like a tank is over the edge of the bridge. Silhouetted in the dark is a big truck with a crane. Surrounding the crane are dark figures of men working while others stand and watch. When the bridge is repaired the armored column will roll east. That is all we need to know. I turn and walk back with my head up in case someone spots me. I rejoin the men and tell them about the road junction and the work the Germans are doing. I explain that when the east road is clear the Germans will turn east. I tell Bear, San Antone, and Pete to watch the house while

Cheyenne and I scout upstream for more tanks. So far we have seen only one half-track and one tank.

"We won't be gone long," I tell the men.

As we move out the going is slow. The creek bed is pitch dark and rocky, making this dangerous ground for stealth movement. The bank next to the road has brush and trees. On our left is a mountainside. After a while we climb the bank, moving on our hands and knees and feeling the ground for loose stones and twigs. In front of Cheyenne and me are German soldiers sitting on the roadside. Some are talking while others seem to snooze. There are tanks, half-tracks, and other vehicles parked alongside the thoroughfare. Ahead the road disappears into darkness, making it unknown what lies beyond. Suddenly two soldiers come by; their hobnail boots crunch and clink with each step they take. They stop and talk to the soldiers in front of us. The two Germans face us as they chat. We freeze. After what seems an eternity they turn and stride down the road with jackboots crunching and clinking. Soldiers in a half-track with a radio on move things, banging and clanging without any care. A motorcycle with a sidecar passes; the men in it are talking loudly. Noisy bunch, these Germans.

A mountain breeze comes, rustling the leaves. We use the breeze and the rustling to cover movements back to the rocky creek bed. This is risky: we could trip in the dark and bust a leg eight miles deep—then we'd be in for it. We start back, taking care to step quietly as we move. We hear German soldiers talking on the roadside as we leave the creek bed. We rejoin the men, who are not bunched up as they keep watch on the house. I tell them we've seen enough for one night. I relay that we're heading back and must hurry. Getting up, Pete trips and falls heavily, hugging his BAR to keep it from clattering on the rocky ground. Nonetheless, the sound travels up the creek bed. A German appears at the side of the house and looks our way. We stay still. Pete, still hugging the BAR, doesn't move. My heart pounds, as the soldier calls back to someone. Then two more Germans appear. Up the canyon heavy motors start. Then the motor of a small car starts. A voice calls. The three soldiers answer back. They talk, take a leak, and then leave. Now the road is filled with rumbling tanks, half-tracks, troop carriers, trucks, small cars, and motorcycles, all moving south. I get my M1 and cartridge belt, then we take off, not bothering about making noise.

Climbing, we pass the man in the lean-to again. Turning left we make sure to keep the North Star slightly behind the left shoulder. Here, the going is rough; it has been a long night. We dogtrot when the ground permits. At the first landmark—where the ridge looks like buffalo grazing among trees— we take a breather. Then we continue on again, dogtrotting. We walk for a while, wading through brush and crossing ravines. Tired, I try to concentrate on the reverse line of march as we move. Looming ahead is the high ground, resembling a wolf's head with its ears up. We rest and drink water before our final leg.

"Ecky," San Antone says from the rear. "Bear's not here." I look back. Cheyenne and Pete follow and glance back too. "I thought he was behind. Could see you guys ahead," San Antone adds. "At the first rest stop, I sat and closed my eyes and didn't look around."

We look back in silence. "Don't think he's been captured. He's too smart," Cheyenne offers.

"Could have sprained an ankle," Pete says. "Maybe he didn't want to slow us up."

I sit, pondering the situation. "We'll wait a few minutes, then we must get the information to Battalion."

We wait and listen, hoping Bear will appear. "Well, let's go," I say, getting to my feet. "Bear's a Creek Indian. Those Creeks are tough. Bear can take care of himself."

"Wait, Ecky. Footsteps," Cheyenne says. Then we spot Bear, who is trotting quietly in the darkness, passing ten yards to our right. He stops, studies the high ground ahead, then moves left and studies it again. Bear glances back at the North Star.

"*Hesci!*" (Hello, in Creek), I say. Bear turns and approaches. I look at him in the dark. "*Chibonni*" (American Indian slang for "boy"), "you had us worried. What happened to you?" He dips his head a little, then looks up. "Y'ah, I know. I was looking for food and wine for us, sneaked to that house. There was a little car at the house close to the road. A soldier was asleep in it. The Germans in the house were asleep too. In there was a table with two bottles of wine. One was full, the other empty. There was a loaf of bread, partly eaten. I took the full bottle and bread, then left. A radio was on in the little car and a man in it was stirring. I moved left so he couldn't see me." He continues: "There were soldiers curled up on the ground sleeping with equipment lying nearby. One called and they began to stir, then I curled up in the bushes next to the road. I heard tank engines, and the man in the car started the motor. Pretty soon tanks and half-tracks came by. The Germans got up, stretched, and went down the road. Some walked past me. They waved and cheered the tanks." And then he said: "Since they weren't looking, I stood up and waved too, giving them the ol' dirty-finger sign. I hid till they all left." Bear smiles and pats the bottle and bread stuffed in his shirt. I look at Bear squarely and say nothing.

"Ecky, I sneaked to that house earlier too," San Antone says apologetically. "Saw a jeeplike car with a soldier asleep in it. I could hear Germans talking in the house. Then I decided to ransack packs of the Germans sleeping on the ground. They had no packs. All they had was a roll bound by a strap attached to a shoulder harness. These things lay on the ground near them." He continues: "Ecky, you know a guy can handle a grenade with the pin out any length of time so long as the lever is held down. Well, took my grenade, pulled the pin, held the lever down, and pressed it in a tight roll. The roll held the lever down. Then this crafty Redskin left, pronto."

We have a good laugh. I shake my head. "You guys are too much. Let's make tracks."

Moving through rough country, we descend to the foothills, then a little farther. Eventually we turn right to keep the North Star behind our right shoulder. After four miles, we pick up Highway 121, turning left there. Now, we dogtrot. It is still dark.

A voice challenges: "Are you one of us?"

"I am one of you," I answer.

Corporal Leading Fox rises and steps forward. "Ecky, they told us you had a patrol out. Everything go right? You guys okay?"

"Y'ah," I say, drinking water. Cheyenne, Pete, Bear, and San Antone drink too. "We found the Germans and got all the information needed. We're okay. Now we have to get it to the captain so he can inform Battalion."

At the company Command Post, Private Keeper, who is on guard, says, "Echohawk!" Keeper, a company runner, wakes Captain Lee. Dug in nearby are the first sergeant and the men who make up Company Headquarters. I tell Captain Lee about the German armored column and that they are moving east. He rings Battalion on the field telephone. I amble to the Second Platoon area. The Morning Star is out. It is signaling a coming new day. Exhausted, I drop in my slit trench and fall asleep.

A hand shakes my shoulder: "Ecky, you wanna eat some bread now?"

It's Bear. The sun has been up by a couple of hours.

"Y'ah, sure," I answer, brushing dirt from my chest and shirt collar. I yawn and stretch.

Bear tears a piece from the loaf and hands it to me. "Did you give any to Cheyenne, San Antone, and Pete?" I ask, chomping on the bread.

"No, not yet. But I will. Thought I'd give you some first. Was afraid we'd have to move out, and you wouldn't get a chance to eat any with your coffee. No telling when we'd get a break to eat again."

"Thanks, *Chibonni*," I say.

Bear heads for Cheyenne's foxhole, carrying the loaf of bread like a football. His pant legs are still pulled out of the lace leggings, and his shirttail is out from carrying the bread and wine. Bear walks a little slow after all the night's running.

A few minutes later Cheyenne joins me, chomping on the bread Bear gave him. "How'd you sleep, Chey'?" I ask, gathering twigs for a fire.

"Out like a light. How 'bout you?"

"Same. Could use more hours, though." A small fire is started for coffee. We have a K-ration can of dehydrated eggs, coffee, and real bread.

After eating, we go to visit Shield Chief, who is near a small rock wall overlooking the platoon area. With him are Last Arrow, Good Buffalo, and Leading Fox. Shield Chief sees us. "*Nawa, six-pettit*" (Hello, sit down). We sit. "How'd you guys do last night?" he asks.

"Y'ah, how'd it go last night?" Leading Fox cuts in.

"Did all right. We found them and went so deep that they didn't even notice us. It was a big armored column. Battalion wanted to know which direction they were moving, either toward us or east. The Germans turned east. Probably going to attack the British."

"Glad you guys made it back okay," Good Buffalo says.

Cheyenne pipes up: "They sure had a lot of tanks. Them German soldiers, when they move around, make a lot of noise." He gives the signs for "noise" and "motion." "A loud bunch."

"By the way," I ask, "what did Major McGee say about the British side tracking us? He was about to say something when my patrol was leaving. I wanted to hear what the major had to say."

Good Buffalo, who attended Central State Teachers College and is pretty smart, speaks: "Major McGee said that Division Headquarters has it that General [Bernard] Montgomery, the British Eighth Army commander, ignored the American boundary line. He crossed over and took Highway 124, which belonged to us. This was when we saw the British—well, Canadians really—cross our front on Highway 124 two days ago." He continues: "This move by Montgomery stopped the American advance. And General Omar Bradley was counting heavily on using Highway 124."

Shield Chief, who attended Bacone Indian College in Muskogee, speaks: "It seemed that according to the major Montgomery had persuaded the British general Sir [Harold] Alexander, commander of Allied forces in Sicily, to give him Highway 124 so he could attempt to encircle the Germans at Mount Etna." He continues: "He wanted the Americans to protect his flank and rear while he pushed up the coast to Messina, across from the toe of Italy. Montgomery then could take Messina, the plum of Sicily. All while the Americans stood on the sideline, watching his flank and rear. None of this has set well with General Patton, who is not one to sit still in a fight."

I turn to Cheyenne: "All this talk about top generals and what they're doing is too much for me."

"Pretty steep for this Indi'n," Cheyenne responds.

"Bureau of Indian Affairs," Leading Fox remarks. "Only I'm in charge now!"

The voice of Sergeant Stone breaks our banter. "Second Platoon! Get off your asses! Let's go!" Cheyenne and I look at Shield Chief, at Sergeant Stone, then back to Shield Chief. Good Buffalo and Leading Fox drop their eyes. Last Arrow shakes his head as he glances at Stone.

"Ecky," Phillip Shield Chief says, facing me. "Some of our guys went to a village searching for food. They found bread and wine. We ate bread and drank wine last night."

Sergeant Stone still sounds off: "I'm in charge now! Second Platoon! Get off your asses! Let's go!"

"Well, to make the story short, the captain busted me for drinking wine and made Stone the platoon sergeant. Now, I'm Private Shield Chief. Hard to believe, huh?"

Cheyenne ponders the front: "It's going to be a long war, a long war indeed."

From here is the start of a new phase of combat in Sicily. General Patton broke loose. We don't know what happened between General Sir Alexander and General Patton, but something did. The Americans aren't guarding anyone's flank or rear is what Medicine Man tells us he heard at Battalion, which is in touch with Regiment. He says the Germans have stopped Montgomery and that Patton is hell bent for leather with tanks and infantry racing northwest for Palermo. He also relays that General Omar Bradley has swung right and is kicking the hell out of the Germans at a place called Enna. With Patton speeding northwest and Bradley blocking the right, it leaves the 45th Division, which is in the middle, free to drive north and cut Sicily in two.

General Troy Middleton, commander of the 45th Division, rotates the three Regimental Combat Teams preparing for our sweep north. One RCT leads, the second passes through the first, then the third rolls through the second. The 45th goes after the Germans like an Osage County wolf hunt. Hounds tear after the wolf. Now and then the wolf whirls and fights, but they tumble. Fur flies; fangs flash before the bloodied wolf turns and runs with the hounds snapping at his heels in hot pursuit. The pace of our advance is grueling.

The July heat is stifling. The dust from tanks, half-tracks, trucks, and antitank guns covers our clothes. Field artillery, command cars, jeeps, infantry, and ambulances pass by occasionally. Sometimes we ride trucks, sometimes we walk. We bypass dynamited bridges and other ruins of war. There are skirmishes along the way as the Germans shoot and run. The 45th keeps up the pressure at all times. Occasionally American planes attack our lead columns, mistaking them for retreating Germans. We take a lot of prisoners during the

continuous advance. They are mostly Italians. However, the Germans we capture are from the crack Hermann Goering Division.

After three days we face a wall of mountains. Here a road sign indicates that
a town—Collesano—is ahead. First Battalion engages the Germans here, forc-
ing their withdrawal eastward. Pursuing them is hard as we climb mountain
roads with sharp hairpin turns, rising and dropping as the landscape dictates.
Bridges are destroyed as well, as are cliffside roads, dynamited by the Germans
in their hasty retreat.

Evening comes when we finally halt. The heat of the day lingers. Tired,
I am called to the CP, where Battalion relates that they want another patrol
out tonight that can return information by morning. I am to take a patrol and
probe north, as we must know where the Germans are at all times. Checking
his map, the captain says the coast is about eight miles from our current position. Since resistance is increasing, he suggests taking a machine gun and all the
men I need. I select six men, deciding on no machine gun, for it's a burden
in this rough country. I eat a supper of dehydrated fruit and water—the last of
our rations.

I visit Shield Chief and tell him we're going out and what the captain said.
He takes his "prayer pipe" and puts it in his mouth; silence for a few seconds.
Then he speaks: "Stay off roads and trails. Go over the mountains where it is
hard for ordinary men. Guide on *Kararíiwari*, the North Star, the one who does
not move. Travel north and south. Then slip behind them. The Germans are
'mechanical soldiers' and are programmed for the front. They won't expect you
from behind. Then you can scout more ground. Listen to the sounds of the
night." Still tired from the three-day march, we drop packs and go at twilight.

The highway that the 179th has been on forks. The main highway continues west. Another road runs slightly northwest. We leave both and head due
north. We dogtrot, traveling north and south. As Shield Chief said, it takes us
over the mountains. It's man-killing but shorter than the other routes. Had
we followed the northwest road, we'd be forever on curves and hairpin turns.
Moving, we rest, sip water, and go again, being careful of our footing in the
dark. We can't afford a busted leg here. I check the North Star and see we are
still on course.

"Ecky," San Antone calls. "Look. Just ahead of us and to the right."

I look. "Goats," San Antone notes. "Let's find the billy. Remember Hank's
Ranch back at Abilene when we were on night maneuvers?"

"Oh, y'ah, in the Texas rough country near Buffalo Gap. Come on, guys,
let's shoo these goats. We'll use the billy like we did at Buffalo Gap in Texas."
We form a line, then move abreast slowly toward the herd of goats. San Antone makes "belly noises" to move them but is careful not to spook them.
The goats mill, then follow the big billy. Then the billy leads them and us to

a mountain pass and safety. We take the pass and leave the goats in peace. The billy saved us time, as we'd have been hours trying to find a pass. Now it's downhill to the coast.

I feel the moist air from the sea, so we must be close. We reach the coastal highway and take a sandy lane that leads to a railroad. Crossing the tracks, we can hear the surf. The lane takes us to the beach, where we wade into the surf of the Tyrrhenian Sea. We sit in the surf and cool ourselves after the arduous push over the mountains. It is a peaceful night, making it hard to imagine a war is going on here. After a rest in seawater, we pull back to the railroad. Nearby is a small train depot that we check and find nothing. On the narrow-gauge track is a lightweight handcar rigged with a bicycle mechanism in the rear. It has handlebars and a board attached on the frame, seating two, possibly three people. Tied to wooden poles is a canvas fly to shade the workmen who use it. We decide to use it to scout the coast, as we can move much faster this way. Close by is a grove of trees enclosed by a low wall. I tell the men to hide here till we return.

We mount with Cheyenne and me riding shotgun and San Antone pumping. With muffled laughter, the guys give the handcar a running shove. San Antone's knees pump as he humps over the handlebars. "Hot dang!" San Antone shouts. "Here comes the MKT, the 'Katy'" (an engine that runs the Missouri-Kansas-Texas line).

I sound off: "Aha-a-ha, San Antone!"

"Take it away, Leon!" Cheyenne adds.

We roll along the dark coast, passing steep cliffs and rocky coves. After a while we approach a crossing and decide to stop. Here I scout a dirt road inland to the coastal highway and find nothing. I feel the green leaves on a low tree branch, noticing fresh dust. The dust is thick from heavy traffic passing by. We return to the crossing and lift the handcar to turn it around. We give it a running shove and jump on.

At the depot, we park the Katy, get off, and move toward the grove.

A voice: "*Hesci!*" It's Bear.

"*Hesci*," I answer. We leg over the wall. The men are sitting together in the dark. They're chewing something. I tell them where we went and that we found nothing besides signs showing heavy traffic. The men say they heard traffic on the main highway after we left, traveling east.

Bear plucks something from a branch. "Lemon," he says, handing me one. "We're in a lemon grove." I chomp into the lemon. Cheyenne and San Antone reach for lemons and tear into them. We're hungry; it makes me wonder what the Brass had for supper. Steaks, probably . . . and plenty of wine.

The sound of motors comes before we spot two vehicles. We disperse quietly. The vehicles turned off the coastal highway and are coming down this sandy lane. They stop several yards away. They shut off the engines, and we hear the Germans talking. Now and then a radio squawks. From the highway comes the sound of traffic. It continues for several minutes as we lie low, listening and sweating. Finally the traffic fades and is followed by the two vehicles starting their engines. They U-turn and head for the coastal highway. All is quiet again and we can hear the surf of the Tyrrhenian Sea. "Let's get the heck out of here!" I say, stuffing my pockets with lemons.

We dogtrot up the sandy lane to the coastal highway and cross it. From here it's straight north and south. I take care to keep the North Star to our backs. After a while, the moist air fades as we ascend the mountains. Tired, we break often, enjoying lemons and water. We move again and come to Billy Goat Pass. Now it's downhill—and not soon enough. After the slog we make it to our lines in the wee hours of the morning. I report to the captain, who is glad to see us back. He asks if there were any problems. I answer: none. I tell him the Germans are pulling back and using the coastal highway going east. Captain Lee rings Battalion to give them a report. Tired, I return to the platoon area. After three days of marching and chasing Germans, patrolling hard miles across the mountains to the north coast and back, my men and I are beat. We flop on rocky ground and fall into a sound sleep.

A hand touches my shoulder; I sit up. It's Private Keeper, the company runner. He says the captain wants to see me. It's dawn and B Company stirs. At the CP Captain Lee and I make small talk. Then he comes to the point: "Brummett, you'll have to go back again. Ships have appeared off the north coast. The ships have not identified themselves. Intelligence suspects a German amphibious landing may be at hand. Regiment must know if there are amphibious landings. I know you had rough going, but you're the only one who has gone there. If anyone else goes they'll lose valuable time just trying to find their way. Soon as you see something, send a runner back."

We remain silent. "The situation is bad, Brummett," the captain says.

"I understand, Sir. We'll go as soon as we get something to eat."

Back in the platoon area everybody is up at the crack of dawn and eating a K-ration breakfast—everybody except my patrol, who are still asleep. They have no rations. I approach Sergeant Stone to ask if he has rations for us. He's eating with Sergeant Turner, who replaced Stone as right guide in the platoon. When asked about rations, Stone says he didn't know that I was out on patrol and goes on eating. I grab him by the shirt collar. "You're going to get my men rations, or I'll knock the hell out of you!" Sergeant Turner drops his canteen cup of coffee and lunges for me. I have Stone by the throat. The three of us scuffle.

Shield Chief comes up and throws Sergeant Turner to the ground, then manhandles Stone. "All right! What's the trouble here?" Stone and I talk at the same time. "Calm down," Shield Chief says. "Stone."

"Well, Echohawk came to me and asked about rations, then jumped me. Sergeant Turner, here, tried to pull him off me."

"Phil," I cut in, "Stone said he didn't know I was on patrol."

"No, I didn't," Stone replies. "We got a new lieutenant takin' Dobbins's place. He didn't say anything about a patrol. Corporal Ingalls, Echohawk's assistant squad leader, should have taken care of that when the kitchen truck came up last night."

"Corporal Ingalls wasn't here when the kitchen truck came up," Shield Chief says. "Medicine Man took him to the aid station, where he was evacuated. Ingalls has yellow jaundice. These men are your responsibility. Know where they are at all times. Especially in tactical situations. See that they have rations, water, and ammo. Check their feet. Check them personally. Now, shape up!"

Sergeant Stone says nothing. There are biscuit crumbs on his mouth. Sergeant Turner picks up his canteen cup and remains silent. Fighting over skimpy rations, just like the Depression years when, back in Oklahoma, a man shot another man in a quarrel over cantaloupes. People were hungry then. Shame, but we're hungry now . . . real hungry.

"I'll send a runner back to find the kitchen truck," Stone offers, trying to make things right.

"Yes, you do that," Shield Chief says firmly. Some of the platoon who had gathered to see what the fracas was all about offer to share rations; I accept. They ask how things went last night. I tell them everything went okay and then wake my men. I have to explain that we have to go back again. I explain why, but the men still take it hard. They realize we're in a tough spot; they'll go.

I go see Corporal Leading Fox and ask if he'd like to go along as a runner since he was a miler on the track team at college. Leading Fox jumps at the chance. Shield Chief and the guys in the platoon bring rations to share with us. They share water too, since they had a refill from the kitchen truck. I thank them and we eat. I mention to Shield Chief that the captain is sending us back to the same place because ships have appeared off the north coast and that intelligence suspects a German amphibious landing. I tell him the Brass needs to know. The captain is sending us again, for he figures that we are familiar with the area. Shield Chief says, "It doesn't make sense. The Americans and British navies are on the south and southeast coast. And Sicily is just over a hundred miles long, about sixty miles wide. Patton is driving for Palermo; he might be there now." Shield Chief puts his pipe in his mouth and studies the mountains. "Go. Be *skiri* [wolf]. *Tus chaticks-si-chaticks* [We are men of men]."

I turn to my patrol: "Well, let's go sink the German navy!"

"There you go," Leading Fox remarks.

We make good time crossing the mountains, since now we don't have to watch our footing or strain to see in dark canyons. On the peaks we can see for miles. After another long slog we reach the Tyrrhenian Sea. Once there we scan the blue horizon and see no ships. At the coastal highway is no traffic. Seeing nothing, we make our way to the railroad and sea. We check the beach for vehicle tracks and other signs, also finding nothing. We listen and hear only the sound of the surf. Back to the railroad we go, where a short distance away is the depot. The handcar is still where we parked it.

"Katy," San Antone says. "Ecky, let's take her again."

Surprised to see a handcar, Leading Fox remarks with a grin: "Missouri, Kansas, and Texas."

"We used it to scout the coast the first time we were here. You want to ride with us, *Tiwat?*"

"Sure. I'm game."

"Ecky, want me to gandy-dance again?" San Antone pipes up.★

"You bet. We'll take Bear this time and leave Cheyenne in charge of the men till we get back."

Leading Fox sits in the middle. Bear and I squeeze in from the sides. San Antone mounts the bicycle part like a motorcycle cop. With horseplay, the men give us a running shove.

"Let her rip!" Bear shouts.

"Go, Katy, go!" Leading Fox yells as we start to roll.

Things look different in daylight. We look to the coastal highway and see nothing. At sea too: nothing. Passing cliffs and rocky coves: nothing. A crossing is spotted ahead; a dirt road leads to the highway. This was as far as we came the first time, and again nothing here. We move again, and though the sun is hot there is a cool sea breeze. After some time, we see bomb craters near the tracks. Inland are houses nearby too. We continue and slowly roll to what might have been a train station that is bombed out. The rails are torn up, and the buildings along the tracks are destroyed.

We stop here. The coastal highway disappears among houses and buildings. We look out to sea again and spot no ships.

"Looks like a pretty big town," Leading Fox comments.

"Hey, Ecky!" San Antone exclaims. "Look out there in the sea. Mines. Floating mines! Floating into the beach!"

"By golly! Mines! This town must be a strategic port."

★A gandy dancer, or section hand, was a slang term used for railroad workers in the United States.

"You know, Ecky, there must be a lot of floating mines out there. And those mines would keep ships from this coast. It wouldn't be possible for the Germans to make an amphibious landing here," Leading Fox speculates.

"Hey, y'ah!" we agree.

"Can't be any Germans here," Bear says. "Heck, let's go up to town for food and wine."

We dismount.

"Ecky, we better turn Katy around just in case we have to make a fast getaway," Leading Fox continues. We lift and turn the handcar around. We hide our bulky cartridge belts under the rubble, taking our M1s and slinging them upside down to hide the barrel. Steel helmets covered with netting could pass for German at a glance. I tell Leading Fox to pull the pant legs out of his lace leggings.

"We'll walk into town like we own the place," I tell the men. "Like when we found that German armored column about a week ago. Deep and behind them, the Germans didn't expect us to be walking among them. We are far behind them now, thanks to Katy. There may not be any Germans in town, but there could be Italian soldiers here. All right, let's go."

We make our way into town. Skinny-legged and barefooted kids gawk at us as we enter. Some follow us with curiosity. Old people who sit in doorways pay us no mind. We meet women carrying on a lively conversation, all talking at once and waving their hands. Leaving the narrow street, we enter a wide road with shops, people, and the traffic of donkey carts, pushcarts, bicycles, and small automobiles. Down the middle of the street is an island of flower gardens, benches, and ornate horse stalls.

People on the sidewalk see us but make nothing of it. Ahead is a vendor with a fruit cart.

"San Antone, you do the talking. We'll buy fruit here."

"Ecky, German traffic coming up behind," Leading Fox cuts in.

"Keep walking; don't break stride," I tell the men.

A German jeep rolls up on our left followed by trucks. A spare tire is on the hood of the jeep. The back seat is cluttered with field boxes, coils of wire, and camouflage netting. With M1s slung on our right side and upside down, we move with pedestrians and don't break stride. The man on the passenger side sees us, then turns and says something to the driver. They glance back. Both Germans look weary and are covered with white dust. On their caps are dust goggles. Ahead is a uniformed man standing on a box in the middle of the street, directing traffic. The man wears a Napoleon hat and is dressed like a toy soldier. Wearing white gloves, he waves the jeep on. The German jeep picks up speed and turns sharply at the next street.

"Ecky, turn in here!" San Antone says as German trucks rumble by. "I'll do the talking." We turn in the building. There is a ticket office here; it's a picture show. We enter to find on the screen Gary Cooper in a World War I uniform. He is sitting on a ledge with a hound dog. In his hand is a book. It's *Sergeant York!*

Surprised, we watch in silence. "Didn't know Gary Cooper could talk Italian," Bear remarks. I tell the guys we'll lie low as the Germans will be looking for us. We'll shoot it out only if we have to, but I don't think that convoy will stop.

"Could be nobody will believe those hombres in that jeep," San Antone says. "They think the Americans are inland and miles away."

Leading Fox cuts in: "I saw a detonator box with a plunger to set off dynamite with in that jeep. It might just be that this bunch is a demolition unit following the main body running from Patton. Their job is to dynamite bridges and roads to slow us down."

"In that case we ought to go out for food and wine," Bear says, perking up. "Heck, I can't understand a word Gary Cooper is saying anyway." Seated next to me is a fat woman eating from a basket held on her lap. She hears us talking and stares at our covered steel helmets and M1s propped between our knees. Big-eyed and nervous, she eats something that looks like an oversized pie. I have never tasted Italian food; smells good. This Indi'n is hungry.

"Okay, let's go."

Outside, there is no German traffic. Ahead and across the way are food carts. We approach the island of flower gardens, benches, and ornate horse stalls. We look in. It's a public urinal! We've never seen anything like this. We relieve ourselves as a young man enters. Taking a leak, he carries on a swoony conversation with his girlfriend over the chest-high stall. We cover our manhood and modestly turn from the girl. "Dang," Bear objects quietly.

The man with the Napoleon hat who was directing traffic enters. Taking a leak, he looks at us. His jaw drops.

"Buongiorno," San Antone says.

"Buongiorno," Napoleon chokes. The man leaves without buttoning up his britches. Walking away like Charlie Chaplin, he glances back now and then. We leave the public urinal. Nearby is a circular flower garden with two flagpoles. One is an Italian fascist flag; the other is Nazi. We haul them both down. I write on a piece of paper and put it in a wine bottle taken from a trash bin. We tie the bottle with the flagpole rope and run it up. Inscribed on the paper: THIS TOWN CAPTURED BY AMERICAN INDIANS, JULY, 1943. We move to the food carts.

San Antone does the talking with no problems. I don't know what San Antone said, but the vendor throws up his hands and kisses him. The vendor chatters happily. We end up with sausage, bread, coffeecakes, fruit, and wine. Returning to the demolished train station, San Antone says he told the attendant at the picture show Americans had captured the town. He gave the attendant American invasion money as proof. The vendor said there would be no charge for the food and wine because we were the liberators of their town. "San Antone, you ought to go into politics after the war," Leading Fox says with a grin. At the demolished train station, we pick up our cartridge belts and decide to eat away from the town and move on while the getting is good. I take the first turn at gandy-dancing. We slip away.

After a while, we stop and eat. The Sicilian fare is delicious. "Beats the heck out of K-rations," San Antone says with a mouthful.

"Amen," Bear adds, taking a swig of wine. "We'll save some food for Chey-enne and the rest of the guys." We take off. We come to the crossing where the inland road runs to the coastal highway and into the mountains. We pass cliffs and approach a bridge spanning a bay. Rolling along, we feel good after a fine meal.

San Antone, at the helm now, sings: "Listen to the jingle, the rumble and the roar as she glides along the woodland by the sea and by the shore." It's "Wabash Cannonball." We pick it up and sing along.★

Suddenly, splinters explode from the railroad ties. Lead cracks and zings off the bridge and clangs into the rails around us. We hump over and lean for-ward; I close my eyes tight. A burst of machine gun fire shreds the canvas fly and kicks up seawater beyond. Helpless, we are sitting ducks moving slow in a straight line. Bullets snap the poles that support the fly, causing the canvas to collapse on us. We pick up speed as San Antone pumps for dear life and Bear sings a stomp-dance song. Reaching the other side of the bay in a hail of lead, we round a bend and escape the enemy fire. Bear switches with San Antone quickly, like a fresh Pony Express rider. We give him a running shove and jump on.

"Now I know how them white guys feel when Indi'ns attack their stage-coach," San Antone says, all out of breath and sweating.

"Got to keep moving as fast as we can," I say, looking to the coastal highway.

"That might have been a German motor patrol." San Antone, his face wet with sweat, says, "I saw two vehicles up there. They had the drop on us from the cliffs, though the highway curved back around the bay. Seemed like they hesitated before firing. Maybe they thought we were civilian railroad workers and decided to shoot anyway."

"The Germans were waiting till we reached the middle of the bridge," Leading Fox says. "And they don't mind shooting civilians. Say, Ecky, that

★"Wabash Cannonball" is an American folk song about a fictional train. The song was made popular by various singers and groups including the Carter Family and Roy Acuff in the 1930s.

could be the rear guard for that truck convoy we saw in town. All were heading east. Now, they can easily drive ahead and bushwhack us again." Moving up a grade, we get off and push till Katy levels off. Pony Express riders change again; this time, Leading Fox mounts up, replacing Bear, whose shirt is wet with sweat. The coastal highway now runs shooting distance from the railroad.

"Think we better stop and leave Katy. If the Germans show up, we'd be leading them to the train depot where Cheyenne and the rest are. We can't take that chance," I say to Cheyenne and Leading Fox. We stop, dismount, and move off the railroad embankment. And none too soon: Katy, though vacated, is fired on from the highway. We stay down as we move.

A few yards down the embankment are boxes. Some are broken, while others are scattered about with clips of ammunition and hand grenades. These are from the Italians. It appears they were dumped from a moving train. After a while, Leading Fox, who has been watching, calls: "No vehicles on the highway. The Germans are gone!"

I make my way up to the tracks. "Let's go!"

San Antone swings into the saddle. We shove the handcar, then board again. With mountains on the right and the sea on the left we roll without incident. At the small depot, Cheyenne and the men come from the lemon grove and meet us. They mention a small truck convoy passing with a German jeep leading. Then a while ago two vehicles passed, bringing up the rear. We give Cheyenne and the men the food and wine we gathered. Hungry, they eat heartily. We tell them we saw no ships. I explain to them at length what happened. They get a kick out of us watching the *Sergeant York* movie while the Germans searched for us.

"Indi'ns have more fun than anybody," Cheyenne says, enjoying the sausage.

"For sure," Leading Fox adds. Well fed and with renewed energy, we start back.

The food gives us strength, and we make better time since we don't have to watch for Germans. We see the mountain peaks at great distance become small as we move at a steady pass up and over the mountain pass. Upon reaching our highway, we find rear echelons of the 179th near a village. When we inquire about the First Battalion, they say everybody pulled out early this morning and is attacking Castelbuono three miles to our east.

"They left us. After all we went through." I grin and shake my head.

"Bureau of Indian Affairs," Leading Fox snickers.

"What's the name of this place?" I ask one of the soldiers.

"Isnello," he answers.

"Thanks." I didn't notice this village, as we went over the mountains and avoided roads during our patrols. We take the mountain highway eastward and catch up with Third Battalion. I think of finding I Company, where there are two Pawnees who are machine gunners, but there is no time. We pass Second Battalion. Cheyenne mentions his cousin Two Hatchets in E Company, yet we don't stop. We enter Castelbuono; it is a mountain town. We see only a few old people. Bent with age, they look at us without emotion as we pass them. They probably eyed the Germans the same way. Finally we overtake First Battalion and rejoin B Company, who has the point. My men from the patrol fall in with the platoon.

I find Captain Lee off the road and under cover; he is glad to see me. I report that there are neither ships nor signs of a German amphibious landing on the coast. M1 shots crack ahead, making the captain flinch. With eyes focused ahead, he says, "Battalion moved out shortly after you left. I still haven't heard any more on the unidentified ships." More M1 fire erupts ahead; however, this time there is no return fire.

A few minutes later we get the order: "Let's go!" B Company advances.

I rejoin Second Platoon and get my pack from the men who kept it while we were gone. The company mountain-goats peak after peak through mountains void of vegetation. This far inland there is no moist air, as the mountains shield it from the sea. We keep going and going until late evening. Finally, we stop and drink water before the order comes down to dig in. Medicine Man comes and checks all the men. Sergeant Stone does not talk to me, nor does he call to help arrange the guard for the night. The kitchen truck grinds up at dark. With blue flashlights, the kitchen crew hands out a three-day supply of K-rations to each soldier and gives refills of water. There is little conversation between the men, who are exhausted. I eat before I settle into my foxhole and drop off to sleep.

Daylight crests the horizon, which means B Company is up for counterattack time. Later Medicine Man calls: "Sick, lame, and lazy." He comes by. "I'say, Echo, heard you were on patrol the last two days and made it to the north coast. Run into any trouble?"

I answer we had none but tell him about the Germans pulling out. I get a K-ration breakfast box and open it.

"Back at Battalion," Medicine Man puts a cigar in his mouth, "they got a report of Germans in landing barges near Capo d'Orlando yesterday, wherever that is. Don't know what happened after that."

"That's why the captain sent me to the coast, to see if there were ships or amphibious landings. He didn't say where, just said the north coast. Well, we reached the coast and found nothing. When we returned, the 179th had advanced. After all that, we had to catch up with everybody. I reported to the captain that we saw nothing. He related that he didn't hear any more on the situation."

"Maybe somebody cried wolf." Medicine Man lights his cigar and puffs. "By the way, I sent your BAR man, Slade, to the aid station. They evacuated him with yellow jaundice."

"When was this?"

"Yesterday. The day before Corporal Ingalls was evacuated with yellow jaundice. That's two of your men out. One guy in the First Platoon is out with it too."

"What day is this? I mean, what's the date?"

Medicine Man puffs on his cigar. "The date I entered on the tag I put on Slade yesterday was the 24th, so today is the 25th of July, 1943. Sunday, in case you're going anywhere."

"Oh, y'ah, y'ah. I was going to the Pawnee Powwow with my dishes and folding chair."

"There you go," Medicine Man says, smiling and showing a perfect set of white teeth. "With all that fried bread, boiled meat, Indi'n corn, and camp coffee it'll be good. Well, glad you made it back okay. I better check the rest of the men in the platoon. *Aho!*"

"*Aho!*" I reply.

Before I forget, I must put the date on my sketch paper. First Battalion will probably be in reserve today, so I might have time to do some drawings. I get sketch paper from my pack and write 25 JULY on a couple of sheets. Then I eat a K-ration breakfast, dehydrated scrambled eggs, cracker biscuits, and have some coffee. As I eat, Cheyenne joins me with his coffee. A few minutes later Corporal Paul Vance, who replaced Ingalls as assistant squad leader, comes up. Vance joined the company when the division was building its ranks to wartime strength at Camp Barkeley, Texas. The three of us chat. Vance asks about my patrol going to the north coast. Just as I start to tell him, Sergeant Stone sounds off: "Second Platoon! Get off your ass! Let's go!"

B Company moves out.

We had the point yesterday. Second Battalion passed through early this morning, followed by Third Battalion. We of the First Battalion are in reserve. The 179th follows a mountain road eastward with the same delays of the previous day: blown-out bridges, cliffside roads dynamited, and now mines and booby traps holding up the advance. The engineers build roads, construct bridges, and clear minefields. Oftentimes they work under fire. In this troubled terrain, they do the impossible through the impassable. The Mediterranean sun burns down on us as sweat pours down my face. I eat a K-ration dinner on the move. I'm so thirsty that I spit cotton. I must conserve water, as we won't see the kitchen truck for three more days.

Afternoon comes when the order to stop comes down. Metal canteen caps clink as men gulp water. I turn to the men, saying, "Go easy on that water!" We get off the road and flop down; no one talks. We're too tired. After a while, B Company leaves the road and moves north up rocky slopes coming to what looks like commanding ground. Here the company stops.

Lieutenant Anson, who has taken Lieutenant Dobbins's place, calls all squad leaders. I meet with Lieutenant Anson. He seems like a good officer. Anson explains to us that fourteen unidentified warships have appeared off the north coast and that efforts to get the ships to identify themselves have failed. Brass believe it could be a German amphibious landing. Lieutenant Anson walks a few paces forward, looks left and right, then says: "Battalion will take up defensive positions here. Just in case Germans from the amphibious force appear." The ground is rocky, and rather than dig we take stones and form stone foxholes. We belly down in them with M1s pointed forward.

Evening comes and I eat another dry K-ration supper. We all lie down and drink water in our holes. As twilight arrives we stand to flex our arms and legs. We all move around but don't stray too far from our stone foxholes. After the guard is arranged for the night, I check the men.

At dark, I visit Shield Chief. With him are Leading Fox, Last Arrow, and Good Buffalo, who are talking about the ships appearing off the north coast today. I gather from them that there were two reports about the possible German landing. The first involved my patrol scouting the coast and finding no signs indicating a possible German assault. The second report resulted in the 179th having to turn, dig in, and face the north coast to meet any amphibious force out there.

"Could have been a communications problem," Last Arrow offers, adding: "It is apparent that we all didn't get the same report, while others didn't get it at all, it seems. Remember back at the beach when paratroopers from the 82nd Airborne were shot down by the Navy and our antiaircraft batteries? That was bad communication."

"Bureau of Indian Affairs," Leading Fox snipes. This expression always brings a chuckle to us.

I ask Shield Chief about the war dance contest held in July at the Pawnee Powwow. He says that, in the last letter from home, his folks think the Ponca could win. Open to all tribes, the contest is exciting. All Pawnee war dancers are in the service. "I like Pawnee war-dance songs," Good Buffalo speaks up. "They tell of brave warriors. I especially like the one called the 'Iron Shirt Song' that tells about a young warrior who kills a man in Spanish armor. In that battle, the Pawnees could not kill the man. Then a boy charges." He continues: "As his arrows bounce off the armor he turns his pony and runs as the enemy gives chase, waving a sword. The Spaniard closes on the right for the kill, but the boy is left-handed. He shoots an arrow that pierces an eye, killing the man in Spanish armor. The boy was fourteen. This happened on the Nebraska plains."

"Good song. Fine history," Leading Fox adds.

"Speaking of history," I join in, "my brother and I visited Jane Blue Hawk when I was on furlough. During the visit, she touched on Pawnee history. When mentioning we were about to go overseas she took my hand, for she has a son in C Company of the 180th. Holding my hand, Mrs. Blue Hawk said that when Pawnee warriors fight a war they will lose one man." I continue: "There is a legend about this. She was speaking in the Pawnee tongue; it was hard to understand her. After leaving, my brother said that what Mrs. Blue Hawk spoke of is true. There was a battalion of Pawnees who served as Army scouts from 1864 to 1877. Called the Pawnee Scouts, they never lost a battle on the Plains. One Pawnee was awarded the Congressional Medal of Honor. In those battles the Pawnee lost only one man.

"A Pawnee also raised the flag on San Juan Hill in the war with Spain. His name was William Pollock, and while he did make it home the war ultimately took him, for he died of what they called in those days 'Cuban fever.' The Pawnees were on the Mexican Border Expedition in 1916 too. However, there was no war and no Pawnee were lost. During the Border Expedition they served with a young officer named George S. Patton Jr.

"In World War I, a Pawnee unit fought Germans in the Argonne Forest. They went on trench raids with a brave officer who never wore a steel helmet named Douglas MacArthur. The Pawnees lost one man to poison gas in that conflict."

We reflect on our Pawnee people and the legend. Shield Chief drums softly on his steel helmet, which is on his lap. Then, in a low voice, he sings the Iron Shirt Song that Good Buffalo spoke of. We listen with one heart. It's a starry night. When he finishes singing, we sack out.

Dawn and up at counterattack time. There is none, nor is there an amphibious landing. We stay put and burn K-ration box tops to heat coffee. With our morning coffee we eat dehydrated scrambled eggs and cracker biscuits in our stone foxholes. Everywhere are barren peaks with no signs of life. The sun climbs higher in a cloudless sky.

Lieutenant Anson comes and talks to Sergeant Stone. Then Stone bellows: "Second Platoon! Get off your ass! Let's go!" Preparing to move, I go to Lieutenant Anson and ask about the situation. Shield Chief comes for the same reason. The lieutenant says the unidentified ships were declared friendly. He explains that they were American minesweepers and destroyers. Anson informs us the 157th and the 180th are parallel to us on the coastal highway. However, mountains separate us, making contact impossible. Each has to fight its own battles as we move toward the coast.

The 179th Regiment resumes its drive with Third Battalion leading. We fight not only German pockets of resistance but also the terrain and Mediterranean heat. Men fall out with heat exhaustion as we move throughout the day. Evening comes, and we again build stone foxholes. For dinner I eat a dehydrated fruit bar and drink water. I have powdered soup, but it takes fire to heat water, and that's dangerous. As the sun sets I notice that these mountains have no darting nighthawks, ring-singing insects, or whip-poor-wills; it is a lifeless place. Tired, we drop off to sleep.

Morning again, and First Battalion leads off the advance. Delays plague us from the get-go. More blown-out bridges and cliffside roads blocked from landslides spurred by dynamite cause us to pick our way over improvised footpaths overlooking steep drops. There are long waits while minefields are cleared too. With this, the Germans have the high ground and advantage as we advance. They bloody our nose when climbing to get them. To outflank them, we have to scale more peaks. By the time we take those peaks, the Germans withdraw, leaving us with casualties and no enemy to engage. But we can take a punch. In the meantime we are pushing them into the northeast corner of Sicily, where sooner or later they'll have to stand and fight us. Then we can get it on and finish this job.

Another day floats by in the Mediterranean heat before the evening brings cooler temps and more stone foxholes. We again eat K-rations—the last of our supply. Low on water, we take care to preserve every last drop in our canteens; water is a lifeline in the Sicilian heat. At dark the kitchen truck shifts gears and rumbles up, bringing water and another three-day supply of K-rations. I check the men; they are tired but still making jokes, which I take as a good sign. Arriving back at my stone foxhole, I remove some rocks and lie down, soon falling asleep.

The sun greets me as I open my eyes for another day of chasing Germans. Today we are in reserve. I prepare drawing paper, as I plan on doing some drawings no matter what. General Patton's Seventh Army is on the north coast, driving the Germans east. General Montgomery's British Eighth Army, on the east coast, pushes them north. It is the aim of the Allies to corral the Germans in the northeast corner of Sicily at Messina. Though pushed hard, they don't stampede—but any day now we know the Germans will paw the dirt and lock horns with us.

The 45th Thunderbird Division spearheads the American Seventh Army eastward to Messina. One sweltering day heats up the next. Each Thunderbird regiment sweeps across northern Sicily like a summer dust devil ahead of a thunderhead billowed by thermal winds. When an alien pocket of cool air is met, a tornado is triggered. It is on a hot, still afternoon when we hear by jeep radio that the 157th has met an enemy force near Santo Stefano di Camastra. This is the alien cool air pocket, and here a tornado is triggered. It's thunder and lightning as the 157th and the Germans clash. Meanwhile the 179th presses forward; its objective is Castel di Lucio just ahead. We pass through a mountain village, where a sign reads San Mauro Castelverde. Beyond there, the mountains are higher.

The going is slow and the heat is fierce. Word comes that Castel di Lucio has fallen to Third Battalion. We advance to peaks overlooking a highway. We stop before squad leaders are called when Lieutenant Anson says to dig in. A map in hand, he tells us the highway is 117. Along 117 is the German defense line. Sergeant Good Buffalo asks about the 157th. The lieutenant answers, explaining that contact is difficult and there is no word.

One of our guys exclaims: "My God, look out there!"

"Mount Etna!" Barely visible on the southeastern horizon, a ribbon of smoke is motionless above the crater. Though far away, I make a drawing, wishing I could paint it. The drawing paper has 25 JULY on it. I cross it out and scribble MT. ETNA, SICILY. 29 JULY, 1943. Quite a sight to see. I think to myself that, from where the American and German dead lay, they might have seen the beauty of Mount Etna in their last hours of life. We stay alert the rest of the day.

The next day a lull comes and I draw more pictures. I make sure to date the paper 30 JULY. Lieutenant Anson informs us that the 3rd Division will relieve the 45th. He says the Germans have been beaten back at Santo Stefano di Camastra. He explains that the 157th has captured a mountain stronghold that they're calling "Bloody Ridge." The 45th waits for the 3rd Division to take over.

At nightfall the kitchen truck comes just so far because of steep peaks. We get a three-day supply of C-rations, which are canned goods and more of a meal than dry K-rations. We eat in the dark. Cheyenne and I each eat a can of cold hash. However, we can't heat the hash because we can't have a fire. After eating, we visit Shield Chief. Leading Fox, Good Buffalo, and Last Arrow are there with him, talking about the situation. We can only guess that Bloody Ridge was a costly battle for both sides. The Germans were set up and waiting. The 157th didn't keep them waiting either. They waded into them. Basically from Colorado, the 157th is a rugged bunch much like us Oklahoma guys.

Grant, Shield Chief's brother, joins us. "Hey, you guys, let's go to the Pawnee Powwow!"

"I'm ready," Good Buffalo responds.

"Me too," says Leading Fox.

"Hot dang, let's go! Can hear them drums now," Last Arrow says.

"Grant, how's everybody in the Third Platoon?" I ask.

"Okay," Grant replies. "Just like a bunch of tired mountain goats. Say, Ecky, heard you took a patrol to the north coast. I take it everything went well."

"Y'ah, no problems." I tell him we made two trips because of the unidentified ships seen off the north coast. I also mention seeing loose floating mines drifting to the beaches.

"Those floating mines were probably cut loose by minesweepers," Good Buffalo speculates. "That was where the minesweepers were seen and didn't identify themselves. Sweeping mines in quiet waters, the minesweepers figured they didn't have to identify themselves."

"Hey, yeah," I add. "Medicine Man heard at Battalion that the unidentified ships appeared off the coast near Capo d'Orlando, wherever that is. But wherever it is, the minesweepers were pretty busy."

Shield Chief speaks: "The Navy is clearing mines from the waters off the north coast. Might ask Lieutenant Anson where Capo d'Orlando is before he has a nap. If it's near Messina that means we're clearing a path toward Italy. We could be getting ready for something big."

Last Arrow pipes up: "If it's something big, I sure hope there are no foul-ups."

"There will be. Bureau of Indian Affairs," Leading Fox says as he nods.

We hear the howl of a wolf from Highway 117. "Haven't heard that wolf in a long while," Cheyenne remarks. "That wolf gets around."

Shield Chief stands and looks to the highway. "*Skiri, tawako kah-kih cha-rah rarut* [wolf says no enemy]. We can rest easy now; let's hit the hay."

"*Aho,*" we reply.

The next day the 3rd Division arrives. We learn that the 1st Division is near and pull back for miles and bivouac near the sea. Close by are the towns of Cefalù and Campofelice di Roccella. A Sicilian comes by selling baked chickens attached to a pole for a dollar apiece. Using the currency from the garrison captured on the first day, we pass it to the man as a gag, for we were told the money was no good. Much to our surprise, he gives us change back. A man from B Company named Benevento, of Italian descent, asks the vendor about the currency. The Sicilian replies that the money is good in the bank of Naples. "Got *damn!*" Benevento exclaims. We search our packs for more money, which we were saving as souvenirs. Dang, we started fires with it and made paper airplanes that we sailed from the cliffs where bridges were dynamited. Most of the currency, in various denominations, was discarded as dead weight. It will always be a reminder that this Indi'n was once a rich man.

The service company puts up showers and we finally get to take much–needed baths. A field kitchen is also erected. We are served hot meals for the first time in three weeks. We put up pup tents, clean our weapons, and swim in the Tyrrhenian Sea. While resting one day the company is called together to join the battalion. Once with the battalion we march to some barren hills. The day is hot as we move. When we finally stop there are a lot of men sitting on the ground there in front of a raised platform. The Brass and rear echelon soldiers in clean uniforms are seated in front. The infantry have the farthest to come and are seated quite a way from the platform. We still wear our grimy uniforms even after our showers. Surprise—it's Bob Hope! With him are Frances Langford and Jack Pepper. Bob Hope is great and brings us all a much-needed moment of joy. We laugh and laugh as he performs, exhibiting the charm and quirkiness that made him beloved by America. When the show is over, we stand, clap, and cheer. There are tears in some infantrymen's eyes. As front-line fighting men, we have respect for Bob Hope, as it takes courage to be here.

After what seems like a lifetime, trucks bring up our barrack bags, which have our personal effects and a clean change of clothing. For the first time in a while we write letters home. As they are completed, Lieutenant Anson, the platoon leader, reads them to see if any need to be censored for intelligence purposes. Mail call also comes for the men from home. Men from New York receive news clips from the *Watertown Times*, where we were stationed at Pine Camp near Watertown in the winter of 1942. This news clip was printed in our division newspaper too; it read:

Watertown Times, Watertown, N.Y., NEWS FROM OLD FRIENDS
   So the 45th is in Sicily. . . . The 45th Division, as all will recall, was at Pine Camp for about two months. They came in early November last fall and remained until the middle of January. They were a rugged, rollicking group. They made the 4th Armored which had preceded them appear as docile as Dagwood Bumstead. It took us a few weeks to get used to them, and frankly speaking, the town was considerably quieter after they were shifted elsewhere. Raw November and December weather never really cooled off their spirits. They cut high, wide and handsome capers on our streets. They broke up a tavern or two. They gave the local police and M.P.s a real workout.
   Yet, we look back with affection upon the 45th. They were fighting men. Woe to anyone who fell in their path. Now, if it is true they are in Sicily, they will find conditions exactly to their liking. If General Eisenhower wants Catania taken, let him shove the 45th into battle. They will deliver any town, mussed up perhaps, but thoroughly conquered.

We get a kick out of the news clip. For it is true: the Thunderbirds *were* a rugged group. The men who enlisted in 1940 when the 45th was called to federal service were basically cowboys, oilfield roughnecks, sunup-to-sundown farmers, and top-notch boxers—the products of Oklahoma Indian schools. A hardy bunch, they came from small towns and were good ol' boys at heart. Of course, there were men from other states who filled the 45th after Pearl Harbor. I remember a fight in a tavern at Watertown. It was a bitterly cold night, the sidewalks were icy, and the roads were even worse. During this the Thunderbirds, police, and MPs slugged it out, swinging nightsticks, slipping, sliding, and tumbling. A jukebox was also thrown through a plate-glass window.

While stationed at Fort Devens, Massachusetts, we got passes to Boston. In a place called the Silver Dollar Bar, one of our guys put a coin in the music box and played "Deep in the Heart of Texas." Then, with the place crowded, he tried to make everyone stand. Then we Indians walked in; all were over six feet. One was a 6'4" Sioux Indian, another a 6'6" Pawnee. A woman at the piano screamed: "Indi-yans!" A fight broke out, and the Indians took on MPs, Boston police, Shore Patrol, sailors, marines, and civilians. It was knuckle junction and the Battle of the Little Big Horn, all to the lively beat and clapping of "Deep in The Heart of Texas." That night in Boston a famous nightclub, the Cocoanut Grove, caught fire. Many people perished; among them was the Western movie star Buck Jones. Like I said, the 45th was a rough bunch.

We have a light work schedule as we continue to rest behind the line. We brush up on scouting and patrolling, also practicing on quickness in hand-to-hand fighting. I take it upon myself to practice throwing my Pawnee knife. There are passes to nearby towns granted as well. One of our men went to Palermo. He told us he saw the catacombs beneath the city. Explaining, he said it was a place where people placed their dead. They arranged them in positions as if they were still living. Some stood. Others were lying down. They were of all ages. He explained that people changed the dead's clothes often and how the temperature preserved the bodies. He said it was like a wax museum. Not having any money, I take drawing paper and sketch the Sicilian coast.

In the evenings, we go to a nearby Sherman tank and listen to the radio. Through the British Broadcasting Corporation in London there is war news and fine music. Then we pick up another wavelength and listen to an American girl who went over to the German side. Known as "Axis Sally" to the Americans, the Germans beam her program to the Mediterranean theater for propaganda purposes. She badmouths our leaders in Washington, saying they are big money men who are getting rich while the men in Sicily are fighting their war. She plays "Home on the Range" for the Oklahoma soldiers of the

45th. She says that we are just country boys who are inferior fighters to the German supermen who defeated the Poles, French, British, and who are now destroying the Russian army. Amused, we call her "Horseshit Sally."

The company forms. This time it's only officers and NCOs. We join Battalion before we march to some stone farm buildings. Entering a barren pasture with few trees, we spot a microphone under a lonely tree, which is cordoned off with a rope. We sit as cameramen move on the ground behind the rope. Nearby are jeeps about, waiting on something or someone.

There is talk that General Patton will speak. A unit of Pawnee Indians served under Patton and General Pershing on the Mexican Border in 1916. The Army moved to stop Pancho Villa's bandit raids into New Mexico. The Pawnees were first to open fire. Patton was a second lieutenant then. Back in 1941 the 45th Division faced General Patton in the Louisiana Maneuvers. There the Thunderbirds made their presence felt by taking Patton's armored units apart. During the maneuvers we Indians made a raft and floated quietly down a river and through their lines, raiding their kitchens and sneaking up from the swamps behind them. Men placed wads of chewing gum on chairs in headquarters tents and stuck signs to the gum paper that read KICK ME. A string of firecrackers were also set off, sounding like blank ammunition used on maneuvers. It caused alarm and confusion among the armored divisions. After wreaking havoc we quietly slipped into the swamps. After Louisiana, one rifle company was picked to go with General Patton on two more months of maneuvers in North Carolina. We heard a rumor that Patton had selected B Company . . . don't know whether it was true, but it made us feel good. It was to be a special maneuver involving tanks and infantry—something the Army was doing to counter the German blitzkrieg.

A command car arrives flying a red flag with white stars. General George S. Patton Jr. steps from the command car. We are called to attention. With swagger stick in hand, wearing a star-studded helmet, and packing a pearl-handled pistol, General Patton steps to the microphone. Words come: "Be seated." We sit back on the ground. The microphone crackles, then is adjusted. General Patton scowls before he speaks. His voice does not fit the man. Earlier, when General Patton spoke to us in North Africa, his language was rough; he cussed a lot, but his points were well made. During that time he also lashed out at the Germans, saying we were going to kick the Huns in the ass and pull out their guts to grease the treads of our tanks. He also stressed the point of looking like soldiers. If we didn't, some German was going to slip up behind and hit us over the head with a sack of shit. This time, postbattle, his speech differs. He praises us, says we fought like veterans. Then General Patton points his swagger stick at us and says: "Born at sea, baptized in blood, your fame shall never die. The

45th Infantry Division is one of the best, if not actually the best division in the history of American arms."

Sitting next to Good Buffalo and Leading Fox, I hear them say, "*Nawa.*" (Pawnee word said after a chief speaks, meaning "Agreed. All is good.") After his speech, General Patton walks to the men. They stand as he passes, inspecting them.

An officer directs the general's attention to us Indian soldiers. He turns and says: "You men have a proud heritage."

Good Buffalo utters, "*Nawa.*" General George S. Patton walks to the command car and gets in. The command car drives off, flying the red flag with white stars.

A few days later we hear that Messina fell to the Americans. The Sicilian campaign finally comes to a formal end. It is August 20, 1943, when the 179th Regimental Combat Team pulls up stakes and moves near San Nicola l'Arena. Once there Major Carl McGee, from our hometown, comes to visit us. We chat and he speaks of the situation in general. Everybody feels something big is going to happen, since the 179th is near two port cities, Palermo and Termini Imerese. It gives thought to what Shield Chief said about the Navy clearing mines off the north coast and clearing a path for the invasion of Italy proper.

Early September comes when we are resupplied with ammunition and issued K-rations. We also have our canteens filled with fresh water before we move by truck to the port of Termini Imerese. We load up on LCIs (Landing Craft Infantry) which hold about three hundred men per boat. We are given three big pills called "pep pills." We are instructed to take one a day for the first three days. The pills are to keep us awake, as the first three days of fighting are expected to be crucial. Not overjoyed, the men guess Italy is our destination. It's midafternoon; out at sea are cruisers, destroyers, minesweepers, and other ships. The port of Termini teems with activity. We pull away and form up out to sea. In the late afternoon there is a German air raid on our convoy. A torpedo plane comes in low and releases a torpedo. We can see the wake of the torpedo coming before it hisses past our LCI and explodes beyond. The American Navy antiaircraft fire is heavy, causing the German plane to break off the attack. Nerves wracked, we wait . . . and wait.

8

Avalanche

Now hardened combat veterans, Echohawk and his men entered into a new phase of the war on mainland Europe. Life seemed to avalanche for the men of B Company as they began to face staunch German resistance and suffer significant casualties. From town to town, and village to village, the Thunderbirds marched onward.

We get under way. Looking back at Sicily, I think of things I saw other than combat. The arid country, giant cactus groves, strange trees, which were found to be olive—and almond and lemon too. Most looked like mesquite trees to us Oklahoma boys. There were the mountains without vegetation, Caltanissetta—"the city of the dead"—and Mount Etna, all truly beautiful.

On the crowded deck, someone calls: "Look out there!" Floating by are dead British sailors in lifejackets. They wear summer whites, white T-shirts, walking shorts, knee stockings, and shoes. On the calm blue sea are black oil slicks that snake lazily by. Orders and maps are issued to officers. The 179th RCT is sailing for Italy and will once again be an integral part of the force attacking the mainland. From the Bureau of Indian Affairs we learn that we are no longer in General Patton's Seventh Army but now in General Mark Clark's Fifth Army. The 179th will be the floating reserve for the main force landing in Italy. The rest of the division is left behind. We will be committed wherever needed, depending on the situation. The ship's radio announces that Italy has surrendered. As a cheer goes up, Shield Chief says it's only whistling in the dark as the Germans won't roll over and give up. Nightfall arrives and gives way to a full moon as we continue to move toward Italy.

Another air raid hits the convoy, and this time it is heavy. The Germans drop flares that light up the night, illuminating the convoy. Thousands and thousands of red tracers go up. Sleek destroyers weave through the convoy, laying down a smokescreen. The night sky rumbles, crackles, and flickers with American antiaircraft fire. Minutes later it rains spent flak. With the air raid over, we try to sleep but are too nervous and scared. Moving about the crowded deck, we strike up a conversation with the captain of the LCI. He's from Newkirk, Oklahoma. I think to myself that it's a small world. The captain said he played high school football against Pawnee in 1939. I tell him I was the team captain in 1939, the year Newkirk beat us. They had a guy named Rossell who returned punts and kickoffs. None of us could stop him.

The convoy moves steadily through the night. Another air raid comes as the Luftwaffe drops flares. As the fireworks start the captain asks if any of us can fire a 20mm gun. Their gunner took flak in the arm and is out of commission. One of our men volunteers. A watch in the conning tower sounds off when a plane is coming in low. The air raid intensifies as bombs explode throughout the convoy. Destroyers continue to lay a smokescreen. From the loudspeaker: "One coming in at nine o'clock. Five hundred feet!" Gunners react, sending their fire streaks out, joining fountains of red tracers rising from other ships. A bomber roars over before it rains more spent flak. When the air raid ends we notice that a ship has been hit at the far right. It blazes red and fades behind the convoy, which keeps moving. Exhausted from fear, we doze. Hours pass as the LCI slows almost to a stop before it resumes speed. We stand and look forward. Ahead is darkness and mist. Our ship turns and heads out to sea. After a while it returns, then pulls up to the beach. Another air raid comes, and once more the German bombers drop flares.

The beach is in a white shimmering light. A gangway is lowered at the side of the LCI. Bombs thunder on the beach and are answered with antiaircraft fire from beachhead guns and ships at sea; this is nerve-wracking. B Company crowds down the gangway like a herd of nervous cattle in an electrical storm about to stampede. In chest-deep seawater, men move toward the beach with rifles held above their heads. As we reach the beach we drop our life-preserver belts and get organized. On the right more men land, probably the Second Battalion. I hear laughter that seems out of place here. Then we see two Indian soldiers. They see us Pawnees and motion in sign language: "Everything is all right. Good." Second Battalion gets organized too.

The First Battalion of the 179th Regimental Combat Team moves forward. The 36th (Texas) Division landed first yesterday. Don't know how they made out. I heard the Germans met them on the beach and it was a bloody battle. As dawn arrives on the beach bulldozers are building an airstrip. Now there is lots of activity as quartermasters are building mountains of supply dumps. At sea is the Navy and all kinds of ships. On this beach are burned vehicles and tanks. Soldiers from the 36th Division lie dead in the sand too. Tracks show they were attacking when they went down. A corporal, without a helmet, has his mouth open like he was shouting. His finger is still on the trigger. The empty brass nearby indicates that the Texans went down with guns blazing. Ahead, on a sand dune with shocks of buffalo grass, is an MG 42 with empty belts of ammunition. Sprawled nearby are German dead too. The 36th Division—we maneuvered against them near Brownwood, Texas. They are tougher than a boot. In the field when they would see us, they would hoot and holler: "There's those blanket-ass Indians. Scared o' cowboys and cavalry!" We would counter with: "If the Alamo had a back door there wouldn't be any Texas!"

Moving out, we spot a signpost reading Highway 18 with an arrow pointing right: Paestum. There we turn left. Everything here is green with vegetation, unlike Sicily. On the far right are mountains. Radio jeeps roll through the column as it advances. American fighters pass over, flying cover for the beachhead. We maintain interval as we head inland.

After about an hour of stopping and moving, the battalion pulls off the highway and enters a green field with trees. We disperse before we wait . . . and wait. While we wait, more Messerschmitts roar in and strafe the beach. There is not much antiaircraft fire, because the fighters have sneaked in low and fast. At the same time, American bombers drone inland on bombing missions. A Messerschmitt climbs after them. One of the German fighters pulls behind our bombers, giving chase. Blue smoke streams from the bombers as their tail gunners open fire. The Messerschmitt is hit and trails smoke before breaking away. Then it flickers with hits from gunfire. Suddenly a British Spitfire flashes by in a vertical dive before the Messerschmitt falls in flames and disintegrates before hitting the sea. The British Spitfire comes inland, flying low. It passes over, rocking its wings at us. All stand and cheer. The Spitfire circles and climbs to join other Spitfires that are flying high-altitude cover for the beachhead. The rest of the day is spent dozing after the sleepless night of German air raids.

Twilight comes, and the 179th RCT returns to Highway 18 and continues its march north. The First Battalion leads, followed by the Second and Third. A moon is out and all is still. I wonder where the Germans are. Word comes from behind: "Counterattack from the rear!" Much of the column breaks from the highway and hits the ground with M1s ready. When the Second Battalion comes up, it meets part of the First Battalion, ready to spring at them. We learn that the original warning was: "Watch for a counterattack from the rear." When the relayed words reached B Company, we got "counterattack from the rear!" We return to the highway and resume the march. After a while we leave Highway 18 and take a road to the right. Moving, I spot a burning bridge; the flames glow red in the dark night. The smoke is heavy and smells of oil as we move closer to the bridge. Once there the battalion fords the river and picks up the road on the other side. Approaching a forest of tall trees that is dark, we hold.

Radio jeeps with small blue headlights pass. Sergeant Last Arrow and I leave to take a leak. Several yards from the road in the dark of the woods is a tank. We take a closer look; it's German. We leave quietly, not wanting to draw attention to ourselves. When we get back, the column has moved on. I hurry forward to tell an officer about the tank. He says it was probably knocked out. Falling back in, we see that the road turns right before intersecting another road lined with big trees. A sign here points left: Persano. The town's buildings are visible in the moonlight; the town is quiet. The night air has a fragrance of flowers. The column snails through the night with frequent stops while scouts check ahead. Medicine Man comes up during a stop to see if the men are okay. He tells us the Second Battalion branched off to the right back at the burning bridge. The Third did too. Shield Chief says the First Battalion is alone now. Then he adds: "It's about like General Custer; he divided his troops in the face of the enemy without knowing their strength."

The First Battalion keeps advancing. We figure we've come twenty miles into enemy territory. Many stars out this night. The Italian countryside is graveyard quiet. The eastern sky lightens to a peach color. *Hupiri-Kucu,* the Morning Star, soon comes out, twinkling with many colors. This is God's messenger, signaling the coming of a new day and awakening all living things.

Day breaks to German 88mm guns tearing the air around us. We dive for cover as the 88s explode on the road. We hug Mother Earth, gasping with fear. I tense up before word comes: "B Company! Move right!" We break right. I check my squad and dig in frantically before ordering the men to point their M1s forward. As we click off safety locks, all eyes are on the immediate front. After the 88 fire ceases, we pull back a few miles and take positions facing southwest. Far to the rear is the thumping of artillery fire.

The battalion commander, Lieutenant Colonel Stevens, appears: "Where's G.I.?" he asks Cheyenne, who is nearby.

"Don't know, Sir." Cheyenne answers. "G.I." is what the officers call Captain Glen I. Lee, our company commander. Colonel Stevens hurries off as artillery fire in the rear continues.

Now there is artillery fire in the northeast. That makes two nights without sleep we've had. The night of air raids at sea and last night's all-night march take their toll. Weary-eyed, I can't stay awake. Then I remember the pep pills we are to take for the first three days. They are supposed to keep you awake and alert. I take one with a drink of water as the artillery fire heard in the distance intensifies. Things seem to be happening—bad things. The battalion commander approaches with a look of panic: "B Company! Let's get those Indians down there!" Captain Lee hurries to Colonel Stevens. I overhear Colonel Stevens say that C Company is under a heavy attack, facing Panzers and infantry at Persano.

It is ordered that B Company is to attack now to provide immediate support!

"B Company! Let's go!" shouts Captain Lee. We move fast. B Company reaches the main road to Persano. It is lined with big trees, some scarred by shrapnel. The Persano sign has been shot up. We hold at the edge of the city.

Platoon leaders are called on the double. They are gone for a few minutes, then return on the double.

Lieutenant Anson, our platoon leader, says nervously: "The First and Second Platoons will attack down this road. Third Platoon will be in reserve, the Weapons Platoon in support. First Platoon will take the left side of the road. The Second, right. Sergeant Eck, your squad will be next to the road. Sergeant Good Buffalo and Last Arrow will be on your right. Move out." Platoon Sergeant Stone, standing near Lieutenant Anson, says nothing. We get in position for the attack. There is no need for scouts, as we know where we are going— and they know we are coming.

We fix bayonets before a voice shouts: "B Company! Let's go!" I lead out before my squad follows. I glance right to see that Good Buffalo and Last Arrow are at the head of their squads.

Taking interval, we advance at high port, bayonets pointing up. Persano is less than half a mile down this road. As we get closer I notice there are trees along the road that have been hit by shell fire. Tank tracks swerve in and out of the ditches. In the ditches too are C Company dead, run over by 40-ton tanks. Some are bound with bandages, perhaps helplessly wounded, while others are crushed; it is a gruesome sight. Halfway down the road we see a tree split down the trunk that was hit by an 88. On a branch is equipment, bits of clothing, and flesh. This is the body of a second lieutenant I knew who was blown apart. There are tank tracks over the body too. Having been crushed, food substance has been forced from the stomach and out of the mouth.

Damn Krauts. We had gone to demolition school together at Cape Cod; he was a fine officer. I try to shake it from my mind and keep advancing.

Reaching the end of the tree-lined road I see an Indian soldier who is dead. His hair is burning and the ground surrounding him is soaked with gasoline. In the right hand is a bloodstained knife. He was a Comanche. Here the road rises and becomes the main street. On the right is an eight-foot wall. I glance right to Good Buffalo and Last Arrow, who maintain interval. Shield Chief, who is now in Good Buffalo's squad, signs to me: "Chin up. Turn right." I turn right, then signal the squad: "on the double." Good Buffalo and Last Arrow shift right too. We run along the wall as we move. A small pipe, with running water, protrudes from the wall, making the ground here soggy. Spotting a staircase, I run to take it.

Atop the stairs, I enter a huge flower garden with a pool and water fountain. Good Buffalo and Last Arrow move down the wall for another opening. Here we can't afford to bunch up, as German artillery has been harassing us since the landing. We belly through a garden of giant goldenrods. Beyond there is a high mesh fence with a street on the other side and two-story buildings. As we evaluate, an 88 barrage roars in. Shells land on the streets and hit the walls of buildings,

Captain Beck of C Company, 179th Regiment, lies dead near Persano, Italy, September 1943.

"Scattered equipment and American dead from Oklahoma lie in the ditch. Here the Krauts hid their tanks in the cathedral. The town looked peaceful." Near Persano, Italy, September 15, 1943.

causing loud explosions and jolting concussion blasts. Shrapnel flies at bullet speed, ricocheting off the sides of buildings and clipping tree branches. We are showered with rocks and broken glass as we hunker down. White clouds of plaster and dust fog the streets. There is a shriek of "jungle birds" that can be heard. Finally the German barrage lifts; though shaken, we keep advancing.

We use the tall flowers in the garden as a blind as we move. I look for an opening in the mesh fence and find one. "A gate! Follow me!" I yell to the men. I spring through and tear across the street, passing the body of an American soldier before enemy fire opens on me. I dive to the curbing. Dirt kicks up along the fence and lead zings off the gate as the Germans zero in on us. The squad is pinned down. I hug the curb, pant, and sweat. I wipe the sweat from my eyes so I can see to shoot. With my face down and arms curved about my head, I soak up the slight breeze. Leaves blow on my hands and shoulders as I find solace in the breeze. I take a look down and realize the "leaves" are American dollar bills. Nearby I see a billfold with more bills scattered about. The dead soldier it belongs to is a C Company man. Lying on his back, he has a leg that is almost blown off and no helmet. There's a big hole in his head above the right eye. Sunlight shines through and into his open mouth. The Germans have ransacked his pack, emptied his pockets, and shattered his M1 rifle. Everyone in the regiment knew him as Slim. He was a rodeo cowboy who was good with dice and always carried a lot of money for the next game.

Someone screams: "Tank!" Approaching on the side street, its steel tracks click and clank as it moves toward us. I think about the C Company men crushed by German tanks and lie still, fearing I might face the same fate. The Panzer draws close, then stops before it fires a machine gun that rakes the flower garden. Our guys lie low. I lift my head and look, spotting a cannon barrel with a muzzle that break-points from the side of the building. However, I can't see the rest of the tank as it sits, motor running. Then the Panzer backs away. The narrow street is flush to the building.

We move forward, staying against the wall of the building. When we reach the side street where the Panzer was we see a building resembling a hotel with palm trees in front. Good Buffalo, Shield Chief, and others rush the hotel. Not going for the front door, they crash through windows before a hot exchange of gunfire can be heard. I follow and race across the side street, crashing through another window. Tangled in a curtain, I land on a man lying down on the floor. I shoot at figures in the dark and reload fast to keep shooting. Return fire comes, and the shots are wild. Plaster flies and glass shatters. Coming in from the bright sunlight, my eyes finally adjust to darkness. I see bodies on the floor; some are propped against a wall. The hotel looks like the garage of the St. Valentine's Day Massacre in Chicago. The man on the floor next to me has his head and chest wrapped with bloodstained bandages. Heavy M1 fire is heard in the next room, but there is no return fire. A Pawnee war cry is heard followed by voices screaming: "Nicht schiessen! Nicht schiessen!" The Germans surrender to us Indians.

Behind them: "Kill the sons of bitches! Kill them!" It is a soldier from C Company, a man named Humble. Now there is no more enemy fire at B Company's front, as the Germans have pulled back. "G'damn, glad to see you Indians," he cries. "Phil, how are you Pawnees doing?"

Phil answers, "We're doing okay."

Shield Chief gives Humble a drink of water from a canteen. "You all right, Humble?"

He takes big gulps and returns the canteen to Shield Chief. "Yep, I'm all right. Them sons of bitches took my shoes and socks. One talked English and said they saw us cross at the burning bridge last night. One of them smartass bastards bragged about how they were going to capture the American beach today. I told him, 'You'll shit too, if you eat regular. We're a wild bunch of cowboys and Indi'ns, and we'll flat get your mean ass.' I gave them some Ex-Lax I had and said 'choco-lot.'"

We all have a chuckle. Good Buffalo says, "When you got to go, you got to go." The German prisoners are herded out. They eyeball us and we eyeball them. They are fresh compared to us.

My squad comes through the gate of the flower garden. I pause to look at the body of Slim before Lieutenant Anson assembles the platoon. He orders a man to take the prisoners back to Battalion. He then checks to see if anyone is hit. Medicine Man comes up to check too.

Platoon Sergeant Stone appears: "All right! Don't bunch up, g'damn it!"

Private Humble shakes hands with us. "Sho' thank you guys. Cain't thank you enough. Reckon, better find C Company, what's left of 'em." Barefooted, Humble picks his way down the street, avoiding bits of stone and broken glass. The late afternoon sun silhouettes him in the shadow of the buildings. He walks with arms extended like a tightrope walker at the circus. Humble sees the body of Slim before he walks to it and kneels. He puts a hand on the breast of the dead soldier and sobs: "Slim . . . Slim." These two were buddies, both enlisted at Oklahoma City in 1940. They were cowboys, who rodeoed together. Both were easygoing and tougher than a boot. Sad day. We move out.

Moving in intervals, the squad is advancing through narrow streets. Word comes: "Hold." Platoon leaders are called. We wait, sipping water in the late afternoon sun. When the officers return we are instructed to pull back to the street that runs parallel to the flower garden. We take up positions near there. Here contact is made with the First Platoon on the left. A few C Company men are with them, who say the Germans overran them with half-tracks and

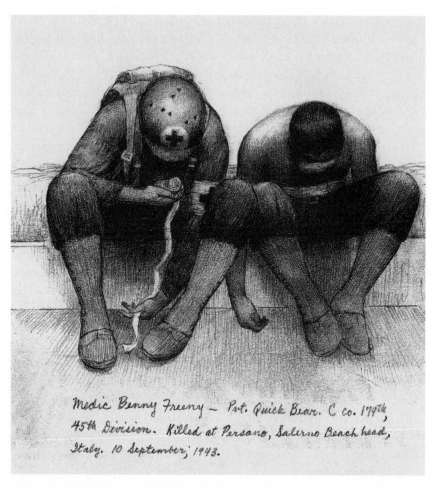

Medic Benny Freeny — Pvt. Quick Bear. C co. 179th, 45th Division. Killed at Persano, Salerno Beach head, Italy. 10 September, 1943.

Medic Benjamin Freeny and Private Dan Quick Bear of C Company, 179th Regiment, lie dead in a shell hole after German SS in a half-track shot them and set their bodies on fire. Near Persano, Italy, September 1943.

Panzers. At the main street and flower garden street is a medic and an Indian soldier; both are dead. Their bodies remain in sitting positions in a shell hole near the intersection. The Indian soldier is shirtless with a bandage around his chest. In the medic's hands are bandages. He wears an armband and helmet that bear a red cross on a white circle. With head bowed, there are bullet holes in the top of the medic's helmet. The Indian soldier beside him has no helmet. He was hit many times in the top of the head. From C Company, the soldier's name is Dan Quick Bear. The medic's name is Benjamin Freeny; he is part Choctaw. One of the soldiers from C Company tells Cheyenne and me what happened. He explains that during the street fighting Quick Bear charged forward and was hit. He continues, adding that Medic Freeny, in an attempt to aid Quick Bear, dashed out and pulled him to a shell hole. While Freeny attended Quick Bear, a half-track full of Germans pulled up beside the men. The Germans leaned over the side of the half-track, shooting Freeny and Quick Bear with machine pistols at powderburn range. Nick Quissio, a C Company man, ran up and shot the Germans in the half-track with a Browning Automatic Rifle before the half-track sped away. When Nick saw Freeny and Quick Bear dead, he screamed and cussed the Germans.

A rage churns inside me. . . . The Indian soldier back there on the ground, doused with gasoline . . . his hair burning . . . the Nazis, cold-blooded killers of an unarmed medic and a wounded soldier. Now we hate the enemy's guts.

Medicine Man comes up and asks if my men are okay. I answer, "Yes." He turns and sees the bodies of Freeny and Quick Bear. Medicine Man steps forward, shaking his head in disbelief: "No, no, no." The Choctaw Indian medic stands in prayerful silence. We do the same; this hits us hard.

Before the moment is over an 88 barrage roars in. It's a German counterattack! We hurry to our positions. As we scurry for cover the German barrage rocks Persano, making the jungle birds screech once more. Panzers appear and begin to fire into buildings, machine-gunning doors and windows as they pass by. As the German machine pistol fires unrelenting lead down the streets toward us, sudden fire comes from a second position. "Second-story window!" someone shouts from behind. I look and see a German with a machine pistol. I aim; my thoughts turn to the Indian soldier with burning hair . . . Freeny and Quick Bear. I squeeze the trigger. Multiple M1s fire at the same time as the German's head snaps. His face is blown off and his gun silenced. His steel helmet catches on the windowsill before it falls on the street, rolls around, and stops. Blood runs down the side of the building, tracing its path. More machine gun fire opens up followed by return M1 fire. As the machine gun fire picks up, German tanks are seen moving into the town. Voices from the rear yell: "Fall back! Fall back!" We once more leave Persano without taking the town.

B Company withdraws to fields with haystacks outside of the town. The September heat is stifling. We all gulp water after the hard day of fighting. I ask myself: *Where's our artillery, where are our tanks, and where is the air support?* Before I finish this thought another Messerschmitt flashes over low, heading left. I wonder if maybe one of our units is attacking on the left. Platoon leaders are called. We wait and check ammo, expecting the Germans to attack again. After a while the platoon leaders return. We are ordered to attack Persano again. This time First Platoon will attack on our left, with the Third—which was in reserve during our first try—attacking on our right. The Weapons Platoon is in the rear. The platoon order is the same as before, though. Good Buffalo,

Last Arrow, and I are abreast. We will avoid the main street, since the Germans have it zeroed in.

"B Company! Let's go!"

We advance, being sure to check our interval regularly. I glance right to see Good Buffalo leading his squad. He walks like a hunter who knows his trail. Beyond him is Last Arrow, who, walking backward, turns to his men and shouts words of encouragement. He then motions for more interval. Sergeant Last Arrow turns, faces the front again, and brings his M1 and bayonet to high port. His men do the same. In short order we all follow and keep advancing. No 88 barrage comes; perhaps the Germans have shifted guns to meet a flank attack. Persano comes alive with small-arms fire as we move closer to the town.

We charge the Germans holding the city, fighting building to building, where we struggle to take the town. Facing heavy resistance room to room makes it hard to keep contact with each other. It is not like fighting in the open. I hear heavy M1 fire in the right front. Good Buffalo's men are advancing. I realize we must stay even with them to protect their flank. I move, and the squad follows behind. Ahead, in the middle of a wide street, is a bird sanctuary—a huge rectangular cage with a screened-in top. Inside it are peacocks and other exotic birds. These are my jungle birds that were screeching. Connecting the cage are beautiful flower gardens. I see nearby a burned Willys jeep. The body of the driver lies close nearby. Farther up the street is another jeep that took a direct hit. Blown to pieces, it is hard to identify the vehicle at first.

Another 88 barrage crashes in as the men scatter to find cover. I drop to the street instantly. Like a crack of thunder, another 88 slams in close by. Concussed, my ears ring and my head throbs. The buildings surrounding me take hits, causing walls to slip and crumble into billowing dust. It rains rocks, plaster, and broken glass around me as I hug Mother Earth. The peacocks give unearthly screams. The exotic birds panic, hitting screens and losing feathers as they fly around their cage. I notice that the flower gardens are walled with stones a foot and a half high. I dart for them and figure it to be better than this open street. The barrage lifts and leaves clouds of dust around us.

Bellied down, I look up and see a dark figure in a window. The figure moves back when I aim my rifle to shoot. More Panzers move into the town, sending everyone scrambling. I break left for a two-story building to seek cover. Seeing a walk-down staircase, I take it, slamming the door at the bottom with a shoulder to break in. A tank and half-track roll up to the building. Germans in the half-track fire through the doorway. Lead whangs and zings, sending glass, plaster, and splinters of wood flying through the air. I crawl across the floor to a back door. It looks like a barber shop, with a linen closet and washroom. I see a window and squeeze through outside. Emerging on a street, I see a half-track has just passed. Germans in the tank have their heads down, heading toward the First Platoon area. The half-track turns right on a narrow street into M1 and BAR fire.

I backtrack and hear the tanks firing. I run past the bodies of Freeny and Quick Bear. I notice that it looks like the bodies have been tampered with. I can't stop, though. I run left on the flower garden street to the platoon area. No one is there. In front of the hotel is a German tank and jeep. I dash to the garden gate as I hear the Panzer coming. Crawling through tall flowers that look like goldenrods, I see a fountain in the middle of a concrete pool. I duck into the pool, hugging the shallow walls. The tank crushes the gate and rolls through tall flowers while shifting gears and turning in tight circles. Clods of dirt fly into the water. My heart pounds. Then the Panzer knocks down the mesh fence before it clanks down the street, dragging metal poles, fencing, clumps of dirt, and goldenrods. I leave the pool running for a shell hole that has made a clearing.

I fly off an eight-foot wall, landing on soggy ground near the water pipe I passed earlier. Beyond I see German tanks roaming the fields, running over haystacks in case men are hiding there. I turn right, running along a wall toward the main street of Persano. Staying close to buildings, I continue to hear Panzers in the streets. I spot a long building that has the look of a palace. Part of it extends over a slope, forming a shelter under which there are stables. Parked here are carts, wagons, and fancy coaches. A tank approaches the front of the building. I get into a stall of hay. To my surprise there are men hiding here. They are First Platoon men. The Panzer turns the corner and rumbles down the slope toward the stables. I run for the open field, diving into a small stream. I belly down in it and I hear the tank crushing carts, wagons, and coaches. While it wrecks the stables, I make a getaway.

Finally I locate the company and join up with Second Platoon. Glad to see them, I notice that a few men are missing from the platoon. Shield Chief checks on me. I explain what happened. He nods, saying that our men fought well but that it is hard to keep contact in buildings and streets. We are ordered to pull back with no tank or artillery to support another attack. Shield Chief tells me to eat so I can get strength back. I realize I didn't eat today. I wolf down a K-ration breakfast with cold coffee. It's midafternoon; in this heat the dust of battle hangs over Persano. The battalion commander powwows with the company commanders. Word comes down that we are to attack again: Persano must be taken at all costs. If they have it, the Germans will use Persano as a springboard to the beach.

We learn that crack Panzer grenadiers are converging on the town. A Company will be on the left; they've been in reserve with remnants of C Company.

Bazooka men are to stay close to the platoon leaders. The .03 antitank grenade men stay ready to make a stand. When B Company rushed to Persano, the heavy weapons company fell behind. Now they're here and ready.

As we attack, D Company rakes the buildings with heavy machine gun fire. They also lay down an .81 mortar barrage to keep Jerry on his toes. Birds at the sanctuary shriek again. When the fire lifts, we advance on Persano. On the left, I see artillery fire. Something's happening there. Men who were missing rejoin the platoon as we move. Small-arms fire slows our advance as we move into the heart of the town. I run into Sergeant Grant Shield Chief coming from the right. He is with Third Platoon. Grant says he is trying to keep contact with us. From the rear a weapons truck from D Company arrives carrying heavy weapons with ammo. Ahead and to the right, Sergeant Ruling His Son crouches at the corner of a building that has an outside stairway. The stairs run flush with the wall to the second floor. He sees us and motions: "come." He points to the stairway.

"Let's go," Grant says. "We can go upstairs where we can see. Can't see anything down on the street."

"Okay," I respond, then yell: "Second Platoon! Let's go!"

Grant and I make a run for it. Small-arms fire increases as we sprint. An 88 hits D Company's weapons truck. The truck explodes, erupting in a sheet of flames. The squad, having tried to follow, lies flat in the street, expecting more 88s to come in. We charge up the stairs, reaching the second floor as another shell hits the wall of the building. The stairs collapse from beneath our feet as we begin to ride it down before crashing in a cloud of dust. Covered with dust, we dash around the corner to a doorway. Grant and I run up another stairway. This time Ruling His Son covers us. At the top of the stairs is a hallway. Pressing ourselves against the wall with steel springs in our backs, we move forward, M1s at the ready. In the last room on the left are footsteps—not jackboots. Grant kicks open the door. Inside is a woman dressed in black. An old man in a dark suit, white shirt, and necktie lies on a couch.

The woman smiles. "Come in, boys. I speak English." She's in her late forties with graying hair. The room's neat. The window offers an excellent view of the main street and bird sanctuary. I can see the burned jeep and the body of the driver, and also see the jeep that took a direct hit, and now, down this main street, D Company's weapons truck that was hit.

The woman is friendly. Her eyes, not so much. She says she's glad to see Americans and asks how many of us there are. She also asks how many are wounded and if we have any tanks. We don't answer. The woman takes a fan, sits on the couch, and cools the old man, as the room is warm. She says the old man is her father and that he is deaf. Though she faces the old man, her eyes follow us.

"The old white woman is a fox," Grant utters in Pawnee without looking at me.

"*Ah-hu, rah ruk, tut*" (Yes, I noticed), I reply. Grant inspects the window. He eyes a cabinet near the window before he pauses. From his pocket he takes a coin and flips it. It clinks and rolls across the hardwood floor. The deaf man turns, reacting to the sound of the coin. Grant nods to him: "Gracias, Señor." The woman's jaw drops. Grant Shield Chief jerks the window curtain down and opens the cabinet, revealing a microphone, radio transmitter, and wires leading to the window.

"All right, woman. You've had it. Let's go," Grant says.

"I do not know what this is about," the woman replies nervously.

I turn to the old man. "Okay, mister. Let's go." They look at each other with fear. Grant destroys the radio transmitter before we leave.

We take them downstairs, where Ruling His Son stands ready. "Who are these people?" he asks. Grant tells him they were directing artillery for the Germans. Mostly the woman. He mentions the microphone and transmitter.

The few men with Ruling His Son, who made it from the street, step up in anger. "Kill her!" one explodes.

Others join in: "She's responsible for the 88 barrages and the burning weapons truck."

Another exclaims: "Town's under attack, civilians get killed. Shoot her. Nobody will know!"

Sergeant Grant Shield Chief keeps them from becoming a lynch mob. He says to let Battalion handle this. The more I think about it, the madder I get, too. However, Grant—the cooler head—does the right thing. During an 88 barrage in our previous attack, near the bird sanctuary, I looked up to that very window. There I saw a person dressed in black, looking out. As I aimed my rifle the figure in the window stepped back. It was that woman. I'm sure she had called fire down on the two jeeps near the bird sanctuary, too. Grant picks a man to take the couple back to Battalion with all the information. Outside the building is the sound of an 88 barrage. We stay put as the building shakes, sending plaster falling from the ceiling. When the barrage lifts, we get outside.

Linking up with the rest of the platoon, we get ready for a German counterattack. The woman and old man are taken to Battalion. More Panzers and half-tracks appear on the edge of Persano. This time the Germans crouch on top of tanks, while those in half-tracks have their heads down. We open fire on the tanks and half-tracks. Germans fall from the tanks and tumble into the streets. Panzers fire machine guns while others fire cannons into the buildings. All lumber like nearsighted buffalo. Dry-gulched in narrow streets, they are hit with bazookas and antitank grenades before exploding. The remaining half-tracks continue to take hits as the soldiers riding them jump, scatter, and fall to M1 fire.

Then the Panzer grenadiers pick up the attack. Wearing gray-green uniforms, they advance in formation with machine pistols. Clomping in jack-boots, they call out things in German. Their stiff-necked leaders shout: "Hands up, Joe! Hands up, Joe!"

"Shit," Leading Fox answers. With M1s, .03s, BARs, tommy-guns, and grenades at the ready, we dig our heels in for a fight. A Pawnee war cry is heard.

Cheyenne yells: "It's a good day to die!" The Creek war cry, the gobble of a wild tom turkey, comes too, followed by the shriek of a gander goose and the whinny of a stud horse. In savage fighting we take Persano once and for all.

It's sundown and the September heat lingers. I think of Freeny (the medic) and Quick Bear (the Indian soldier with burning hair). The C Company men, dead, glance through my mind. Like at a funeral there is a fragrance of flowers, but it is mixed with the smells of cordite, burning rubber, gasoline, oil—and the odor of burning flesh. Smoke from the fighting shrouds Persano. All is quiet, except for the unearthly cry of a shell-shocked peacock at the bird sanc-tuary. At twilight, I eat a dehydrated fruit bar for supper before I visit buddies in other platoons. I see Sergeant Bob Shultz of First Platoon. We talk about the burning bridge and Persano. He mentions crossing the river at the burning bridge before the column took a highway through a wooded area and stopped. There Last Arrow and I left the column to take a leak. This was when we saw the German tank sitting in the woods. It was dark, so we slipped away and went back to tell an officer, who said it was probably knocked out. Bob says he and another guy left the column too, and saw soldiers moving toward the burning bridge on a side road. Knowing we were the only troops pushing inland that night, he wondered who they were. Well, now we know that they were Germans, for they had infiltrated Persano and beyond. No wonder things were so bad.

I see Medicine Man making his rounds to check on the men. "Say, you re-ally racked up the crack Panzer grenadiers today," the Choctaw medic remarks with a smile. "You bloodthirsty Redskins gotta hold down these massacres. Save some German white-eyes for the British."

The BAR man pipes up: "Medicine Man, what's the word back at Battal-ion?" Medicine Man takes a dead cigar out of his mouth and puts it in his shirt pocket. "Well, the Third Battalion at the right got hit with tanks. The Second took it on the chin. It sure staggered them, but they didn't go down. Our guys stood toe to toe and slugged it out with no tank support. The Germans circled

behind the First Battalion and took Persano. C Company hit Persano to run
the Germans out and was mauled. B Company jumped in feet first . . . well,
you know the rest."

"No tank support," grumbles Leading Fox. "Bureau of Indian Affairs."

Turning toward Cheyenne, Medicine Man says, "Hey, Cheyenne, how
would you like to go to a Cheyenne Sun Dance?"

Cheyenne answers: "I'm ready."

Medicine Man sits down cross-legged. "You Cheyenne dance three days
and nights without sleeping and eating, right?"

Private First Class Gilbert Short Nose Curtis answers: "Right. During meal-
time, women place food before the dancers. The dancers don't eat but look at
the food for spiritual strength and keep dancing."

"Cheyennes are tough," I add.

Cheyenne chuckles. "Don't know about that. This Cheyenne feels like he
has been run over by a herd of buffalo. Say, changing the subject, when pulling
back, I passed by the bodies of Freeny and Quick Bear. I noticed the Germans
had put rifles in their hands. Wanted to make it look like Freeny and Quick
Bear were armed when killed."

"The Geneva Convention doesn't mean anything to the Germans," Medicine Man fumes.

I speak: "And that Indian soldier, his hair burning. There was a smell of
gasoline on him. He might have been wounded and still alive."

Medicine Man stands. "If I ever see Germans mistreating our wounded, I'll
take off this Red Cross armband and do like we do in the Choctaw Nation
when it comes to handling troublemakers: take a piss-elm club and beat the
gotdamn hell out of the bastards." Cheyenne and I look at each other, then at
Medicine Man; we have never heard him cuss before.

Private First Class Moses Bowlegs glares at the front, with arms at his sides
and fists doubled. Then he sits.

"I knew Benjamin Freeny since 1940," Medicine Man says, composing
himself. "He was part Choctaw and had a brother named Bennett. His brother
was a medic, too, attached to A Company. . . . This is hard to take, especially
since it was an atrocity."

Word comes: "B Company! Let's go!" The battalion withdraws under a
moonlit night. B Company takes positions in what looks like a kafir cornfield.

Sergeant Grant Shield Chief appears with a canteen cup in hand. "*Tiwat,
cutur lakets-kaw tit?*" (Cousin, have any coffee?)

I answer, "No."

Grant says, "Let's go over to the right. Matlock and his men are digging
in there, maybe they got coffee." I take my canteen cup, hopeful they'll have
some joe. I walk past our guys, who are sleeping. Moving right through the

dark field, I hear digging. We approach men who are digging. To our surprise they are Germans! Armed only with our canteen cups, we do a "to-the-rear" march. Moving quietly, we gather some men and capture the Germans. Surprised, they offer no resistance. We take all eight of them to Battalion. There we learn that they are part of a group infiltrating for an early morning attack. We also find out that a tobacco factory is near and that we're in the middle of a tobacco field. The company withdraws to tighten the line. Weary, we try to sleep, but harassing German artillery fire keeps us awake throughout the night.

Dawn comes and we are up for counterattack time. This time the counterattack comes. It starts as we ride out another German 88 barrage in our foxholes. When it lifts, ten Panzers attack. Behind the tanks, German infantry follows. From behind us, and overhead, whooshing sounds are heard. Clouds of dust rise: it's American ordnance! At last we have artillery support, which rains down on the enemy. It bolsters our spirits. The attacking Panzers are hit, sending turrets, steel side plates, bits of steel, and tracks whirling through the air. The German soldiers following the tanks disappear in the explosions' clouds of smoke and dust. Some make it through, only to meet our BARs and light machine guns, which cut them down. What few are left weave and stagger before being picked off by M1 fire. When the dust and smoke clear, tanks are aflame. The fields and trees around us burn. The German dead and wounded lie out there in the burning grass. We cease fire.

We pant and perspire like boxers after a hard-slugging round. I do a quick check of the squad; everyone is okay. I check my ammo and notice I'm low. I feel my body shake. The sun is now up. Hungry, I eat a K-ration breakfast of dehydrated eggs with a cracker biscuit. I daydream I could make a fire for hot coffee.

Medicine Man comes to check on the platoon. "Everybody okay? The government hospital is now open. Broken arm, '88 fever,' green apple two-step—but first you got to fill out forms in triplicate."

Shit! Another counterattack hits. Medicine Man takes off as we all sink into our foxholes to escape the German artillery. All around us are explosions that shake the earth, sending clods of dirt raining down. The rumble of tanks is heard approaching our position. I take a quick prairie-dog look and see infantrymen huddled behind the approaching tanks. Waves of friendly artillery whoosh overhead and explode on the Germans, making the Panzers burst into flames. Bodies cartwheel around the Panzers, leaving only a few tanks to break through. They fan out on our front. A bazooka fires at one rolling toward our right flank. The rocket shell streaks above the ground, hits a rise, and sails over the tank. An antitank grenade fires, hitting the turret with a glancing blow, sending the grenade flying end over end. The Panzer swerves. Another antitank grenade fires, hitting the rear of the tank—the engine. Still moving, smoke billows from the tank's rear. Finally the tank goes up in flames. The crew scrambles out with clothing afire. Screaming, they are shot down by M1 fire. The other Panzers withdraw.

Messerschmitts pass over treetop high, heading for the beach. We stay low in our holes. My heart pounds like the hoofbeats of a runaway horse. The day grows hot as artillery fire erupts all along the beachhead line. I have a K-ration dinner, a small can of cheese, and a cracker biscuit. I have powdered lemonade but can't spare water, so I throw it away.

A runner comes up and tells Lieutenant Anson something. Then the lieutenant calls out: "Second Platoon! Let's go!" Platoon Sergeant Stone parrots the same. We move a quarter of a mile to a road where we come to a stop. "Second and Third Squad, move up to that road bend. First Squad, here in reserve. We are to protect the left flank and dig in. Okay, move out," the lieutenant says.

Sergeant Good Buffalo and I move our squads for the road bend about a hundred yards away. Trees with communication wire hung in the branches line the road, with sunflowers at the edge. A small road connects from the left, coming from the west. Beyond is the road bend. Here, we dig in. Then Good Buffalo and I scout ahead, where we come to another road bend. As we move closer we see in the road a knocked-out German half-track. Ahead of it are woods where the sound of Panzers moving about moans from its depths. We return and then send a man to inform Lieutenant Anson. I tell our antitank men and bazooka men to get ready fast. Suddenly a tank appears. It is yellowish and muddy brown. On the front of the tank are spare tracks. Buttoned up, the Panzer stops to check things out. Shouldering a bazooka, our bazooka man eases up from his slit trench. The loader slips a rocket shell in the rear of the tube, then taps the bazooka man on the helmet: *loaded*. The antitank grenade men take aim. "Wait till he gets closer. Make sure we get a hit," Good Buffalo cautions. "Aim for the tracks."

Behind, on the road linking from the west, comes the sound of vehicles. One is a white panel truck. Another vehicle looks like an ambulance, painted olive drab. They park, and lucky for them they are not seen by the Panzer because of the road bend and trees. On top of the "ambulance" vehicle are racks holding tripods with cameras. On the side is a sign: Pathé News.

A Navy officer in cotton khakis alights from the panel truck. Getting out of the news truck, too, is a man with a handheld camera. Fresh and looking well fed, the men stride forward. The camera man calls: "Hey, you soldiers! We'd like to take pictures!"

The Navy officer adds: "Yes, some of you stand up and wave!"

"Hell no!" one of our guys answers. "There are German tanks just up the road. Get down or you'll get us all killed!" They register shock before both run. The Navy officer sets fire to the white panel truck with a flare. Then he hops in the news truck. They spin out and speed away in a cloud of dust.

Still buttoned up and with a limited view, the German tank pulls back without incident. We breathe easy but stay ready—we know they are close. A runner comes and reports that the platoon will return to the company. We all saddle up and move out.

Upon returning to the company, we learn the 157th is now on our left trying to relieve the pressure. We hear the Germans are bringing in more tanks and infantry in an effort to break through to the beach. The First Battalion will hold this ground: Second and Third Battalions are up to their ears in Germans. We are told we could get hit any minute, so we don't attempt to rest. Everyone works to improve his foxhole. Some guys have pick mattocks and others have shovels. We exchange tools as we work. A shovel can scoop but can't hack the ground. A pick mattock can't scoop but can hack the ground. We scoop, hack, and sweat.

"Jerries! Jerries!" one of our men shouts: five tanks at our immediate front, followed by a company of infantry. The Panzers fire machine guns at our lines, sending the men scrambling for their holes. An American 105mm M101A1 howitzer barrage thunders into the advancing Germans in response. The scene is an explosion of dust, smoke, flying rocks, shrapnel, wheels, tracks, and turrets. Our machine guns open up and fire until the smoke and dust clear. The Germans are forced to retreat. Tanks are blown apart and burn where they were hit. Dead and wounded Germans lay on the ground ahead. Some convulse with pain; others cry out. A few Germans get to their feet and raise their hands. We take twelve prisoners.

The squad leaders check the men. No one is hit. Captain Lee calls the platoon leaders. Something's up . . . and it ain't good. We seat the prisoners on the ground. In this situation, we can't spare anyone to march them back.

Medicine Man comes to check the platoon. "Hey, you Indi'ns are soft on captives. In movies the heathen Redskins tie them down spread-eagle in an ant pile, then leave."

"Don't tempt me—I'm a paid-up heathen," Last Arrow remarks.

Medicine Man turns to Shield Chief: "These Germans don't look tired at all. And they appear arrogant as hell."

Shield Chief speaks: "This bunch was probing for a weak spot. When they find one, the Germans will make an all-out push to break through to the beach. This is probably why the captain called the platoon leaders. Medicine Man, what do you hear at Battalion?"

"The situation is bad," Medicine Man says, lighting up a cigar. "Colonel Hutchins, the regiment commander, had called for air support. Air Command said none could be spared. General Mark Clark, the Fifth Army commander, had toured the beach with newsmen. He reported conditions satisfactory and morale high."

"Baloney," Leading Fox scoffs. "A Bureau of Indian Affairs report."

"His morale is high. He probably had ham and eggs, pancakes, and hot coffee for breakfast," Last Arrow adds.

The German prisoners chatter and sing. Last Arrow approaches them: "Hands on your heads!" he barks, motioning with his hands.

A blond-headed German stands: "Come now, Sergeant. We Germans will soon capture the American beach. You haven't a chance." Then he says something to his men; they snicker. Last Arrow looks at the man, grins mischievously, and walks to Leading Fox. He speaks with him in a low voice. Leading Fox moves back to San Antone, the Comanche, who lies in some bushes. He talks to San Antone, who looks at the Germans and nods. Leading Fox returns. He signs to Last Arrow "yes," then puts his hand to his forehead and clutches hair.

The prisoners start to sing as the German officer lights a cigarette. Last Arrow steps up to the blond German: "I warn you. Tell them to put their hands on heads, and be quiet."

"Foolishness, Sergeant," the German spouts with arrogance. "We shall crush you Americans with our superior infantry and tanks. In a short while you will be my prisoners. Ponder that."

Sergeant Last Arrow answers: "But you won't be alive in a short while. Of course you know of the Geneva Convention. Well, the Geneva Convention doesn't mean anything to us. We are American Indians." The blond German pales. He tells the others before the singing stops and their jaws drop.

Last Arrow turns from the officer. He winks at Leading Fox, who nods to San Antone. Then the Comanche gives a piercing war cry and comes running with a knife in hand. He tackles the officer, downing him hard.

Leading Fox shouts: "No scalp um! No scalp um!" He dives on San Antone.

Last Arrow swan-dives, dramatically, joining the melee. "No! No!" The Comanche clutches a fistful of blond hair and presses the blade to the man's forehead. Leading Fox and the German strain to hold back the knife. The man's eyes bug out as veins swell on his temples. Last Arrow struggles for a half nelson. There's a thrashing of arms and legs as they wriggle about. The shriek of a Comanche war cry makes the German prisoners look as though they are about to have heart attacks.

Finally, the Comanche is restrained. Sergeant Last Arrow reprimands him: "*Oologah Muskogee Tulsa Tahlequah!*"★ It's hard to keep from laughing. The officer is seated next to his men. With hair rumpled and shaken, he sits silent, his

★These are the names of various towns located in Oklahoma.

pupils dilated. Now with hands on heads, the German soldiers do not move. It's all quiet on the Western Front.

A few minutes later, we chat with San Antone, who says he almost blew the charade when Last Arrow bawled him out by naming towns in Oklahoma. Last Arrow grins: "I'm a Potawatomi and can't speak Comanche. I had to say something. By the way, San Antone, didn't know you could act. That was an Academy Award performance."

San Antone shrugs his shoulders. "I want to thank my producer, I want to thank my director and supporting cast."

"Hey, heard you Indi'ns caught some live ones." It's Private First Class Francis Brave, a six-foot-plus Sioux Indian from McCloud, Oklahoma. We have known him since mobilizing in 1940.

"*Aiay*, Brave! Long time, no see!" Leading Fox says.

The rest of us greet him. "Good to see you," Last Arrow says. "Last time we saw you was when you were arresting Ay-rabs in North Africa for robbing our soldiers."

Brave, who was Military Police, looks us over: "You guys okay? You've seen a lot of fighting since hitting Sicily. Everybody okay?"

"Y'ah, we're okay," Shield Chief reports.

"Good," Brave replies. "Phil, heard you got busted for drinking wine."

"Y'ah, what the heck—"

"It's bullshit. All soldiers drink, including the Brass. Even General Grant drank. Abraham Lincoln knew it. And he was president then. Well, I'm here to collect prisoners, boys."

Last Arrow nods to the prisoners: "Be our guest."

The big Sioux Indian lumbers toward them. They register fear. "Anyone speak English?" Brave thunders.

"I speak English, Sir," the officer bleats.

"Line up, keep your hands on heads. March!"

They are marched back where a two-and-a-half-ton truck waits with a load of German prisoners. The truck driver and Brave cram the prisoners in the overloaded truck. They try to squeeze the officer in, but he can't fit. Brave says to the driver: "Pull up, turn around, and come back. When I yell 'now,' hit the brakes." Returning, Brave shouts: "Now!" The driver brakes. Bodies thump into each other. The giant Sioux Indian grabs the officer by the collar and seat of his britches, pitching him headfirst up and into the truck like a bale of hay. Stuck headfirst, with legs up and kicking, the officer gives a muffled cry: "Geneva Convention! Geneva Convention!" The truck grinds gears and pulls away.

"Poor fellow," Last Arrow comments. "Everything's happened to him and General Custer. Thanks to us heathens."

Lieutenant Anson returns and assembles squad leaders and Platoon Sergeant Stone. Lieutenant Anson says the Second and Third Battalions are fighting off counterattacks and have taken casualties. He explains that we can't evacuate their wounded and that the Germans have pushed back the 157th at the left. We are to fix bayonets in order to save ammunition for a final stand.

"What about tank support, Lieutenant?" Good Buffalo asks.

"When the Germans took Persano the first time, their tanks pushed to the burning bridge and blocked our tanks and artillery. That's why we didn't have tank and artillery support. This way they could hold Persano as a jumping-off place to the beach without facing American tanks and artillery. Persano is the key to the beach. Right now, the Germans have the key."

We remain silent.

"Lieutenant, what's the name of the river at the burning bridge?" I ask.

"Calore," he answers. "There are two rivers. The Calore meets the main river, Sele, forming a fork. The Sele flows to the sea. Above the fork about three miles near the Sele is Persano. According to the map, Persano is on high ground overlooking a plain between the Sele and the Calore. The Germans are expected to drive down the plain, a corridor, for a breakthrough."

Evening comes and I eat a dehydrated fruit bar for supper. I save a cracker biscuit for tomorrow—*it's sure to be a long day*, I think to myself as I stuff it away. Two officers and a chaplain show up. From Corps Headquarters, they tell us we will likely be overrun in the morning. They instruct us to take everything from our pockets and billfolds that identifies our unit and explain that in the event we are overrun, we have dog tags in plain sight. If captured give only name, rank, and serial number. Before departing, the chaplain says, "God bless you, men." After they leave I remove a small Bible from my shirt pocket, given to me by Chaplain Theus of Oklahoma City back in 1941. On the first page is "B Co. 179th Inf." I tear it out and keep the Bible and place it with a notepad with drawings in it.

Twilight comes and I don't know what to think. No one in B Company talks surrender. We speak with Shield Chief about the possibility of "surrender." He makes the sign for "bad," then looks at us for a few seconds. Then he explains: "But we must follow orders, for we are soldiers." He pauses: "We are also Indi'ns, born warriors. Pawnees, *Chaticks-si-Chaticks*—Men of Men. We will see what morning brings."

Shield Chief has his prayer pipe in hand, but it isn't lit. "Remember the legend spoken by the old ones of the tribe that only one Pawnee will die in every major battle they are in. We won't all die, so come morning, fight like Men of Men. Try to sleep tonight. Sleep heals the body and strengthens the heart." Phillip Shield Chief puts the prayer pipe in his mouth and draws on it prayerfully, as though it were lit.

Harassing German artillery erupts across our front as men hurry to their holes. Last Arrow, Good Buffalo, and I decide to scout around. Last Arrow goes left. I take the middle. Good Buffalo takes the right. It is a starry night and there is a light breeze. I move quietly as fog rolls in. A wolf call comes from afar, but this time yipping follows. The yipping is a warning that the enemy is near. Ruling His Son, scouting too, creeps past enemy outposts. I keep moving and come upon a German vee trench, with radio, coils of wire, field equipment, and blocks of TNT. Everything is German, but the TNT is American, about the size of a brick. I find it odd that there are no Germans around. Radio men must be off in a bull session with buddies. I string the TNT with the wire before wrapping the wire around an ankle. I quietly dismantle the radio and begin to crawl away, dragging the TNT wire. I don't have to walk with my arms full, and I'm able to snail past the German outposts with the wire around my foot. Using the breeze to cover rustling sounds, I return safely back to our lines. The TNT will be put to good use come counterattack time. The harassing fire goes on all night. I get little sleep.

Dawn comes and we're bright-eyed and bushy-tailed for counterattack time. Taking a pair of GI socks from my pack, I knife a hole in the toes. I then take a grenade from one of the men and place it in the sock, passing the safety ring through the hole in the toe. I then press a block of TNT behind the grenade, wrapping the sock with some of the wire I brought back. I half-hitch the wire through the safety ring, which protrudes from the toe, and then take my grenade and do the same. The loaded socks are strung on the wire a few feet apart. Like roping a horse, this could be whirled and then slung into the tracks of a moving tank.

We are almost out of bazooka shells and luckily save two .03 antitank grenades. Desperate, we realize that we must stop the tanks. A heavy 88 barrage rains down on us as our slit trenches fog with dust. After several minutes, the German barrage lifts. Panzers and infantry begin their approach. I do a quick double-check of the wire, grenades, and TNT. From our rear, a sudden American 105 barrage slams in with a deafening sound. As the barrage finally lifts, we look forward and see the German tanks knocked out and aflame. A few of the German infantry stagger through smoke and dust before BAR and light machine guns cut them down. The remaining Germans retreat quickly. We do a quick check of our men to see if anyone's hit; everyone is okay.

Minutes later the Germans attack again, but once more BARs and machine guns cut them down. The Fourth Platoon hits them with a 60mm mortar barrage and we stop them again. Shaken, I once more check the squad. Wide-eyed, they've weathered the storm. Medicine Man, staying low, comes up to check on the platoon. There are calls for medics in the other platoons, as men are hit. *I hope no one was killed.* I decide to eat the cracker biscuit I saved yesterday evening for breakfast. There is no coffee this morning, but the morning sun feels good. I stay in my slit trench, making sure to keep my head down, and stay alert.

"B Company! Let's go!" I unhook grenades from my makeshift antitank weapon and return the one I borrowed. We pull back and join A, C, and D Companies. When the First Battalion is formed, we move out. The afternoon heat is fierce; each solder follows the man in front of him with the all-important interval. We're like a long line of wildebeest from Africa, plodding through heat waves in a documentary movie. Now and then the column moves like an accordion as it stretches and closes. Then the battalion stops before companies separate and dig in.

We are thirsty. Nearby is a creek bed that Shield Chief volunteers to take a few men to. He takes a pole to attach the canteens to with their covers on so they won't rattle. I go along in case he runs into any Germans. Shield Chief follows the creek bed, reading the ground as he moves. "Lots of people passed here. Americans. Germans." Then Shield Chief moves from the creek bed for a look; we follow. We spot an artillery outfit and men digging in.

Shield Chief waves to an officer.

The officer calls back: "Phillip Shield Chief! Good to see you!"

"It's Hal Muldrow," Shield Chief tells us. "He's a battalion commander."

We've been acquainted with Lieutenant Colonel Muldrow since 1940; we served together in the Oklahoma National Guard. He and Shield Chief chat. Colonel Muldrow points to the front, and to his howitzers, which have barrels leveled. The colonel takes the canteens from Shield Chief and has them filled from the unit's water supply.

I walk up to thank Colonel Muldrow. Shield Chief says, "Sir, you remember Sergeant Echohawk."

"Oh, yes," Colonel Muldrow responds, smiling. "Last time I saw you, you were a corporal during maneuvers at Pitkin, Louisiana."

"Pitkin, Lousy-aha, Sir."

"Right," the colonel grins.

"Thank you for the water, Sir." Shield Chief says. "We better get back. Don't want to miss the massacre party. Our guests may arrive early. We want to give them a warm welcome."

"There you go," Colonel Muldrow chuckles as we leave.

Shield Chief tells us what the colonel said, explaining that the beach was in jeopardy. The colonel had told Shield Chief that we had to bring up clerks, cooks, and truck drivers to plug the line. Muldrow said his unit was also about out of ammunition. That is why he had lowered the barrels. He set fuses for five hundred yards to explode in the faces of advancing infantrymen, which is called "red firing." But Colonel Muldrow called it an old Civil War trick. It will be a punch in the mouth the Germans won't forget. After that the breeches of the howitzers are destroyed. Then everybody is to fight to the last man. The 155mm howitzer shell is big—it weighs about 95 pounds. It is lobbed into the enemy lines with devastating impact. Colonel Muldrow will destroy not only the German infantry but also a good part of the Italian landscape in the process. I glance back, seeing Colonel Muldrow walking among the men digging in. His people—the Chickasaw—served as an ally of the Confederacy under General Jackson and in the Civil War.

Returning to the company, everyone is improving his foxhole. Evening comes and I'm hungry. I try to stay alert, but three days of fighting without sleep is telling. The sound of heavy fire is heard on the left. I figure maybe the 157th is trying to regain lost ground. From Colorado, they're a fightin' bunch.

I doze.

"B Company! Let's go!"

I wake up; it's dark. We pull back from the front, tired and sleepy. No one talks. It sounds like packhorses plodding through the night as we move along the sandy ground. The company halts and is ordered to disperse. Beyond, we see the sea, where, parked nearby with interval, are tanks and other vehicles. We are issued water and rations. Hungry, we tear into the K-rations. Lieutenant Anson calls the squad leaders and says we are in reserve at a critical point in the line where the Germans could break through. He explains that we are to brace for the worst.

We dig in as an air raid begins. Above, German bombers drone as thousands of glowing red tracers rise from the beach. They fountain into the night sky, racing toward the enemy bombers. At sea, transports, heavy landing craft, gunships, destroyers, and cruisers also open fire. The heavens flicker and rumble. On the beach there is a chain reaction of bomb flashes with heavy explosions. The Americans on the beach take a pounding. Beachhead attack. Guns fire continuously, making spent flak fall from the sky. Pieces of flak the size of apple cores to hatchet blades hit the ground everywhere. We make sure to keep our steel helmets on. We sit, lock arms around knees, and make ourselves as small as possible. A slit trench is no protection from falling flak. I see men crawl under parked vehicles. Some of us crawl under a tank with the crew buttoned up. When the air raid finally ends there are ammo and gasoline dumps ablaze. The beach is quiet again.

As quiet sets in I begin to fall asleep. Right as I begin to doze off another air raid moves in. The antiaircraft fire at night over Salerno beachhead is a giant spectacle. Beautiful—but you don't say it because men are being killed. Beauty like this shouldn't be the cause of death. The beach is again bombed heavily. As the German bombers drone inland and circle for another pass, a plane with a different-sounding motor follows. Red tracers appear before the bomber is hit, making it fall from the night sky in flames and explode into fiery pieces.

We gape at the sight. Shield Chief says a British night fighter made the kill—a Beaufighter. Equipped with radar, they were built in 1940 to be used at night in the Battle of Britain. Beaufighters patrol the skies at night over the beach; by day it's the American Mustangs and British Spitfires.

It again rains flak as we crawl under vehicles. When the raid ends, we return to our foxholes. The bombers return again as more antiaircraft fires into the air. More gasoline and ammo dumps are hit. They explode, making the beach glow red with fire. Spent flak falls and clangs on top of the vehicles we are under. After a long and exhausting night at Salerno beachhead, we finally drop off to sleep.

Morning comes and we are ordered to move forward. We cross a river and follow it to a burned bridge. There we find American dead who have .03 Springfield rifles, with grenade launchers attached, in their hands. Scattered about are antitank grenades. We dig in along the river and build a small fire for coffee. It is our first hot coffee in days. I eat a cold K-ration breakfast. The flowing river with trees along the bank is peaceful. However, no birds sing; if they were, it would be like home. Machine gun fire erupts, sending us diving for slit trenches as the fast-firing German gun whirls like a riveting machine. Another rings out, raking our front, producing cracks and zings as lead rounds hit near us. I take a quick prairie-dog look and see Germans wading the river and firing machine pistols. The machine pistols have short barrels—not too accurate. Bullets strike the ground, raising cotton balls of dust in the air.

Last Arrow and Good Buffalo raise and shout: "Let 'em have it!" I do the same. We all open fire. Some Germans fall, thrashing in the water, while others whirl and splash for the bank as we keep dropping them. The Germans who escape our onslaught disappear in the woods. I reload and get busy improving the slit trench before they hit us again. Messerschmitts pass over, streaking for the beach. American Mustangs respond and jump them. The enemy fighters climb sharply with Mustangs on their tails—a real dogfight. We can't see them, but we can hear the motors and their guns. The German infantry attacks again. This time they are ferocious as they fire machine pistols and shout things in German. They keep coming. The attack is fantastic. Our Fourth Platoon's light machine guns mow them down. BARs, M1s, .03s, tommy-guns, .45 automatics, and grenades stop them dead in their tracks. Things fall quiet as the moving river carries German dead downstream.

There is a lull, and I learn no one has been hit. The firefight really heated up my M1. I decide to clean it, losing the ejector spring in the process. I tell Cheyenne about it and pass word that I'm going to the Battalion Aid Station to get a wounded man's rifle. I won't give up my rifle, though, as it was one of the first Garand M1s issued to us in Texas. The sights and windage are zeroed in for my kind of shooting.

Trotting back, I meet an American half-track rolling toward a support position that points me in the direction of Command. I head for B Company's Command Post to ask where the Aid Station is. As I approach the CP an 88 explodes nearby with a loud boom. I hit the ground. I look down and notice my shoe is blown off. With heavy dust around I call for a medic. The company commander is also hit. Captain Glen I. Lee, from Pawnee, Oklahoma, is given first aid. He has a bandage wrapped around his head as he is helped onto the stretcher. As he is carried away, Glen looks at me, dazed, and says: "See you back at Pawnee."

At the Battalion Aid Station I find a rifle, remove the bolt, and leave. The half-track I met earlier is backing into a draw. It grinds back and forth to where its 75 will be level with the ground. One of the crewmen directs the driver. Dust rises as the half-track moves. *Not good,* I think, so I move away quickly. Minutes later, German shells bracket in. Diving for cover, I see the American half-track erupt into flames. Metal parts and tracks whirl into the air and fall to the ground. A steel helmet drops to the ground and rolls; it looks like there is a head in it.

I move back into the squad area, where I take my M1 and insert the new bolt. Cheyenne asks about that explosion. I tell him a half-track was moving around, raising dust. The Germans spotted the dust and hit the half-track. Cheyenne says Lieutenant Anson wants to see me. I report to him immediately. Anson instructs me to take my squad up the river about a quarter of a mile to guard the right flank and that I am to take the platoon's bazooka and extra men along. The squad moves out.

Upriver, we see American dead with Springfields that have grenade launchers attached. Lying about are antitank grenades. The ground is torn by shell fire from tanks. We follow an oxcart trail across the barren ground; I signal "hold." I check the gullies ahead, returning to find the men dozing. We've had days without sleep, and all those air raids last night only made it worse. Three Sherman tanks rumble from the right rear. They have markings like the British, with white circles. In Sicily, American tanks had white stars on them. I wave at the man in the turret of the first tank; some of my men wave too. The tanker waves back. I remember the men killed back there by Panzers—and think of what could happen ahead. I shout: "Go back!" The tanker doesn't hear, as his motor's too loud. I position the men where to dig in. The ground is hard, so they dig a little and lie down to snooze. The three Shermans return. They are in a hurry, buttoned up, turret guns pointed to the rear. Most of the men remain asleep.

Time passes before different tanks appear across the gullies. "British tanks!" the BAR man calls out. "They are coming back!"

Cheyenne snaps back: "You guys were asleep! The British came back a while ago. Those tanks are not British!"

With that, I stand and take a good look. "They are not Shermans!" I note. The men get to their feet and look.

Black crosses on the tanks. "Germans!" The men scatter.

Cheyenne and I stay. I yell to Private Wintsell, who transferred from an artillery unit. I tell him to get artillery fire. I shout for the bazooka and antitank grenade men. They come running. Cheyenne and I are on a knoll near an ox-cart trail that leads to some gullies. On the right side of the trail is a rundown barbed wire fence. Behind, for a quarter mile, the land is flat and treeless.

Eight Panzers approach. In the first tank a man stands upright in the turret. Scared, I lie low and think: *If I run, the men will run too. Then the German tanks will machine-gun and crush us like they did C Company's men at Persano.* Wearing earphones, the German in the turret looks my way. I stand and shoot, hitting him in the face. His earphones fly as he drops. The tank stops and the rest follow. They mill and rumble into the gullies before the lead tank backs up.

Houston Cox, the antitank grenade man, and I crawl forward. Bisby, the ammo carrier, follows behind us. Cheyenne covers us as we move to position ourselves. A tank emerges from a gully at the left front and rumbles across our front about thirty yards away. Cox fires an antitank grenade, causing an explosion. The tank wobbles into a gully. Nearby, the bazooka man cries in panic: "This damn bazooka won't fire!" He and the ammo carrier run for it. Suddenly I see another tank coming up the oxcart trail. We fire as explosions shake the earth, causing dust to rise. With a clanking noise, the Panzer disappears into a draw.

"We're out of grenades!" Bisby cries. As the tanks pull back, I remember the American dead with antitank grenades back there. I tell Cheyenne I'm running to the river and to take the antitank grenades from the dead we saw there. I consider my route, thinking: *If I run across our front straight for the river I can move downstream and find our dead. If I run to the rear, then to the river, I might not end up in the right place.* Realizing that I would lose valuable time searching if I went through the rear, I decide to cross our front.

As I jackrabbit across our front, my shoe flaps from being partly shot away. Suddenly small-arms fire kicks up dust around me. I figure it is probably the German tank crew and try to keep moving. When I finally reach the river, I turn downstream, where I find our dead. I stuff my shirt with antitank grenades and grab a web cartridge belt. I dash back across the front and am fired on again. I make it back to our position, where Cheyenne says that Cox and Bisby took off. Chey' explains that they didn't think I'd make it back, but they left the .03 Springfield. They say it is useless now. An incoming 88 barrage is heard before it thunders on the oxcart trail. As we flatten out, a shell hits the barbed wire fence. A strand of barbed wire hits my steel helmet. I also take splinters of wood in the right arm and shoulder. I can't hear very well, but I can hear the loud motors of Panzers. Cheyenne and I ready the antitank grenades and .03 Springfield. I frantically search the web cartridge belt for blank rounds used to launch the grenades and find none. Desperate, I pull the pins and throw the antitank grenades at the tanks bearing down on us, hoping they'll explode—but they don't. We fire M1s at the slits. From the rear an American artillery barrage explodes on us and the Panzers. The ground shakes as Cheyenne and I hug Mother Earth in a storm of steel. We can hear the German tanks withdrawing as the 105 barrage lifts.

We move back. A heavy-caliber machine gun fires at us. It comes from an American tank destroyer way back there who seemingly mistakes us for German soldiers attacking with Panzers. The .50-caliber slugs explode in the nearby dirt. In the open, I chance it and stand. I turn my left shoulder forward, waving frantically. I point to the shoulder, hoping they're watching through binoculars and can see my shoulder patch. They cease fire. Then the German tanks spot the American tank destroyer and open fire on it. The American tank destroyer races back across the plain, raising a column of dust, swerving now and then to avoid hits as the German tanks keep firing. Exploding mushrooms of dust follow the American tank destroyer as it barrels away with our last hope of support.

"Ecky, look back there!" Cheyenne shouts. I look and spot a huge German tank near a stone house about half a mile away. We run as the ground here is bare, giving us no cover. We come upon our men down flat and not moving. They've seen the big tank too.

"We'll form a line and relay word back," I tell Cheyenne. "Maybe we can get fire on that tank. Let's hope someone behind us will pick up the call. Worth the try."

"We got to do something. When that big tank comes, the others will come too. It will be bad," Cheyenne says.

"Hey, you guys!" I yell to the men. "On your feet; form a line looking back," I say. "We will take up a wide interval so we can relay word to the rear. On the double!" The men form a line with an interval of fifty yards. "Wider! Hundred yards!"

The men move quickly. "That thing's comin'. Got dog! It's a Tiger tank with an 88 gun!" Cheyenne exclaims.

I call to the men at the head of the line: "Tank. Immediate front. Eight hundred yards. Near stone house!"

The word is relayed back.

"Seven hundred and fifty yards!" The Tiger tank seems as big as a locomotive.

"Six hundred!" That big thing keeps coming.

"Five hundred and fifty!" I hear other tanks rev their motors and am scared.

"Four hundred and fifty . . . four hundred!" An explosion with a mushroom of dust appears close to the tank.

"Three fifty!" A hit. Smoke rolls from the Tiger tank. It backs up with dust exploding nearby. The Tiger reaches a stone house and moves behind it. A column of smoke rises from behind the house as the other Panzers retreat. The men cheer wildly. I don't know if a mortar or artillery observer brought that fire. All we know is that a Tiger tank was put out of action—and the Panzer attack was stopped. We stay ready. For we all know they could come again.★

Evening comes as my squad withdraws and rejoins the platoon. Lieutenant Anson and Sergeant Stone meet us. I tell them about the nine German tanks; their eyes widen. The lieutenant asks if anyone got hit. I answer, "No." Both mention hearing barrages and seeing the tank destroyer run to avoid enemy fire. Lieutenant Anson says we have no company commander and that Lieutenant Lancaster, who was second-in-command, got blown out of his foxhole and was evacuated. The lieutenant studies the front, then instructs us to tighten our line. Immediately, Sergeant Stone turns, walks to the men, and bellows: "All right, gotdammit! Let's be improving those foxholes!" Later, I search a knocked-out half-track nearby for ammo and grenades. I see a tommy-gun with a full clip and take it. We are just about out of ammo.

As night falls a few of us visit Shield Chief's slit trench. He's glad to see us. Medicine Man joins us. "Say, Echo, heard you shot a German riding in the turret of a tank."

"Had to do something," I reply.

Cheyenne pipes up: "Really dropped him. The tank stopped."

Medicine Man continues: "The guys think he was the tank commander 'cause their attack stalled. Knocking out one tank, and blasting another, made them think we had antitank guns."

The bazooka man cuts in: "That's when my bazooka didn't fire. Guess the batteries got wet or something crossing the river earlier. I took off."

Bisby perks up. "Nobody wants to get squashed by Panzers. When firing our last antitank grenade, we took off too!"

Some men lie on their side smoking, with raincoats over their heads. This way the glow of a cigarette can't be seen at night. They talk of Panzers following

---

★For his actions in halting the advance of the German Panzer column, the Army awarded Brummett Echohawk the Bronze Star.

an 88 barrage, and our 105 barrage, and mention Cheyenne and me shooting at the slits of the tanks where the driver looks through. An M1 slug through there could ricochet inside and hit somebody or even hit the tank ammo. Wintsell, who was sent back for artillery fire, made contact, as the American barrage came at the right time. The Germans couldn't break through, so they called for support. And that's when the Tiger tank showed. I listen to them talk but can't hear well. Drained, I fall asleep sitting up.

When I wake, everyone is sacked out. I return to my hole as German shells pass over, whizzing toward the rear trying to knock out American artillery. American shells whiz back, trying to knock out German artillery. A starry night; I doze off again.

Cheyenne wakes me. "Ecky, outpost man came in. He says the Jerries are moving around across the river. He told Lieutenant Anson. Now Anson wants everybody up and on alert." Beyond the river, a Roman candle arcs into the night sky, falls, then burns out. My M1 with bayonet is handy at the right side of my slit trench. I also hold the tommy-gun I took from that knocked-out half-track. The Roman candle is a signal of some sort. I hear footsteps in the immediate front. They are hobnail boots! I cut loose with the tommy-gun; it flashes and kicks rapidly, ejecting brass with sparks as M1 fire joins in. There is no return fire, and we spot dark figures running for the river. It was a German patrol, probing for a weak spot in the line. My heart pounds as it grows quiet again. I hear the faint sound of planes in the distance and look up. The motors roar in a dive as thousands of red tracers stream down in the dark. These are American planes strafing German positions. Before the Germans can hit back with antiaircraft fire, it's over and our planes escape. Probably P-38s, twin-engine jobs, noted for diving and strafing. I was hungry; now I'm not. I was scared, too; now I'm not. Too tired and sleepy to care.

This September night is noisy with big shells approaching like freight trains. Passing over and streaking forward, they glow red. As they become smaller and smaller they disappear before the impact, flash, and rumble is heard. It's the American Navy shelling German positions. The bombardment jars the whole Italian peninsula, it seems. Timber along the river burns as the countryside is flooded with red light from the inferno. The night air is filled with smoke and dust. Exhausted, I sink into my slit trench and fall asleep to the sound of shelling.

I dream I'm in Pawnee, Oklahoma. It is a funeral being held at the small weather-beaten house where I was born. Pawnees often have funerals at the home of the deceased. A casket is open, but covered with a veil, and an American flag is under a mulberry tree. A mockingbird at the top of the tree flies up and down, singing. I climbed the tree many times as a little boy, where I viewed the horizon, dreaming of seeing faraway places. All I saw were buffalo grazing. They belonged to Pawnee Bill, a Wild West showman who had buffalo on his ranch. Old men sing a warrior's song. There is crying.

Good Fox, the tribal spokesman, steps to the casket. Speaking in the Pawnee tongue, he says:

> A tall tree has fallen. It leaves an empty place in the forest. Birds and animals mourn. A soft breeze whispers words of comfort. Tears of rain will fall on the empty place. The sun will shine there. A green shoot will appear. It becomes a tree. Life in the forest begins again. In *Tirawa's* plan, no life is ever lost. These tears are not ones of sorrow. They are tears of honor I shed for you. You were a warrior—men of men.

I must have been killed at Salerno. My body shipped home. My face is powdered. Wax on my lips. I lie with my hands folded. *I'm not dead . . . I'm not dead.* I open my eyes: the "casket" is my slit trench. The veil covering is a mosquito net worn over the steel helmet for camouflage. I pull it over my face at night to protect against mosquitoes. The powder on my face is dust from the Navy barrage. The wax on my lips: dryness from not drinking enough water.

Not fully awake, I hear a voice: "Look at the dawn sky. *Hupiri-Kucu,* God's messenger, signals the coming of a new day. All will be well." It is the voice of my father, who died before the division came overseas. He sings the Pawnee Morning Song.

I wake up. *Hupiri-Kucu*—the Morning Star—above the Italian mountains reflects like a signal mirror. Beautiful. The dream tells me I was about to crack up. Three days of fighting with no rest, seeing men killed, and almost getting killed myself has taken its toll. I think back to seeing bodies of our guys crushed by German tanks and what happened to my friends Freeny the medic and Dan Quick Bear. There was also that earthshaking Navy barrage.

It's a wonder anyone is sane.

As the sun rises I stand. My legs and back are stiff. At the right, Corporal Leading Fox rises from his slit trench. Rubbing his ankles and knees, he says: "Now the foot bone connected to the ankle bone." Singing, he raises his hands, "Hallelujah! Hear the word of the Lord!" He shuffles forward. Guys laugh and join Leading Fox in "Dry Bones."

"Hey, what's going on?" It's Shield Chief.

"After that Navy barrage, it's great to be alive," Leading Fox replies.

"Hallelujah!" others sing out.

"I'll buy that," Shield Chief says.

"Me too!" Sergeant Last Arrow adds. "But let's get to our holes. It's counterattack time." We move to our holes, but no counterattack comes. I uncoil and wolf down a K-ration breakfast.

Medicine Man approaches. He has a canteen cup of K-ration coffee and biscuit crumbs on his lips. "Say, how's things on the reservation?" He smiles, showing his perfect white teeth.

Sergeant Good Buffalo answers: "Well, on the reservation all is well with the FBI, full-blood Indi'ns."

Shield Chief cuts in: "Medicine Man, what's the latest from Battalion and Regiment?"

"First off"—Medicine Man takes a sip of coffee—"Second Battalion is near. We were pulled back 'cause Regiment wanted them clear of the Navy barrage. I got to see my medic buddies attached to the Second Battalion who said that when they landed on the first day an Indi'n soldier charged onto the beach and drove a feathered lance into the sand, shouting: 'Christopher Columbus, we are here!'"

We all laugh. Fitting after Columbus's visit in 1492—but nothing a general would say at this landing.

Medicine Man chuckles. He tells us E Company got a hoot out of this. He says the soldier's name was Two Hatchets. I tell them we in B Company know him.

"Two Hatchets, a Cheyenne, has a cousin here."

Cheyenne pipes up: "That's me!"

Medicine Man sips the last of his coffee. "They said Two Hatchets chased a lot of screaming chickens in Sicily for feathers. Figured he would use a lance like a true Cheyenne warrior."

"Amen," Cheyenne voices with pride.

"I second the motion," Leading Fox adds.

Medicine Man goes on: "The 157th is fighting like a junkyard bulldog and pushing the Germans back. No word about the 180th. Well, about the Big Brass, some battalion officers listened to our tank radios, which pick up BBC London at night. They heard BBC announce that General Montgomery and his British Eighth Army are rushing up the boot of Italy to rescue the Americans at Salerno."

Sergeant Last Arrow scoffs at that notion: "Montgomery wants all the glory, just like in Sicily when he wanted the Americans to protect his flank while he captured the important cities. Didn't turn out that way 'cause General Patton broke loose after that."

Leading Fox joins in: "Compared to Patton, Montgomery rushes like a turtle."

"This guy was a replacement. I believe he was from Wisconsin. He was a handsome man. Had a hero look about him. He had a friend that wore a mustache like Clark Gable. Both wanted to be in the 'Indian Company.'" October 1943.

While there is a lull I decide to go back to the aid station to find a right shoe. My shoe is torn by shrapnel. I tell Cheyenne where I'm going and move out. Back near Battalion Headquarters, I find a soldier's packs on the ground. I ask a soldier at Battalion who the packs belong to. He explains, saying that they had belonged to replacements and guys returning from hospitals who were caught in a barrage that killed most of them. He continues, offering that the Grave Registration Unit removed the bodies. The packs are full, with one blanket roll and an extra pair of shoes attached. I take a right shoe that looks like my size. I notice the name on the pack: Private Anthony Cematarro. He was in my squad for a while before coming down with yellow jaundice. I feel sad and return to the platoon.

When I return to the platoon I see Private John Seely, who was hit in Sicily, and has returned to duty, talking to the BAR man. I also see Pete Miller and Cheyenne. Seely and Miller are buddies. Pete is 6'3" and Seely is short. Together they look like Charles de Gaulle and Mickey Rooney.

I greet Seely: "Hey, Seely! Welcome home!"

"Sergeant Ecky! Glad to be back!"

Seely has a bugle, tied with a cord hanging around his neck. I glance at it: "What you got that thing for?"

He fingers the bugle like a child with a new toy. "When B Company attacks, I'm going to blow charge." We look at the bugle, look at Seely, and then look at each other. John Seely, who is very young, beams.

The order comes down, "B Company! Let's go!" We move out.

The First Battalion joins the Second and Third Battalions. According to the angle of the sun, the 179th is heading in the same direction taken yesterday. Something is up; we walk at a fast pace. The Fourth Platoon, lugging heavy weapons, has difficulty keeping up. After a while, the column stops. We learn that we are to plug a gap between the American VI Corps and British X Corps. We dig in. The 179th advanced twenty-two miles inland three days ago; now we are pushed back to within four miles from the sea. The Germans are wolves that have a buck deer at bay.

The Germans smell blood and move in for the kill. Now, the buck deer lowers its horns as the Germans strike the 179th with a seemingly infinite supply of Panzers and infantry. The 157th on the left is hit hard. We take a heavy barrage before an American counterbarrage shields us. Light machine guns of the Fourth Platoon open up before everybody starts shooting. Shells flash and thunder as shrapnel flies. The ground shakes as it begins to rain clumps of dirt. Through the din, we hear a bugle. I take a quick prairie-dog look and see a bugle poking above the ground. On his back in a slit trench, Private Seely sounds *charge*. Stuttering but spirited, the bugle sounds loud. *He's something else*, I think. I sink down and begin to hear German tanks. The American barrage intensifies. Bleeding, the wolf pack breaks. The Germans fall back, leaving burning tanks, wounded, and dead scattered on the battlefield. However, we do not go untouched. The 157th Regimental Combat Team and all three battalions of the 179th RCT suffer heavy casualties in this fight.

Evening comes and the September heat lingers. Some of us are out of ammo and grenades. Low on water and tired, we eat a cold K-ration supper.

Medicine Man joins us. We ask for the latest. Weary, he perks up: "First, want to tell you a funny story." He clears his throat. A happy tone comes to his voice: "There is the Shah of Iran. Before, he was known as the Shan. He had a castle and a harem of beautiful women. One day, the Shan went off on a state visit and left his sons in charge. Upon returning, he found his sons living it up and in bed with all the beautiful women. Then the fit hit the Shan." *Ugh*—we laugh as some are slow catching on. Medicine Man is just trying to lift our spirits.

Medicine Man continues: "Well, the shit hit the fan for all of us. The Germans about had our scalps. They are a determined bunch. A while back, I met some Second Battalion medics who said E Company was in a hot shoot-out. The enemy stopped shooting about fifty yards away from them and approached, waving a white flag. When they got close, the Germans dropped the white flag and started shooting. E Company didn't buy that." He continues: "For the country boys from Beggs, Oklahoma, it was a turkey shoot; they killed them all.

"Now, about the Big Brass. You'll be happy to hear that General Mark Clark moved his headquarters and staff from their ship to the beach now."

"Great news, I'm sure," Leading Fox says. "Where did General Clark come from? He wasn't in Sicily. Wasn't in the North African campaign. Thought General Patton would command troops landing in Italy."

"Not after he slapped that soldier in the hospital back in Sicily," Shield Chief says. "The soldier was there for his nerves, but General Patton called him a coward. He got in hot water in Washington, and the press wanted General Patton's scalp. And, about General Mark Wayne Clark. In 1942, when the British fought the Germans in Egypt, General Clark made a secret mission by submarine near Algiers where he met with an important French general. General Clark wanted to make sure French troops did not oppose the Americans when invading French North Africa at Casablanca." He continues: "Since the Germans defeated France in 1940, they had the French under their heel. General Clark saved American and French lives and helped the Allied cause. With Americans advancing from the west and the British from the east, they pushed the Germans out of North Africa."

"Oh," we say.

Having attended Bacone Indian College and Oklahoma Baptist University, Phillip Shield Chief has a lot of smart under his warbonnet.

"Well, General Clark must be okay, then," Leading Fox says, signing "good" to Shield Chief.

I join in: "The best generals we got are General Troy Middleton, our division commander, and General Raymond S. McClain, the artillery commander."

"Say, speaking of General McClain," Medicine Man comes on. "Heard some artillery guys back there say General McClain drove a truckload of artillery shells under fire to one of his units that was about to be overrun, and that the unit was out of ammo too. General McClain from Oklahoma City is a brave and caring man."

"All squad leaders!" bellows Platoon Sergeant Stone. "All squad leaders!" Last Arrow, Good Buffalo, and I meet with Sergeant Stone and Lieutenant Anson, our platoon leader. Lieutenant Anson has just returned from a meeting of platoon leaders and First Lieutenant John Heller, the new company commander. We are to double the guard tonight because the Germans may try a night attack. Battalion expects them to launch an all-out attack in the morning regardless. Anson continues explaining that the American beachhead is in danger of being lost. He shows fear, as does Sergeant Stone. We squad leaders return to positions and fill the men in on the situation. We dig in deeper and improve our defensive positions.

Night falls; back at the beach more German air raids start. We can hear the antiaircraft fire in the distance. Now and then German bombers pass over, circle, and return to bomb the beach again. Though tired and sleepy, we stay alert for a possible night attack. Dawn arrives, and we are bleary-eyed come counterattack time. We have our bayonets fixed and keep all eyes on the front.

Sun's up and no German counterattack comes. I eat a cold K-ration and burn a K-ration box, using twigs to heat a cup of water for hot coffee. I keep watch and stay ready. Midmorning comes; it is a clear day. American bombers drone inland. Mustangs flash over to strafe the enemy before us. British Spitfires patrol the skies over the beachhead for bombers. We hear Corporal Leading Fox singing "Dry Bones" as he rises out of his slit trench and rubs his legs. Other men stand and move about to get the kinks out of their legs and backs. We stay put the whole day. We guess that the Germans have pulled back, bloodied and bruised like us. The Salerno beachhead has been costly for both sides.

During the evening I eat a dehydrated fruit bar for supper. Cheyenne and I go visit Shield Chief's slit trench. Good Buffalo, Last Arrow, and Leading Fox are there, talking. I didn't have to go through an 88 barrage, face Panzers, or fight off fanatic German infantry today; it feels good. Medicine Man drops by, and we hear the latest. Battalion gets orders and rumors from Regiment. Regiment gets things from Division. Division from Corps. Corps from Fifth Army. And the big chief at Army Headquarters is General Mark Clark.

As a joke, I ask Medicine Man: "What's General Clark going to do with us now?"

"Funny you ask that, Echo," Medicine Man replies. "Battalion and Regiment have it that General Clark called a meeting of his generals. During the meeting General Clark talked of evacuating the beach. The two division commanders and a high Navy officer objected. General Walker of the 36th Division and General Middleton of the 45th got their feathers up. General Middleton

D Company (heavy machine gunners), 179th Regiment, crosses the Volturno River, Italy, October 19, 1943.

left the meeting in anger, saying, 'Put food and ammunition behind the 45th. We are going to stay!'"

We look at each other. We are grimy, exhausted, and beat up. But if they attack again, we'll do as Will Rogers said to the Germans after World War I: "If you birds try that again, we'll give you the other barrel." We think about what General Middleton said about leaving food and ammo behind the 45th, and stay we did. The battle for Salerno beachhead had been won.

We fight steadily from Salerno. By night, we Indians run patrols behind the German lines. By day, we shoot it out with them for villages, river bends, olive groves, and for high ground terraced with stone walls and grape vineyards.

Here the fighting is hand-to-hand and savage. I make very few sketches during this period of intense action.

I get wounded in November before ending up in a hospital. While recovering at the 33rd General Hospital in North Africa I come across my Cheyenne friend Two Hatchets. We are glad to see each other. Seriously wounded, he tells me that things at the front are bad. He explains that the Pawnee Company is fighting day and night with few replacements and no rest. He mentions one hill—he gives the number of the hill—and that it had to be taken. Battalion wanted Sergeant Phillip Shield Chief and his men to take it. They crawled to the German stronghold on steep rocky ground. Up there were shell-torn scrub cedars. It was a cold night, and he says loose rocks slipped just as they got near the top. He says they heard Germans cock their machine pistols and machine guns. Shield Chief gave a Pawnee war cry—and they charged with bayonets. Two Hatchets describes the situation and how, during this charge, a potato masher hit his chest and his legs. Grenades were going off all around him. He says Shield Chief killed a German officer and others before going down from machine-pistol fire at close range. It was a whirlwind fight, as they said. The Germans ran, leaving dead and wounded behind. Two Hatchets says we were shot up too . . . then somebody went to get Medicine Man. It was freezing cold, and Medicine Man had chills with high fever and was waiting to be evacuated. He grabbed his aid bags and came running to help the men.★

Medicine Man gave Shield Chief first aid and put a tourniquet on his arm. While Medicine Man was dressing Shield Chief's wounds, some Germans snuck up and shot him with machine pistols. Medicine Man winced, then grabbed a cedar club and charged like a wounded grizzly bear. Later our medics found him badly wounded and barely alive. Two dead Germans lay near our fallen Choctaw medic. One had his face clubbed in. The other had been strangled and had an ear bitten off. Then Two Hatchets's voice weakens to a whisper: *We fought well. . . . It was a good day to die.* A nurse comes over and tells the wounded Cheyenne that he should not talk, and try to rest. Emaciated, he is a mass of bloody bandages.

Tears come to my eyes as I drift off to sleep.

After a while I am awakened by the sound of dog tags rattling. It is medical aid men who are attending to Two Hatchets's wounds. Two Hatchets is in and

---

★In November 1943, north of Venafro, Italy, Echohawk sustained wounds from a German artillery blast, leaving him unconscious and stranded on a mountain ridge. Coughing blood and suffering from a concussion, Echohawk managed to retreat down the mountainside, where he eventually reached the safety of a field hospital.

"Damn mountains." Pawnee Indians fight in the mountains near Venafro, Italy, November 1943. Monte Cassino lies ahead.

out of consciousness, and I hear him singing what sounds like an old Cheyenne song. Then I hear one of the aid men: "This man is dead." The Cheyenne warrior looks peaceful as he lies still. He sang his death song; more tears come.

I am a few days off crutches and now walk with a cane. I throw away the cane and go AWOL. I hitch a ride with some Arab locals in a three-wheeled truck across the North African desert at night. The next day, I stow away on a plane to Sicily and do the same from Sicily to Naples. On the plane into Naples is Bill Mauldin, a fellow Thunderbird. Once there he hides me out in his apartment-studio. I show Mauldin my sketches; he is impressed. Later, I am arrested as an Army deserter, for I have no papers and am out of uniform. Still determined to get back to the company, I fight six MPs and an officer in what turns into a knock-down, drag-out brawl. I land in a tough stockade bound by heavy wire juiced to electrocute a man. A .30-caliber machine gun guards the place.

But the Great Spirit is with me: an Oklahoma general happens by. He sees me and gets me out. Then heads roll as he chews out the Naples military authorities for holding one of his fighting Thunderbird Indians. The general gives me money and passage on an LST bound for Anzio. The Holy City of Rome is twenty-five miles from Anzio.

Anzio is anything but holy; it is an inferno.

9

The Anzio Abscess

To the Allies, the attack at Anzio was critical for breaking the stalemate that developed in Italy as they pressed north. For Adolf Hitler, the attack represented a practice run for the inevitable Allied invasion of northwest Europe that was bound to take place in the near future. He knew that he had to "Lance the Abscess" that was the Anzio Beachhead. Upon receiving word of the landings, the German field marshal Albert Kesselring immediately dispatched some of the most renowned German troops to counter the attack, including components of the 4th Parachute and Hermann Goering Divisions, in addition to other units from Yugoslavia, France, and Germany. By the end of D-Day at Anzio, thousands of German troops were gathering for an attack on the beachhead, setting the stage for one of the bloodiest battles of the war. It was here that the Thunderbird Division earned their moniker as "The Rock of Anzio." *

In late 1943 the war in Italy had become a stalemate, with Allied troops facing staunch resistance from the Germans along a string of defensive positions known as the Gustav Line as they advanced north across Italy. Extending from the Tyrrhenian Sea on the west across the peninsula to the Adriatic Sea on the east was the Gustav Line. Within this German line were mountains and rivers and other natural defensive positions. Using the landscape to their utmost advantage, the Germans stalled the Allied advance for many months from December 1943 until the following June. The Gustav Line crossed Highway 6 to Rome at the crucial road that followed the Liri Valley near the ancient abbey at Monte Cassino. This abbey, sitting atop a mountain, overlooked the entire Liri Valley corridor, offering the Germans a defensive position to halt any advance on Highway 6 toward Rome. One of the bloodiest battles of the war would

---

*In this chapter Brummett Echohawk looks back at Anzio, jumping between past and present tense to relate to the reader a sense of the immediacy that was life on the Anzio Beachhead. He reveals the struggles that American GIs faced on a daily basis during the Battle of Anzio, fighting both the conditions and the enemies that surrounded them.

be waged in this valley, costing the Allies more than fifty thousand casualties before a breakthrough occurred in the spring of 1944.

To break the stalemate, the Allies pressed to outflank the Gustav Line by striking the town of Anzio to the south of Rome. Although outflanking the Germans by sea had been brought up before, Anzio was basically the project of Prime Minister Winston Churchill, who insisted that Allied generals take action to end the growing stalemate. Sitting nearly thirty miles southwest of Rome is Anzio. Conquered by the Romans following its founding by the Volsci people, the town traditionally served as the strategic harbor and getaway for Rome's elite, including Emperor Nero, who built a home there in ancient times. Lost to time by the Middle Ages, Anzio became less popular through the centuries.

Winston Churchill called this World War II beachhead in Italy the "cat's claw." Adolf Hitler called it "the abscess on the Italian coast." The Americans called it the "end run." The Willie-and-Joe infantrymen cared little for what it was called. To them it was going to be just another beachhead for the taking. For Hitler, lancing the abscess was as much about making a statement to the Allies as it was about holding ground in Italy. German leadership recognized that, if the landing could be halted and driven into the sea, the Allies might rethink the inevitable invasion of Northwest Europe, making this perhaps the most important beachhead of the war for the Germans.

The Allies' Anzio venture came to be called Operation Shingle. The British had euphoric projections about it. The Honorable Sir Harold Alexander, commander-in-chief of the Allied army in Italy, echoed the words of Churchill about Anzio: "It will astonish the world." General Alexander added that "it will certainly frighten Kesselring" (Field Marshal Albert Kesselring, the German commander-in-chief in Italy). He even went as far as suggesting that it would probably make Operation Overlord unnecessary if the mission panned out to be an overwhelming success. Overlord, then, was the code name for the coming cross-channel invasion that largely became known as D-Day.

Less optimistic, the Americans saw sobering problems at hand. One was the availability of landing craft, as they were needed in England for the massive assault to come on the beaches of Normandy. Another was raising enough troops. Important, too, was time, for many landing craft slated for Anzio were to be withdrawn on February 15 and sent to England in preparation for the Allied landings during Operation Overlord, which was to occur near June 1.

In a top-level conference on January 9, 1944, General Alexander stated that the operation would take place nearly two weeks later—on January 22. Major General John Lucas, who had been assigned to lead VI Corps, which was to land at Anzio, protested the target date, as it gave him little time for rehearsal. The American general was overruled. But Lucas managed one rehearsal near

Naples that proved fruitless. A navigation error caused the big ships to stop miles out to sea, which in turn caused the assault craft to take hours reaching the shore. The landing was a snafu, leaving many questioning how the show would play out for us. Many of the LSTs (Landing Ship, Tanks) opened their doors too soon. Forty vehicles sank into the sea. Ten howitzers were lost, and several men drowned. Lieutenant General Mark Clark, commander of the US Fifth Army, whose superior was General Sir Harold Alexander, was furious.

It was January 19, two days before the landing at Anzio. The French Expeditionary Corps, the British Eighth Army, and the US Fifth Army staged attacks along the Gustav Line. In miserable weather and rough country, the French gained little. The British failed to make a dent as well. The Germans holding the Rapido River staggered the 36th (Texas) Division with 1,500 casualties. The Allied strategy was to break through and contain the bulk of the German army. Later, Lucas's VI Corps would land behind the Germans at Anzio, twenty-five miles from Rome. With a breakthrough, the Fifth Army was to link up quickly with VI Corps. But now the Allied drive was stopped cold. It was January 20. On that day, Lucas boarded the command ship USS *Biscayne*, knowing that a rapid link-up by Fifth Army was no longer possible. For General Lucas, the picture was dark. A visit from General George S. Patton Jr. didn't brighten the picture any, for General Patton said: "John, there is no one in the Army I'd hate to see get killed as much as you, but you can't get out of this alive . . . of course you might get wounded. No one blames a wounded general."

January 22, 1944

The VI Corps landed unopposed on the beaches. Making up the VI Corps were the British 1st Division with reserves and the American 3rd Division, 504th Parachute Infantry Regiment, 509th Parachute Infantry Battalion, and three Ranger Battalions. In floating reserve were the 1st Armored Division and the 45th "Thunderbird" Division. On this day 36,034 men came ashore with little resistance. However, the enemy awaited us and prepared by flooding troops in from other theaters where German forces were fighting. Everything seemed to be going as planned; however, this would be the calm before the storm to come.

January 23, 1944

An American liberty ship was sunk. The British destroyer *Janus* also went down, sending balls of fire into the surrounding waters. A German torpedo bomber hit the *Janus*, sending it to the ocean depths in less than a half hour. The next day, Luftwaffe torpedo bombers scored another hit, sinking the

"Men of B Company brewing coffee, tense moments. Watching to see which way German fighters will go. Will they come for us or the battalion next to us, or will they head for the beachhead. Watch. Heads up." Anzio, Italy, 1944.

British hospital ship *St. David*. This ship had been one of many to ferry British soldiers from the beaches of Dunkirk following the German invasion of France four years earlier. It was marked and illuminated according to the International Red Cross as it sat off the coast. The Germans seemed to have it out for our aid stations throughout the fighting at Anzio. When the going got tough, the Germans liked to play dirty.

January 24, 1944

British motor patrols probe inland and draw fire; the enemy is out there observing all of our movements, waiting for the moment to strike. German air raids continued to increase, leaving many of us wondering where our planes are during the German bombardments.

January 25, 1944

Sustained rain and gales battered the beachhead all day, making our ships drift ashore from the storms. The offloading of supplies was also disrupted as a result of the weather wreaking havoc on the supply ships ferrying the loads critical to establishing a defensive stronghold on the beach. Word came down that General Alexander was apprehensive about the situation, while General Lucas was deeply worried. With the rain continuing, Willie and Joe's slit trenches filled with water, a problem that sustained the Anzio campaign for many Thunderbirds. For ol' Willie and Joe, nature became a second enemy on the field of battle at Anzio.

January 26, 1944

Lucas notes in his diary: "I want an all-out Corps effort but the time hasn't come yet and the weather will not help matters. Bad for tanks. I might be able to move soon." Field Marshal Kesselring tightened the noose around Anzio with troops from northern Italy, southern France, Yugoslavia, the Adriatic, and some from the Gustav Line. General Lucas stored supplies and prepared for a German counterattack that we all knew was to come. It had happened in Sicily and at Salerno too. A strong counterattack came, nearly pushing the Americans into the sea. General Mark Clark warned Lucas about sticking his neck out: "I did at Salerno, and got in trouble."

January 27, 1944

Message from General Sir Harold Alexander to General Clark: "All efforts should be concentrated on full-scale coordinated attacks to capture Cisterna and Campoleone followed by a rapid attack on Velletri."

January 28–February 6, 1944

Churchill prods General Alexander in a cable: IT WOULD BE UNPLEASANT IF YOUR TROOPS WERE SEALED OFF AND THE MAIN ARMY COULD NOT ADVANCE UP FROM THE SOUTH.

General Lucas readies a two-pronged attack. The British were to take Campoleone, a position that was key to extending the beachhead perimeter. The Americans on the right would take Cisterna, which would offer a springboard to Velletri, where German escape routes from the south could be cut off. The Anzio Beachhead was roughly nine miles deep and seventeen miles wide. In the planning stage, the company commanders of the Grenadier Guards met with a tragic accident. They were to meet officers of the Scots Guards concerning a start line and artillery reference points. In a jeep that night, they took a wrong turn and drove into the enemy lines. All were killed. The attack was delayed.

For the American Rangers, the delay was fatal. They had been waiting to move on Cisterna by crawling up a prominent ditch leading from the Mussolini Canal. It would have placed them under the noses of the Germans holding Cisterna. They didn't get the green light until January 30. During the delay, the Germans had reinforced Cisterna. That night, the 1st and 3rd Ranger Battalions crept forward with rifles, grenades, and courage. Out of 767 American Rangers, only six returned.

The 2nd Ranger Battalion attempted a rescue but failed. The loss of Darby's Rangers killed the morale of the Allied forces. Their loss, coupled with an attack by the 3rd Division being repulsed, made the situation near desperate. At Campoleone, the British were also mauled. The two-pronged attack by Lucas was blunted and fell short. "I had hoped we were hurling a wildcat on the shore, but all we had got was a stranded whale," Winston Churchill said. Allied casualties were up to 6,500 killed, missing, or wounded.

February 7–10, 1944

Near the village of Carroceto, which was held by the British, was a complex of brick buildings called "The Factory" by Allied forces. A highway, the Albano-Anzio road, ran from Anzio through Carroceto and The Factory. From here it led to Campoleone, then to Albano, joining Route 7 to Rome. Carroceto and The Factory now came under a German attack. The positions at both Carroceto and Campoleone fell, thus turning over the twin keys of the gate to the sea. Now that the Germans held the keys, Anzio lay ahead. It was February 10, 1944.

VI Corps Brass confer. The Factory is the issue. The British explain the situation, then focus on Lucas, who turns to General William Eagles, commander of the 45th "Thunderbird" Division, and says: "Okay, Bill, you give 'em the works." It was to be nothing fancy; the order got the show on the road for the Allies. With a downpour and deep mud, this would be a Willie and Joe show; artillery and tanks could not be relied on in such arduous conditions.*

The First Battalion of the 179th Regimental Combat Team of the 45th Division is given the task of taking The Factory. As a member of B Company, First Battalion, this Indian had recently returned from the hospital after being wounded in November. My return to the regiment proved to be a fight in and of itself. Sergeant Last Arrow and I are called to the Command Post. It is midnight, and it is raining. The captain fills us in on the situation at hand; his demeanor reflects the seriousness of this mission. He tells us that we are to take

---

*Willie and Joe featured in Bill Mauldin's satirical drawings from 1940 until 1946. Mauldin, who entered the military as a member of the 45th Division, was a lifelong friend of Brummett Echohawk.

"This is the misery of Anzio. Wait. Wait. Wait. Attacks are all waiting. I am scared all the time, but I never let anyone know." B Company before an attack in the rain. Anzio, Italy, February 9, 1944.

a factory. He uses a blue flashlight to focus on a cellophane-covered map. We'll have tank support—although I know better than to count on it with the soggy conditions plaguing the area. The captain pauses and looks at us. Battalion, he adds, wants two Indian sergeants to lead the attack at 0600. I am Pawnee. The sergeant at my side is a Potawatomi. We are it.

"Dead 'Jerries.' German dead near the Mussolini Canal." Anzio, Italy, February 11, 1944.

Sergeant William "Last Arrow" Lasley takes Panzer grenadiers at The Factory near Anzio, Italy, February 11, 1944.

February 11, 1944: Predawn Hours

We alert the men. They are in two-man slit trenches with a shelter half stretched over as protection from the rain. Some sit outside, hunched over in raincoats and steel helmets, for their slit trenches have long filled with water.

B Company moves out. There are many replacements. A few, like Last Arrow and myself, have been Thunderbirds since the division mobilized in 1940. At the start line of the attack, we wait. While it is still dark, the rain has stopped momentarily. It is brass-monkey cold. In the rear, the sound of tank motors roar to life. Then American artillery opens fire from behind. Word is passed on to fix bayonets; it is time.*

At 0600 Sergeant Last Arrow and I start forward. The men follow close behind at the ready. We maintain interval and slosh through mud, which slows our advance and makes noise as we squish in and out of sodden patches of ground. It grows light in the east as we continue to advance. After a while

---

*According to Warren P. Munsell in *The Story of a Regiment: A History of the 179th Regimental Combat*, it is stated that the odds for failure in the February 11, 1944, attack were a thousand to one against success.

"A German mortar and 88 barrage. This is the worst feeling a man can go through. It is a helpless feeling. The loud, ear-splitting explosions and concussions are terrifying beyond all words. There are no brave men here—only desperate men hugging Mother Earth." Sketch completed at Anzio Beachhead, 1944.

The Factory, which is silhouetted on a black horizon, comes into view. Just as we catch our first glimpse of The Factory, a German artillery barrage rocks the ground around us. We hug Mother Earth. Sergeant Last Arrow hollers: "Move!" I shout the same. We move as the mortar barrage continues to hit us.

We hit the ground, struggling to stay upright in the chaos of the German barrage. "Move! Keep moving!" Suddenly, blue tracer bullets from a German machine gun streak to us. At the left front, another gun does the same. They whirl like riveting machines, shooting 1,200 rounds per minute. From the left rear, red tracers sail forward, challenging the German gunners. It's D Company from Norman—the heavy weapons unit. Pitching in, and blazing away, on the left is A Company from Oklahoma City.

B Company from Pawnee presses forward. The dark fields are alive with knee-high, crisscrossing tracers. Last Arrow and I shout above the din: "Don't lie down! Run!" Later we gain a road two hundred yards from The Factory. Splattered with mud, we pant like winded prairie wolves.

Sergeant Last Arrow yells: "Go!" We charge forward with bayonets. American tanks don't show as they bog down in the sea of mud, becoming sitting

The Factory, near Aprilia, Italy. Image courtesy of the 45th Infantry Division Museum.

ducks for German artillery. The tanks, now destroyed after taking hits, burn for hours as the fight rages on. At The Factory, we now stood toe to toe with the German Panzer grenadiers to slug it out.

For hours The Factory battle raged on, with Willie and Joe taking the stronghold only to lose ground to German counterattacks minutes later. A real shootout. German infantry chased us out of there, only for the company to regroup and retake the ground immediately. This characterized the day's fighting; throughout, The Factory changed hands numerous times.

The Germans continued to fight, running us out of The Factory once more, with Panzers followed by infantry moving in to secure the German ground. Sergeant Last Arrow urges me to help organize another attack before the Germans settle into the area and take hold. I tell the sergeant I had seen movement in one of the buildings we must bypass to take the objective. Sergeant Last Arrow smiled assuredly to me, saying, "Oh Brummett, we can make it," with gold teeth glimmering, a relic of his time as a boxer in Indian country. I agreed to another charge.

The final attack was here. Only eleven of us whoop it up and charge toward The Factory again. On the right, and near what looks to us like a gashouse, Last Arrow yells and peppers away with a tommy-gun. I fire into the buildings in a similar fashion. Then—from where I suspected the enemy might have been hiding—machine gun fire erupts. Coming from the direction of the gashouse, the machine gun mows us down. As a round hits me I dive for a watery cow

"*In The Factory area, one of the bitterest fights of all.*" *Thunderbird hit by German sniper fire. Anzio Beachhead, February 1944.*

path. It is only inches deep, but it is enough to provide some sort of cover. I struggle backward like a crawdad; we have been slaughtered. I make it back to a roadside ditch. My sides heave like an eared-down bronc from the machine gun. I hear mortar shells fire as they rustle like dry leaves, then explode where Last Arrow and the men are down.

They had us. Tears come.

Corporal Harold Morgan and Sergeant William "Last Arrow" Lasley in traditional American Indian regalia, July 1942. During their training across the United States, American Indians of the 45th Division often performed traditional dances before large crowds of spectators. Courtesy of the Oklahoman.

I swallow down what has happened and reach for grenades and see holes in my raincoat. The grenades are gone; I lost them in all that running and crawling. American mortar fire crashes around the gashouse. I crawl down the ditch looking for more of our men and find no one. At a road junction, I finally come across components of A, B, and C Companies who are pinned down. The men who try to keep things moving I recognize as being from "Okie City," including sergeants I went to judo and bayonet school with in Abilene.

One thing is noticeably not good: they are bunched up and noncoms, exposing themselves in an effort to rally the men. It can't be helped. The Jerries spot them, sending in another 88 barrage. I crawl back toward the gashouse in an effort to move away from the line of fire.

Then a captain jumps into the ditch. He asks for Bill. I tell him; his jaw drops and he is silent. The captain is crouched with a tommy-gun over his

Portrait of Sergeant William "Last Arrow" Lasley, who was a Potawatomi Indian from Fairfax, Oklahoma. A Golden Glove boxer before the war, Lasley died from German machine gun fire near The Factory at Aprilia, Italy, on February 12, 1944.

shoulder. He wears a look of desperation. He is trying to link everybody and tells me we need support in a bad way. Rattled, the captain turns to leave before he suddenly splashes face-first into the ditch; a single bullet from the heating ovens of hell kills him.

The barrage lifts at the road junction, but shells continue to fall harassingly. I turn for the junction once more. An 88 explodes in front of me, almost blinding me and bursting my eardrums. It tears a gap in the ditch facing The Factory. I zip across the smoking gap. While I pause for a breath I hear a man crawling from behind. I turn to look, and before he screams "Medic! Medic!" I help him with his first aid packet. He has taken a bullet in the side while crossing the gap. A medic bounces across the road to us, answering the wounded's call for help. He pulls off his muddy gloves and wipes his hands under his jacket before reaching into his saddlebags and taking out sulfa powder, gauze, and scissors. He is upright on both knees as he works on the wounded soldier. I hear a slapping sound and turn to suddenly see the medic topple across the wounded man. A sniper drilled him through the mouth.

Sensing the seriousness of the situation, I move on, keeping low to avoid the German fire. At the junction a frantic cry rises for a bazooka men. Someone yells: "Flak truck!" An armored vehicle sputters from The Factory. Brave men with M1s and tommy-guns blaze away, then duck. The flak truck sprays the ditches. The fire sweeps over, churning up the road as rounds slap the muddy surface. The vehicle races back to The Factory, with American artillery thundering after all the way. Our men fall back.

The road junction is riddled with shell holes. In the ditches is cumbersome and discarded gear. Sprinkled throughout are empty M1 clips, empty brass, and traces of blood. I pass the dead as if not to disturb them. At the junction I turn for our lines.

Five American tanks rumble up the road. I can't say I'm glad to see them— not this close—for the tanks draw tremendous fire. A man's head protrudes from the turret of the lead tank. I shout at the tanker to get away. Other infantrymen scream the same. The roars of the motors drown out our pleas. I have one thought: *Get the hell away from that tank.* It's too late, though, as an 88 belts the lead tank. There is no explosion as expected, but a vibrating thud; these are armor-piercing shells. The man in the turret gathers himself and jumps. A hail of bullets catches him on the way down. The tank rocks with another hit before smoke boils up. More AP shells thump the road banks, glance, and sputter like giant fan blades. One tank has its turret blown off; its motor keeps running, causing vapor to rise in the cold air from the exhaust.

I move to the right of the junction to avoid any more tank traffic. Now I hear the roar of Panzers. To my right front I can also hear machine pistols. I

"A man out of B Company 179th was hit in the belly. Under savage arms fire and a barrage, a medic heard his call and gave the wounded man first aid. As the medic rose above the ditch level with his bandage and gauze a German sniper hit him in the cheek. Bullet passed clean through. Both men hugged the ditch in pain. The medic was pulled to safety and survived; the other man died." Near The Factory, Anzio, Italy, 1944.

dogleg it on all fours as fast as I can for the road junction. I scramble over the dead without thought as the Germans start to close in. I spot a small culvert full of ice and water. Here I peel off my pack fast before reaching inside my breast pocket to take out some spicy German photographs. I throw them as far as I can, then slither into the culvert. The ice cracks and the water comes to my mouth.

I hear nothing but my heart pounding as I slouch in the icy water. I try to get my mind off fear and freezing. I think about the spicy pictures I just threw. I took them from a Kraut at Venafro. He had wild pictures of him and his girlfriends . . . a real Romeo, you could say. We used to pass them around and roar laughing. He had other pictures of him and his buddies on a Panzer holding up cans of beer. One was marked POLAND 1939. He had some taken in

Russia too. He was an old pro, one of the Nazi "supermen" that beat the Poles and French. I remember this Jerry wore a Clark Gable–type mustache when he and his gang jumped us Pawnees. I put an M1 slug into his chest. Indians win battles sometimes.

I hear burp guns and "Hands Up! Hands up!"

"Nicht schiessen!" A pair of German jackboots sloshes by the opening of the culvert, sending water rippling to my face. I don't move or breathe for fear of being detected.

My body is numb with cold. I must lie in the water, as the culvert is too low for me to rise on my knees. I do half pushups slowly to keep warm and fight off hypothermia. The water in front of me is bloody. In the strains of doing pushups my hand tears again. I shiver so hard that the water ripples with each convulsion. When things outside seem quiet enough, I pour out of the culvert. I am numb all over—but alive.

I crawl stiffly for the junction again. The dead men's packs have been ransacked by the Germans. Scattered are personal effects: a pipe, a pair of eyeglasses, a busted deck of cards, a harmonica, and a folded-to-pocket-size, well-worn copy of the *Daily Oklahoman*. *Damn Kraut-head bastards*, I think to myself.

I crawl for our lines, as there is no cover in the front of The Factory. The countryside is bleak as I pass dead milk cows. They are bloated and mud-splattered. I glance back at The Factory. It is on a broad hill that overlooks the main highway leading from Anzio. After the day's fighting it is dead, jagged, and torn. It looms against the wintery sky like a forbidden Castle Frankenstein. My hands swell from the frostbite. Everything's quiet as I make my way back to the Allied line.

For the next several months I recovered from my wounds suffered during the battle for The Factory at the Evacuation Hospital back at the beach. I touched up sketches I had done and tried to get my mind off the death of Last Arrow and the others. Our big Sioux Indian MP happened by after bringing in prisoners. We embraced and shook hands. We were glad to see each other, but we were both sad, for we knew that our Indians were all but gone. The Evac facility was a tent hospital. The Anzio Beachhead was compact everywhere with men, ammo dumps, armor, vehicles, ack-ack guns, and an airstrip that took a steady pounding. Men appeared to walk in a crouch with shoulders hunched up, ready to duck incoming enemy shells; it became known as the "Anzio gait." As the big Sioux and I talked, we noticed not far away a formation of men. They were Thunderbirds. I asked what they were doing. The big Sioux said they were awarding medals for bravery. He said they were just "new men and officers." I thought about Short Nose, Shield Chief, Medicine Man, Last Arrow, and the rest. Medals never meant much to us.

"The Anzio Beachhead Kamerad!" Captured Panzer grenadiers near The Factory. Anzio Beachhead, February 1944.

The big Sioux reached into his pack and pulled out some pemmican his folks had sent him.* He gave some to me, shook hands, then left. I drew a picture of a Red Cross nurse during a late afternoon air raid. I got acquainted with a dark-eyed nurse. I liked her, and she seemed to have a special affinity for checking on me. She was fascinated by the drawings I had done under fire. That night the Germans hit the beachhead with a heavy air raid and fire from a railroad gun we called the "Anzio Express." The tent I was in took a hit. The dark-eyed nurse I liked was decapitated.

---

*Pemmican is a mix of dry lean meat such as buffalo, elk, or deer mixed with fat to form a nutritious food that can last up to a decade.

"Jerry prisoner captured on the Anzio Beachhead near The Factory." Drawn on Red Cross stationery at 93rd Evacuation Hospital, March 3, 1944.

German K5 Railway Gun. Allied Soldiers nicknamed these guns "Anzio Annie" and the "Anzio Express" due to the express train–like sound the shells made as they came in. Image courtesy of the 45th Infantry Division Museum.

Anzio was a nightmare—a complete nightmare. Back at the 17th General Hospital near the Bay of Naples, I lay in bed and covered my head, trying to blot out all that was Anzio. I kept seeing Sergeant Last Arrow in my mind as he fell from the German machine gun fire. He was not a Pawnee. He was a Pota-watomi—but damn was he brave. He went down fighting. I could not help him, for I too was hit. The Germans kept pumping lead into him long after he was down, and with his last spark of life he kept up his war cry. I try to think of better times we had together, like when Last Arrow and other Indians in the division put on powwows as we traveled across the country during training. And then there was that pretty, dark-eyed nurse. To me, she was noticeably scared but tried to hide it. I felt sorry for the beachhead nurses. Women have no place in a combat zone, and especially a place like Anzio. They were angels for many of the men and lifted our spirits with their compassion and bravery.

My spirits were brightened some when I met the movie actress Madeleine Carroll. She was with the British Red Cross. The 17th General was a combina-tion British and American hospital. Madeleine Carroll noticed me touching up my combat sketches one day. Fascinated, she brought me more drawing paper. We became acquainted, and she suggested that war correspondents see them, as they were some of the rawest depictions of combat she had seen. Through her, my drawings were published back in the States. Newspapers featured them as the first front-line drawings of the war done by an infantryman. This was my first break in what was to become a long career in art for me.

I met an Indian soldier out of our outfit. He said that a Cherokee named Jack Montgomery was awarded the Congressional Medal of Honor at Anzio. Montgomery, a lieutenant of the 45th Division, destroyed a force of Germans preparing to attack his unit. With great courage, he killed several Germans and took many prisoners.

I never saw Madeleine Carroll again, as the 17th General Hospital was struck by a German air raid. After all the fighting I had been through, I did not panic. I grabbed my steel helmet, crawled under the bed, and rode out the storm. At the same time, Mount Vesuvius erupted. The entire city of Naples was veiled with volcanic ash as well as the smoke from German air raids.

By the time the stalemate at Anzio set in while waiting for the breakout, most of the Pawnee Thunderbirds I marched off to war with had long been wounded, killed, or captured. However, the Thunderbird Division had held the beachhead at Anzio despite the Germans throwing everything they had at us.

Angered, Adolf Hitler ordered his generals "to lance the abscess" and destroy the Anzio Beachhead by pushing the Allies into the sea. For the next several weeks, German divisions continued to arrive in the days following the battle for The Factory. From Germany came the Führer's special unit: the Berlin-Spandau *Lehr* Regiment. Hitler insisted that this regiment of dedicated Nazis lead the attack to drive the Allies back. Field Marshal Kesselring now had 125,000 troops at his disposal to crush the Thunderbirds. But we went on the offensive—like we always did.

0600, February 16, 1944

The day dawned with the largest artillery barrage yet seen exploding on the center of the Allied lines. Positioned there, and taking the full blow, was the 179th RCT. Following the barrage came Hitler's spirited Nazi regiment. Four hundred and thirty-two American guns fired a counterbarrage with tornadic fury. As they had done before, against all odds and in all kinds of weather, Willie and Joe rose to the challenge. In the first hours of the knock-down, drag-out fight, the Berlin-Spandau *Lehr* Regiment broke. "They were thrown back disgracefully," Field Marshall Kesselring wrote later. Other German units thundered forward and did not falter. On the left of the 179th was the 157th.

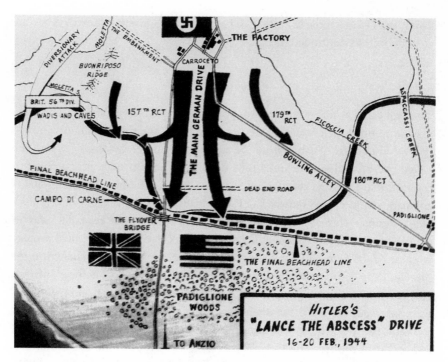

Brummett Echohawk's hand-drawn map of Hitler's "Lance the Abscess" drive (February 16–20, 1944).

Both Thunderbird regiments took a pounding but never stopped fighting back. By weight and numbers, the Germans pushed the two regiments back one mile.

General Sir Harold Alexander complained about Lucas to General Clark: "You know the position is serious. We may be pushed back into the sea. That would be very bad for both of us, and you would certainly be relieved of your command."

February 17, 1944

Dawn. The weather cleared briefly as the sun rose in the east. Forty German planes dive-bomb the 179th. Almost as quick as the German planes had come and gone, another German counterattack began in earnest.

Waiting in reserve behind The Factory are Panzer divisions, ready to bull through the first break in the Allied lines. Allied planes then roared in from above, dropping 1,100 tons of bombs on the attacking Germans. All beachhead guns fired a storm of steel at the advancing infantry. Two Allied cruisers at sea poured salvo after salvo into the area in front of The Factory. Briefly the German attack is halted, yet after this devastating storm, and taking terrible losses, the German attacks resume. They are as fanatical as before. Yet we are as stubborn; we continued to hold.

February 18, 1944

The rain came again, grounding support from the Allied air forces. The Germans continued their relentless advance, surging down the Albano-Anzio road without the threat of attack from the air. They hammered a gap deep into the Allied line 2.5 miles wide and a mile deep. American counterattacks failed to regain the lost ground throughout the day. Back at the beachhead hospital, I am marked "duty" and returned to B Company. The front flashes and rumbles like a summer electrical storm. Up the Anzio road, about six miles, was an overpass we called the "Flyover." Adjoining the Flyover was the final protective line. If the Germans could cross the Flyover, it would be all she wrote. As the Germans continue their attacks we fear the worst. To reinforce infantry troops on the front, all rear-echelon soldiers like cooks, clerks, and mechanics were summed up for the last-ditch stand soon to occur.

Night falls as the heavy rain continues. A crisis exists; you can see it on faces and feel it in the air. The Germans threaten the Flyover, inching closer and closer to the line of our last stand. At B Company, some platoons are overrun, unable to stall the relentless enemy. Now the situation began to grow dire. Enemy barrages continue as fierce as ever. The barrage spared none, leaving one cook brought up for the last-ditch stand dead from a direct hit. In place of his slit trench was a huge shell hole—no body to be found. Soggy walls of the slit trenches caved in from the concussion of the blast. After a near-hit, we find ourselves helping each other dig out. We cough and spit mud but continue to rise and fight back, holding the line with every attack.

Chaos ensued as the Germans, in long overcoats, swarmed forward. Flares fired, lighting the area, allowing the red tracers from American machine guns to zero in on the approaching enemy. Meanwhile the rumbles of beachhead artillery flashed, rumbled, and pulverized the front, catching many of the enemy in their advance. What few Germans made it through the Allied barrage could be seen in the eerie flare-shadows dancing between the light and rain. Accurate rifle fire dropped them and stopped the few that continued their advance. We later found out that Sergeant Charles H. Johnson, of Pawnee, burned out several machine gun barrels that night holding off the German attack.

By the next day the crisis was over. The German drive had collapsed and the Allies held the line. Exhausted, but still game, the Americans mounted a counterattack and swept the field. The back of the German army at Anzio was now broken. The Albano-Anzio road was all shell craters now. Across the

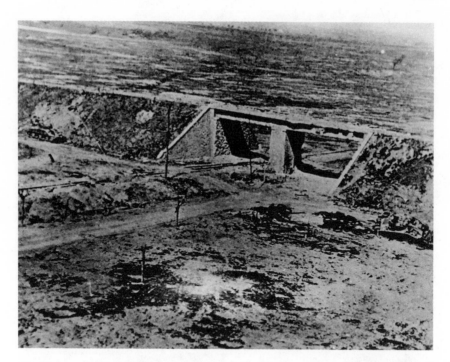

The Flyover—the "Last Stand" position at Anzio. Image courtesy of the 45th Infantry Division Museum.

front were burned vehicles and tanks. Mother Earth, too, was gutted. On her bosom lay four days of carnage. This place was later referred to as Compo di Carne—the Field of Flesh.

Hitler was enraged and ordered another attack. Field Marshal Kesselring's army had no spirit. Following orders, Kesselring hit the US 3rd Division holding the Cisterna front. The 3rd, one of the best divisions in the army, kicked the daylights out of them—leaving little hope for a German victory at Anzio.

February 22, 1944

General John Lucas was relieved. General Lucian Truscott, who commanded the 3rd Division, replaced him. Lucas blamed the British all the way to Churchill. General Lucas believed he was right about the powerful counterattack, and felt it was his victory. At this point, it could have been that "the stranded whale" was a shark that the enemy could not handle. Since the southern front, over sixty miles away, couldn't support the VI Corps at Anzio and the Germans could never muster an offensive strength, the gun barrels cooled. There were grass fires but never the forest fire we had all expected.

"Infantry advances at Anzio. Sergeant Charles Hooker Johnson of Pawnee, Oklahoma, going on patrol with green replacements at Anzio Beachhead. They walk and slide in mud past a dead German soldier. Sergeant Johnson [and] I grew up with each other. We played together as kids and were both on the football team in school. He was a damn good sergeant." February 4, 1944.

May 23, 1944

The Allies finally broke out at Anzio. Both sides suffered high casualties—more so for the Germans, though. There were twenty-two Congressional Medals of Honor awarded for service at Anzio. One of the recipients was a Thunderbird and Cherokee Indian named Jack Montgomery from Sallisaw, Oklahoma.

Lieutenant Colonel Ernest Childers, C Company, 180th Regiment, 45th Infantry Division, attacks a German machine gun nest in September 1943 near Oliveto, Italy. On this day Childers killed two enemy snipers, attacked two machine gun nests, and captured an artillery observer. For his bravery he received the Medal of Honor, becoming the first American Indian to receive the award since the Indian Wars of the nineteenth century.

Montgomery joined the Army in 1937 and served as a lieutenant in the 180th Infantry Regiment. In late February 1944, Montgomery repeatedly attacked German positions near Padiglione, Italy, where he killed nearly a dozen Krauts and took many more prisoner. Another American Indian lieutenant in the 180th received a Medal of Honor too. Ernest Childers, a Muscogee (Creek) Indian from Broken Arrow, Oklahoma, singlehandedly captured multiple German pillboxes and apprehended an artillery observer near Oliveto, Italy, in September 1943. Salerno and Anzio solidified the Thunderbird Division's reputation as one of the most respected infantry units of the entire war.

By June 4, 1944, the Americans had taken Rome, with the Thunderbirds being the first Allied soldiers to arrive at the Vatican. Pope Pius XII gave a public thanks to God for sparing Rome from the destruction the war produced in many areas around the world.

Lieutenant Colonel Ernest Childers, Medal of Honor recipient, approaches German positions before an attack near Oliveto, Italy, September 1943.

Following the battle, the Soviet leader Joseph Stalin sent a message to Churchill congratulating him on the Allied victory and praising the determination of the Allied men during the long, hard-fought battle. During one of his famed Fireside Chats, President Franklin Roosevelt also paid homage to the victory at Anzio and Rome, explaining to radio listeners that there was "one up and two to go." As for Willie and Joe, one of our good ol' boys from the Panhandle drawled: "We broke 'em from suckin' eggs."

With leg and foot wounds, and having taken concussion hits that left me with internal injuries and a partial loss of hearing, I was returned to the States, where I was furloughed home to Pawnee, Oklahoma.

At home I met Phillip Shield Chief, our platoon sergeant. He had lost an arm. I also saw Sergeant Good Buffalo from the platoon. He had suffered a wound in the temple and ear.

With tradition, the Pawnee tribe honored us as true warriors. We were also accorded another honor: awarding us a warrior's name. A song was composed in our honor. The Pawnee ceremony was held far out in the country under brush arbors. It was summer now—a stiflingly hot season in Oklahoma. On a hill, not far away, I spot Indian ponies grazing peacefully. The old chiefs, as well as elders of the *Ahrooks-pakoo-tah* (Warrior's Society), brought the American flag into the circle. Immensely patriotic, the Pawnee Indians rose to their feet. The drummers and singers sang the Pawnee Flag Song. In fine beadwork, buckskins, and eagle feathers, the chiefs and elders stood erect, though some were bent with age.

The three of us Indian Thunderbirds stood at attention. I swelled with pride. My combat art was being published all over the country. And now my tribe was honoring me as a full-fledged warrior.

Then the singers paused and took up a slow drumbeat and wailed a slow War Song. The old ones bowed their heads. I saw Shield Chief's family and relatives cry.

I turned to Good Buffalo and asked: "Whose War Song is that?"

He answered: "Grant Shield Chief's."

I listened to the wailing song and the low drumbeats that throbbed like the human heart. Grant was Phillip Shield Chief's brother. He was a sergeant in our Third Platoon.

Then Good Buffalo turned to me and whispered: *Grant was killed in southern France.* My chin dropped as tears came. The Legend had proven true: the old ones said one of us would go. It was Grant. And I had done a sketch of him. Sniffling, I stood erect and gazed at the American flag snapping at the summer breeze. The low singing continued. From the distant hillside came the whinny of a stud horse. My thoughts went back to Sicily and Italy—and our bayonet charges. Then from the peaceful fields of the Pawnee Nation came the sweet call of a bobwhite.

Postscript

Mark R. Ellenbarger and Trent Riley

For his service in World War II, Brummett Echohawk earned a Combat Infantry Badge, a Bronze Star, the Army Commendation, two Invasion Arrowheads, a Purple Heart with two Oak Leaf Clusters, and a posthumous Congressional Gold Medal. His combat sketches completed in the trenches of Italy gained popularity around the world, appearing in the United States Army's weekly *Yank* magazine and achieving syndication in more than eighty international newspapers. Echohawk's wartime work propelled his career path as a professional artist for the remainder of his life.

Although some of Echohawk's closest friends suffered serious injuries during the war, many returned home to Indian Country, where they lived long lives. In 1940, when the National Guard began mobilizing for war, Phillip "Shield Chief" Gover qualified for an exemption for having a family back home. Despite his exemption, Gover passed on the opportunity to remain stateside and instead chose to lead his men into battle, becoming the *Raáwiirakuhkitawi'u* (Leader) of the Pawnee war party. After suffering serious wounds near Venafro, Italy, Gover returned home to Oklahoma. One of Echohawk's proudest works of art was a portrait of Phillip Gover wearing traditional Pawnee regalia. The painting hangs prominently at the 45th Infantry Division Museum in Oklahoma City today. Gover and Echohawk remained close friends for the rest of their lives, with Echohawk speaking at Gover's wake in 1992.

Grant Gover, the brother of Phillip Gover and a close friend of Brummett Echohawk, made it through the campaigns of the Mediterranean before dying in action on November 1, 1944, during the invasion of southern France. As Pawnee legend foretold before the war, Grant Gover would be the only Pawnee killed in action who marched off with the 45th. The US government posthumously awarded Grant Gover a Congressional Gold Medal for his use of Pawnee language in combat, along with other members of B Company, including Phillip Gover, Chauncey F. Matlock, Brummett Echohawk, and Master Sergeant Floyd E. Rice.

Gilbert "Cheyenne" Curtis survived the war after sustaining wounds and receiving a furlough. Curtis and Echohawk remained friends for the remainder of their lives. Sergeant Floyd "Good Buffalo" Rice, whom the men also called "Flop," returned home to Pawnee, where tribal elders honored him as a decorated warrior. Floyd "Good Buffalo" died in 1956.

Captain Stewart Dobbins from Ohio was killed in action at The Factory near Anzio on February 11, 1944. Assigned to the company in 1942, the men of Second Platoon all liked Dobbins and considered him to be an intelligent and capable leader. Thunderbirds of Company B who fought under his leadership never forgot him and continued to visit his grave at the Sicily-Rome American Cemetery in Nettuno, Italy, after the war.

Moses Bowlegs, known to Echohawk and his squad as "Medicine Man," provided laughs in addition to medical care for the men of B Company throughout the war. While Bowlegs was treating Phillip Gover following an injury, two Germans soldiers shot and wounded him. Finding him barely alive, members of B Company were shocked to discover that he had fought back his German attackers, leaving their corpses as a reminder to all of the fighting spirit of the company from Indian Country.

Sergeant William "Last Arrow" Lasley, a Potawatomi Indian, was one of the top boxers in Oklahoma before the war. His boxing exploits regularly appeared in Oklahoma newspapers during the 1930s, during which time he earned the title of Golden Glove. Echohawk remembered him as always having a sense of humor when things were rough, approaching deadly situations with an unflinching bravery. Last Arrow died from machine gun fire during the Battle of The Factory near Anzio on February 11, 1944. Oklahoma newspapers reported Lasley missing in action as late as June 1944—four months after he was killed in action. He left behind a widowed wife and friends in Fairfax, Oklahoma. Like other men Echohawk served with, Last Arrow never had the chance to live a long and fruitful life in peace, instead living and dying as a true warrior on the field of battle.

After his return home, Echohawk studied at the Detroit School of Arts and Crafts and at the Art Institute of Chicago. He later attended the University of Chicago for a brief period and also studied journalism at the University of Tulsa. Following his studies, Echohawk became a staff artist for the *Chicago Daily Times* and *Chicago Sun-Times*. There, he made a name for himself working as an illustrator. Echohawk's illustrations appeared in various newspapers, including his popular comic strip, titled "Little Chief," which appeared regularly in the *Tulsa Sunday World* in the late 1950s and early 1960s. Echohawk's work appeared in other magazines and publications, including the cover of *Western Horseman* more than sixteen times throughout his career.

In the early 1950s, Echohawk met the love of his life, Mary Francis McInnes-Echohawk, while attending a sketching class at the Philbrook Museum of Art in Tulsa, Oklahoma. They were married until her death in January 1986.

Echohawk's subject matter, centered on the American Indian and the American West, became a trademark of his artistic works. His impressionistic and realist style garnered the attention of many in the art world. The Pawnee knife he carried throughout the war became a tool he frequently used when painting his impressionistic works. Echohawk explained his impressionistic style: "Bold strokes applied by a Bowie knife bring out the vibrant spirit of the subject—as opposed to showing a picture . . . or copy of the subject." His pursuit of the truth—by revealing impressionistic works focused on historical subject matter—became a trademark of Echohawk's fine art. Over the span of his career his works appeared in museums around the world, including in England, Germany, India, and Pakistan. Beyond his work as an illustrator and fine artist, Echohawk also put time into special projects of various sorts, as was the case when he assisted Thomas Hart Benton with the mural *Independence and the Opening of the West* at the Truman Memorial Library in Independence, Missouri. One of Echohawk's projects of which he was most proud was a mural aboard the US Navy cruiser the USS *Anzio*. Using vivid detail, he applied imagery from his memory and combat sketches to create a touching montage honoring the men and women who held the beachhead at Anzio. Echohawk also designed the flag of the Pawnee Nation. The design of the flag reflects that in peace and war Pawnee Indians are always courageous and loyal to America, symbolizing the ethos Echohawk lived by.

In the early 1990s, Brummett Echohawk began putting his story on paper, deliberating over the process and the difficulties that telling it presented. The writing process was painfully slow for Echohawk, as he struggled to describe what he experienced and the friends he lost. He knew this historical record would serve as a monument to his service and, most important, the service of his fellow Thunderbirds. Writing page after page, he contemplated the project and detailed in his daily journal the difficulties he faced. With other pursuits calling him toward his art career, Echohawk never had the opportunity to see this written work through to publication prior to a debilitating stroke. He passed away in 2006 after a long and successful life. When people met Brummett Echohawk, they saw the flapping of the Thunderbird's wings and the flashing of its eyes, for they stood before an honored warrior who, in the traditions of old, proved himself.

Chaticks-si-Chaticks—Men of Men.

Dramatis Personae

The most dangerous of all American soldiers is the Indian. . . .
He is an army within himself. He is the one soldier Germany must fear.
—1918 German World War I report

Chaticks-si-Chaticks—*Men of Men*

Cheyenne (or Chey')—Gilbert "Short Nose" Curtis. Private First Class, B Company. Known as "Cheyenne," he was a full-blood Cheyenne. He was the grandson of a famous warrior, Chief Roman Nose.

Good Buffalo—Floyd "Good Buffalo" Rice. Sergeant, Third Squad. Also called "Flop" by the men. A Pawnee, he had ramrod-straight posture, a barrel chest, and a slight paunch. He was a college wrestler and football player.

Grant Shield Chief—Grant "Shield Chief" Gover. Sergeant, Third Platoon. Grant Gover, the brother of Phillip Shield Chief and a close friend of Brummett Echohawk, was also a former quarterback.

Last Arrow—William "Last Arrow" Lasley. Sergeant, First Squad. He was a Potawatomi Indian from Fairfax, Oklahoma, and a Golden Glove champion boxer before the war.

Medicine Man—Moses Bowlegs. Private First Class, B Company. A Choctaw medic known to Echohawk and his squad as "Medicine Man." He had a round face, full lips, and narrow slits for eyes. When smiling, his eyes appeared to close. Moses Bowlegs provided laughs in addition to medical care for the men of B Company throughout the war.

Shield Chief—Phillip "Shield Chief" Gover. Platoon Sergeant, Third Platoon. At thirty-seven, Shield Chief was the oldest man in the company. Powerfully built, he had been a college quarterback. Intelligent and well respected, this Pawnee had been employed by the US Indian Service in his civilian days. Enlisted despite qualifying for an exemption for having a family back home.

Other American Indians

Sam Bear—A Creek Indian who served with Brummett Echohawk, he used a wild tom turkey call during charges. He accompanied the men during their scouting mission to the north coast of Sicily when they utilized the Katy Line handcar. Little more is known about him.

Sergeant Louis "Ruling His Son" Eaves—Often performed scout missions for B Company.

Leonard C. Leading Fox—Corporal, B Company. A Pawnee who served with Brummett Echohawk in the same company, he had previously worked for the Bureau of Indian Affairs. He accompanied the men during the scouting mission to the north coast of Sicily when they utilized the Katy Line handcar. Leonard Leading Fox was a graduate of the Pawnee High School and the Haskell Institute.

Chauncey Matlock—Sergeant, B Company. Matlock was among the many Pawnee Indians in B Company. Except for his burr haircut, Sergeant Matlock resembled the chief on the Indianhead nickel.

Gilbert Santana—Private, B Company. A Comanche from San Antonio, Texas, he was known to his fellow soldiers as "San Antone."

Two Hatchets—Cheyenne's cousin and Brummett Echohawk's good friend, who served in E Company.

Other Men

Stewart Dobbins—Second Lieutenant, Second Platoon; later became captain. An intelligent man from Ohio.

Robert Stone—Right Guide Sergeant, Second Platoon. Stone served in the National Guard prior to 1940. A sunup-to-sundown farmer, he was tough as a post oak and mean as a jersey bull.

Glossary

Native American Terms and Phrases

A-a'e—ay, kiddi didde didde, kidde didde didde!—Pawnee war cry

Ah-hu, rah ruk, tut—Yes, I noticed

Ah-ka—An expression of lament or disappointment depending on the situation

Aho—An old Indian expression for "agreed"

Ahrooks-pakoo-tah—Warrior's Society

Atius Tirawa—Supreme Being, Father

Chaticks-si-Chaticks—Men of Men

Chaticks-takah ta kitti wis—White man who cheats

Chibonni—Boy

Chu-wat—Girls

Hesci—Hello, in Creek

Hupiri-Kucu—Morning Star; he is a messenger from God, signaling the coming of a new day

Ka?—What?

Kah-kih—No

Ka-ka-ti-ra-ita—I don't know

Karariiwari—North Star

Ka-rusu-terit?—Did you see that?

Kitte kesu toddi?—What are you doing?

Nawa—Pawnee word said after a chief speaks, meaning "Agreed" or "All is good"; a Pawnee greeting

Nawa, tiwat—Hello, cousin

Oologah Muskogee Tulsa Tahlequah!—Towns in Oklahoma (gibberish spoken during a prisoner encounter)

Raáwiirakuhkitawi'u—Leader of the Pawnee war party

Ra-ri-pa-ku-su—Soldiers

Ru-ra-chi-ra-u—All right

Siks-a!—Come here!

Six-pettit—Come, sit down

Skiri—Wolf

Skiri, tawako kah-kih cha-rah rarut—Wolf says no enemy

Suks-ti-wata—Watch over the little boy

Ti-ku-skipi—I am sleepy

Tirawa—Supreme Being, Father

Ti-ros-a luri-hi-ru pa-huh—He is far behind the hill

Tit kotit, tawit!—Killed three!

Tiwat—Nephew/cousin

Tiwat, peduski tah-kah, pahetuh!—Cousin, tell that white boy, quiet

Tudahe—Good

Tus chaticks-si-chaticks—We are Men of Men

Uh-dee—An expression of disgust

Uks-kotit! Retsu-kih!—Kill them! Use knife!

Wees!—Hurry!

Wees-kah-chuh!—Hurry up!

Wuh—An Indian expression that applies to a comical situation

Weapons and Vehicles

.03—The decades-old M1903 Springfield 30-03 bolt-action rifle, carried by many US infantrymen during the war, had power, accuracy, and range, and was deadly in the hands of a skilled sniper. Commonly referred to as the "Oh-three." The 30-03 was remanufactured in 1906 to 30-06.

75—The standard 75mm howitzer used by the US artillery in support of ground operations.

88—The German 88mm antitank gun that was used in a variety of capacities; it was one of the most effective heavy weapons deployed by any side during the war.

AP—Armor-penetrating shells.

bangalore torpedo—An explosive inserted into connected pipes and typically used to clear paths through barbed wire or other enemy obstacles during an attack.

BAR—Browning Automatic Rifle. An automatic rifle with devastating power, it was carried by the "BAR man" in the squad during close attack and typically chambered the .30-06 Springfield round.

half-track—A large hybrid vehicle with truck wheels in front for steering and tank tracks behind for propulsion; on the field of battle it could transport personnel, weapons, and supplies cross-country over rough terrain.

M1—Named after its inventor, John Garand, the M1 Garand, a .30-caliber semiautomatic rifle, was the standard-issue rifle for the US military during the war.

Messerschmitt—Recognized for its production of prominent German fighter planes used in World War II, Messerschmitt AG was a German aircraft manufacturing company. Allied soldiers referred to most German fighter planes as "Messerschmitts" rather than by a specific model. Germany's advanced fighters were comparable to the American Mustang and British Spitfire, among other Allied models.

MG 42—The Maschinengewehr 42 was a general-purpose machine gun designed in Nazi Germany and used by German forces during the war. It chambered the 7.92 × 57mm Mauser round and continues in service.

Panzer—German tank.

potato masher—German hand grenade. A foot-long stick with a tin can–shaped explosive on one end, it resembled the common kitchen utensil.

Index